FAMILIAR STRANGER

An Introduction to Jesus of Nazareth

Michael J. McClymond

WILLIAM B. EERDMANS PUBLISHING COMPANY
GRAND RAPIDS, MICHIGAN / CAMBRIDGE, U.K.

For Dr. Stewart and Arleen Ensign
in gratitude for your hospitality and friendship

Wm. B. Eerdmans Publishing Co.
255 Jefferson Ave. S.E., Grand Rapids, Michigan 49503 /
P.O. Box 163, Cambridge CB3 9PU U.K.

Printed in the United States of America

08 07 06 05 04   7 6 5 4 3 2 1

Library of Congress Cataloging-in-Publication Data

McClymond, Michael James, 1958-
    Familiar stranger: an introduction to Jesus of Nazareth / Michael J. McClymond.
        p.   cm.
    Includes bibliographical references (p.   ) and index.
    ISBN 0-8028-2680-6 (pbk.: alk. paper)
    1. Jesus Christ — Person and offices.   I. Title.

    BT203.M338   2004
    232 — dc22

                                    2004040355

www.eerdmans.com

Contents

Preface   vii

Jesus   1
  A Thumbnail Portrait

Piles of Books   7
  A Short History of Jesus Research

Sources and Methods   26
  What Can We Know? How Can We Know It?

The Palestinian Context   44
  Geography, Politics, Economy, and Religion

The Forerunner   62
  John the Baptist

The Central Message   67
  The Kingdom of God

The Man of Power   82
  Healings, Exorcisms, and Other Works of Wonder

The Teacher   93
Sayings and Parables

The Public Figure   109
Career and Controversies

Approaching the End   120
The Final Week

A New Beginning   129
The Resurrection

Wisdom, Apocalypse, and the Identity of Jesus   133
Some Historical Reflections

Thinking Outside the Boxes   139
A Critique of Contemporary Images of Jesus

Notes   153

Index of Subjects and Names   199

Index of Scripture and Other Ancient Literature   207

Preface

At the time of his death, Jesus of Nazareth was a figure known only to certain Jews in Palestine. Today by contrast, nearly everyone in the world has heard of Jesus. Printed literature, global travel, and the mass media have transmitted some basic information about Jesus to seven billion people. In a sense, the whole world knows Jesus. Yet this most familiar of persons continues to be unfamiliar. Those who have heard of Jesus, and even those who worship him, are often unacquainted with the teachings and stories presented in the Gospels and the possible interpretations of these sayings and doings. Moreover, the enormous effort by scholars to study the life of Jesus — an academic industry in itself — has made Jesus both more accessible and more distant. Recent research has emphasized some basic features of Jesus' life that were overlooked in the past. As scholars have investigated Jesus' social, cultural, and historical context, Jesus has come to appear more human than ever before. In the newer literature, the backdrop for Jesus is not the heavenly scenes and angelic choirs of traditional church art, but rather the fishing villages, dusty roads, political struggles, synagogue services, and religious debates of first-century Palestine. Jesus now appears as a Jewish peasant from Galilee, and that has made him seem earthy and human and approachable. On the other hand, Jesus' culture sets him apart from many modern readers. Those who live in traditional societies in Africa, Asia, and Latin America may feel more kinship with this Galilean peasant Jesus than those residing in Western societies.

The close of the second millennium and start of the third is an exciting time to reconsider the life of Jesus. Most scholars today have greater confidence than they did a generation ago regarding our ability to piece together the essential features of Jesus' life. Despite many points of disagreement, which crop up repeatedly in the pages that follow, the areas of consensus have begun to widen. Jesus was a Jew — that is certain. While hardly an earth-shattering revelation, this simple assertion forces one to read Jesus' life in a rather different way than was characteristic in the past. From the middle of the second century until sometime in the twentieth, Gentile Christians interpreted Jesus so as to leave out his Jewishness. Another basic point: Jesus preached "the kingdom of God." This is another truism, yet it opens up a rich field for interpretation. In some way, the "kingdom" ties into nearly everything that Jesus said or did, and, correspondingly, the meaning that one attaches to "kingdom" affects everything else that one says about Jesus. Furthermore, Jesus taught in parables that made his rich and powerful hearers feel like outsiders, and the poor and powerless feel like insiders. The research of the last generation has permanently altered the picture of Jesus that prevailed throughout much of Christian history, which — with notable exceptions — had little to say regarding Jesus' Jewishness, his proclamation of the kingdom of God, and his approach to the marginalized of his society.

Much of the burgeoning literature on the life of Jesus is quite technical, and that makes it unappealing to the average reader. Some books apparently intended for a lay audience have devoted ten or fifteen pages to the minute and meticulous dissection of a single saying from the Gospels — a level of analysis that is appropriate for professional biblical scholars and exasperating for everyone else. Terminology is also a stumbling block. Scholars need to use a specialized vocabulary to advance their research and to discriminate accurately between opposing points of view. Yet many terms used in the scholarship on Jesus are not familiar, and the discussion becomes hard for most readers to follow. Yet another obstacle arises from the infighting that is characteristic of academic research, and especially biblical scholarship. (Readers might assume that people who study the Bible for a living are nice folks who get along with one another. They might be surprised to drop into an academic conference where biblical debates are conducted like gladiatorial contests!) Generally speaking, scholars are inclined by temperament and by training to emphasize their *differences* from other scholars. But when disagreements are exaggerated, it is hard for the layperson to see the forest for the trees. Imagine a mayoral debate where the candidates, rather than covering the entire range of issues, spent half their time discussing the number of dogcatchers who were out on the streets and the other half evaluating the merits of one elementary school.

Sometimes the scholarly debates on Jesus are just as narrowly defined and removed from the concerns of laypersons.

This book provides a summary of recent historical research on the life of Jesus. If there is something distinctive in the work, it consists less in originality — which is hard if not impossible to achieve in this area — and more in the effort toward comprehensiveness, balance, and brevity. After showing the manuscript to a number of biblical scholars who approach the life of Jesus with differing historical and theological assumptions, I found to my surprise and pleasure that my presentation won favor with all of them. Readers must decide for themselves if I have been fair-minded and faithful in presenting and evaluating the various points of view on the issues, but I can say that this has been my aim throughout the text. For the most part I have accentuated the widely accepted points about the life of Jesus, such as those mentioned above, and have given less attention to issues that are doubtful, obscure, speculative, or imponderable. Many questions about Jesus cannot be answered from the historical sources we possess. Much as we might like to know about Jesus' adolescence and early manhood, there are no reliable accounts or data on this matter, and so the books that promise startling new revelations regarding the "missing years" are founded on wishful thinking.

Though I have steered clear of technicalities in discussing the life of Jesus, I have also tried to avoid "dumbing down" my presentation. Many issues in the study of Jesus are complex and cannot be simplified beyond a certain level without distortion. The most challenging sections of the book for lay readers will probably be the second and third chapters, which treat the history of Jesus research and the sources and methods used for study. The fourth chapter, on the first-century Palestinian context, includes helpful background information but is not absolutely essential for understanding what follows. Those who want to get only the "bare bones" might read the short first chapter and then jump ahead to the fifth chapter on John the Baptist and the subsequent chapters on the major themes and periods of Jesus' life.

The notes to the chapters are informative and yet not necessary reading for those who are interested in the main flow of the book. They provide documentation and give references for further reading on particular topics. The notes allow the reader to follow some of the major scholarly debates on Jesus, with arguments, quotations, and bibliography that would prove cumbersome if included in the main text. Unless otherwise indicated, all biblical quotations are taken from the New Revised Standard Version. Following the usual convention in academic studies of the Bible, I generally refer to the collected books of the Hebrew scriptures as the "Hebrew Bible," rather than the "Old Testament," since the former designation is one that both Jewish and Christian scholars find acceptable. For the same reason, I refer to dates as "common era" (c.e.) and "before common era" (b.c.e.).

Something needs to be said at the outset regarding the vexatious issue of "faith and history," as it is called, and my stance in approaching it. The academic study of Jesus leads into certain ineluctable questions: What sort of relationship exists between the "historical Jesus" uncovered by scholarly inquiry and the "Christ of faith" who is preached on and believed in by Christians? Are these one and the same, or are they distinct from one another? If they are distinct, then is the historical Jesus irrelevant to Christian faith? Does research on Jesus' life have any bearing on what people choose to believe? Does historical inquiry undermine an attitude of trust and faith in the Gospels and their message concerning Jesus? Alternatively, could academic research serve to support and encourage the attitude of faith? Obviously these are large and deep questions, and entire books could be devoted to considering and answering them. Recently the eminent New Testament scholar Luke Timothy Johnson has registered his grave reservations about the entire enterprise of historical Jesus studies. He argues that the effort to reconstruct the life of Jesus has resulted in "the discrediting of the gospel portraits of Jesus," and given rise to "fantasies and abstractions" that are "incapable . . . of galvanizing human lives." They present Jesus as "a dead person of the past" rather than a Living Lord.[1] Rarely has a biblical scholar written as pointedly on this matter as Professor Johnson, and yet his outlook is widely shared by the rank and file of the churches, who typically view historical Jesus studies as irrelevant to faith or as destructive to it.

If you are among those who turn up their noses at Jesus research, then I hope to change your attitude with this book. Though I share Professor Johnson's concerns, I cannot agree with his proposal to separate the "Christ of faith" from the exigencies of academic investigation. Sound historical scholarship, in my view, is not antithetical to faith. My position is that the "historical Jesus" is neither identical to, nor wholly detached from, the "Christ of faith." The Christian message claims to be based on actual events in history connected with the birth, life, teachings, works, death, and resurrection of Jesus of Nazareth. Consequently one cannot isolate or insulate the "Christ of faith" from historical arguments, claims, and counterclaims. To do so would be to turn the Christian message and Jesus himself into a pretty story and nothing more. On the other hand — and here I am in league with Johnson — the "historical Jesus" is an academic construct that does not include all that believers say they believe or think or know regarding Jesus.

A simple analogy may help. Imagine a woman, whom we will call Marie, who was born and lived and died in the city of Chicago. More than thirty years have elapsed since her death, and yet Marie was a remarkable woman — a wife, mother, coworker, and friend to many, and so she endures in the memories of many people and in the form of written documents and a few published accounts concerning her. Those who knew Marie, if they so desired, could assemble themselves in an effort to reconstruct "the historical Marie." Now would the "historical Marie" established by reliable memories or textual sources be one and the same with Marie as she was experienced by those around her during her life? Of course not. It is likely that only a small portion of her character and conduct would have passed into the documents and the memories of her. Now this analogy can be applied to the "historical Jesus" and "Christ of faith" if we observe that Christian faith claims to be a form of direct acquaintance with Jesus. Multitudes of people say they "know Jesus" apart from any process of historical inquiry and certainly without having read a book like this one. (The Danish philosopher Søren Kierkegaard said that from the standpoint of faith, everyone is Jesus' contemporary. In terms of faith, there is no distinction then between the first century and the twenty-first century.) Hence there is a rough correspondence between the "historical Jesus" and the woman Marie as reconstructed by investigation and research, and, on the other side, the "Christ of faith" and Marie as known by direct acquaintance during life. Believers will not equate the historical Jesus with the Christ of faith, even as Marie's family and friends will not identify the historically documented woman with the person they have known. On the other hand, just as Marie's own children might gain new insight into their mother by reading an account of her life based on documented accounts, so Christian believers can profit by studying the literature on the historical Jesus.

This book is intended for Christians of all traditions and denominations — Roman Catholics, Protestants, Evangelicals, Anglicans, Orthodox Christians, Pentecostals, Charismatics, and nondenominationalists — and for Jews, Muslims, Hindus, Buddhists, Confucians, Taoists, adherents of new religions, agnostics, atheists, spiritual seekers, and those who fit into none of the above categories. It might be put to use in college, university, and seminary classrooms, and also in church-based study groups or book discussions.

I would like to acknowledge the helpful suggestions and corrections of David Noel Freedman, whose erudition in biblical studies saved me from error more than once. Robert Gundry also read the manuscript in its entirety and provided incisive commentary. Thanks are due to my research assistant, Chris Crain, who helped by supplying sources and checking references in Judaic texts. Michael Farley procured books for the final revisions, and made many helpful suggestions. Keith Smith, with lawyerly tact and skill, convinced me to rethink my chapter on the resurrection of Jesus. All remaining errors of fact and interpretation are entirely my own.

I wish to convey my heartfelt appreciation to the Atlanta gang that read through the text and gave me feedback during my year as a Visiting Scholar at Emory University. Included in the group were Chuck Fell, who organized the meetings, Jeanne Fell, Keith Smith, Marni Bender, Dr. Jonathan Lace, Kathy Underwood, Melanie Benedict, Mary Beth Cox, and Ron Moolenaar. I am also indebted to my graduate seminar at Saint Louis University, including Dr. Bill Shea, Dr. Belden Lane, Michael Farley, Jonathan Barlow, Father Andre Mhanna, and David Miros. Though I failed to follow through on many of their suggestions for revising this book, that is not their fault. People with Ph.D.s are a stubborn lot.

A final thought for this preface: Those who feel a familiarity with Jesus may find that much becomes unfamiliar and downright strange to them as they read and study further. Conversely, those who feel unfamiliar with Jesus may discover a growing sense of familiarity. Both the followers of Jesus and those who are not his followers may benefit if the familiar Jesus becomes a bit stranger and the strange Jesus becomes a little more familiar.

Jesus

A Thumbnail Portrait

As a basis for what follows, we may begin with a brief chronological survey of Jesus' life. A few events of his life are all but indisputable, and there are some equally secure facts regarding the aftermath of his life. Together these form a solid foundation for understanding Jesus and his influence. Here are the most essential points:

> Jesus was born around 4 B.C.E., before the time of the death of Herod the Great. He spent his childhood and early adult years in Nazareth, a Galilean village. He was baptized by John the Baptist. He called disciples. He taught in the towns, villages, and countryside of Galilee, and apparently not in the cities. He preached "the kingdom of God." He taught in parables and was known for effecting remarkable cures, including exorcisms. He associated with the disreputable people of his society and had female as well as male followers. About the year 30 C.E. he went to Jerusalem for Passover. He created a disturbance in the Temple area. He had a final meal with his disciples. He was arrested and interrogated by Jewish authorities, specifically the high priest. He was executed on the orders of the Roman prefect, Pontius Pilate. His disciples at first fled. They saw him again (in some sense) following his death. As a consequence, they believed that he would return to found the kingdom of God. They formed a community to await his return and sought to win others to faith in him as God's Messiah.[1]

It is possible to expand on the above points.[2] His family was Jewish, as is clear from the names of his parents (Joseph and Mary) and his brothers (Jacob, Joses, Judas, and Simon).[3] (Traditionally, the brothers have been interpreted as Jesus' stepbrothers, half brothers, or kinsmen.)[4] Jesus' father was a building artisan or a carpenter (Matt. 13:55), as Jesus himself may have been prior to his public career. Jesus' mother tongue was Galilean Aramaic, or perhaps a Hebrew dialect that had survived in Galilee. Like many of his contemporaries, Jesus presumably could speak some Greek, yet the sayings that the Gospels attribute to him in Greek derive from an Aramaic original; Aramaic was the language he used in his public discourses. No reliable information exists regarding his education, yet Jesus may have been able both to read and to write.[5] One Gospel passage (Luke 4:16-20) speaks of him reading aloud in the synagogue.

It is possible that virtually all of Jesus' active ministry, with the exception of the last few weeks, occurred in Galilee during the reign of Herod Antipas. How often Jesus traveled to Jerusalem remains unclear, since the synoptic Gospels seem to speak of only one journey to Jerusalem and the Gospel of John speaks of multiple journeys. Jesus was apparently not an urbanite. The cities of Galilee — Sepphoris, Tiberias, and Scythopolis (Hebrew Beth-Shean) — do not figure in the Gospel accounts of Jesus' activities. Doubtless Jesus knew of Sepphoris, which was only a few miles from Nazareth, but he may have regarded his own mission as centered on the Jews of the villages and small towns in Galilee. Nazareth itself was a small village of less than two thousand tucked away in the hill country, not bordering the Sea of Galilee. Yet Jesus taught principally in the towns and villages on the sea, and fishermen were among his first followers. Rural images frequently appear in the teaching recorded in the Gospels.

When Jesus was a young man, perhaps in his late twenties, John the Baptist began to preach a message of repentance in light of the coming judgment by God. John's message was "apocalyptic" or "eschatological" — two terms that refer to the whole constellation of beliefs about the end of history and the transformation of the world, including the afterlife, judgment, the resurrection of the dead, the Messiah's reign, and the final states of heaven and hell. (These words are defined and characterized more precisely in the chapter entitled "The Central Message.") Jesus heard John and felt called to accept baptism at his hands. All four Gospels point to Jesus' baptism as a decisive and life-changing event. Jesus "saw the heavens torn apart and the Spirit descending like a dove on him," and he also heard a voice saying "You are my Son, the Beloved" (Mark 1:9-11). Herod Antipas had John the Baptist arrested because he had criticized his marriage to

Herodias (so say the Gospels) and/or because he feared that John's preaching might lead to insurrection (so says the Jewish historian Josephus). At about this time Jesus began his public ministry. While John had worked outside of the settled areas, Jesus went from town to town and usually preached in synagogues on Sabbath days. He called a small number of people to be his disciples, including a group that became known as "the Twelve." Unlike John, Jesus not only preached but also healed the sick. The crowds may have gathered to see miraculous healings, yet they stayed to hear Jesus teach in parables and explain the "kingdom of God."

Jesus was known among his contemporaries for exorcism or the casting out of demons. Yet this activity on Jesus' part does not imply that his special authority came from his psychological ability or supernatural power. On the contrary, the sayings connected with the exorcisms indicate that Jesus viewed them as the visible sign of a victory over Satan and the beginning of the rule or kingdom of God. "But if it is by the Spirit of God that I cast out demons, then the kingdom of God has come to you" (Matt. 12:28). This suggests that Jesus viewed himself as the mediator of God's rule.

The announcement of God's kingdom was one of the most important aspects of Jesus' career, one that he took over from his kinsman and predecessor John the Baptist. Yet Jesus' emphasis seems to have been different from John's. Unlike John, Jesus did not stress a future coming of God for judgment but rather a call to participate here and now in the kingdom of God. The difference between Jesus and John is shown in that John's disciples fasted while Jesus' did not (at least during his lifetime; Mark 2:18-20). The parables of Jesus were central to his proclamation of God's rule, in that each parable expressed a particular aspect of God's rule. They were not illustrations of timeless truths but statements through which God's kingdom became a living message for Jesus' hearers.

In Jesus' parables it becomes clear that the coming of God's rule is God's own act and that human action does not determine how or when it arrives (Mark 4:26-29). Moreover, God's kingdom contradicts human notions of right and wrong (Luke 16:1-9), religious standards of value (Luke 18:9-14), and the idea of just rewards (Matt. 20:1-16). God's love exceeds all expectations, as in the famous parable of the prodigal son (Luke 15:11-32). Characteristically the parables of Jesus involve an element of surprise. The stories begin within the framework of customary ideas but often conclude with a twist in the plotline and an assertion of unconventional wisdom.

What kind of farmer would do nothing during the entire growing season, allowing the weeds to sprout up with the crops (Matt. 13:30)? Or when did a rich man ever invite hooligans and street people to his lavish party after the distinguished guests declined the invitations (Matt. 22:10)? Or what father would be so undignified as to run down the street to embrace an unworthy son who just squandered his entire inheritance (Luke 15:20)? Jesus' parables underscore the mystery and incalculability of God's kingdom.

Jesus affirmed and emphasized the command to love one's neighbor (Mark 12:31), which already held a central place within Judaism (Lev. 19:18). Yet he rejected a practice of loving others because they love you, or loving only the people of one's own family, social, or ethnic groups. Indeed Jesus commanded love for one's enemies (Matt. 5:44). Thus he taught that power and force are not the way that God's kingdom will be established (Matt. 26:52-54). What is more, the person who wants to follow Jesus must be prepared to suffer, and even to lose his or her life (Mark 8:34-35). Discipleship means to give up one's security (Luke 9:62), one's possessions (Luke 14:33), and one's identification with family and kin (Luke 14:26).

Jesus' itinerant ministry probably lasted from one to three years, and was concluded by his visit to Jerusalem during Passover (Matt. 21-27; Mark 11-15; Luke 19-23). Jesus rode into the city on a donkey, and some people hailed him at that time as the "son of David." When he went into the Temple precincts, he confronted the moneychangers and those who sold doves to be used in Temple sacrifice. The high priest and his advisers decided that Jesus was dangerous and had to die. After Jesus shared a final meal with his followers, he went apart to pray, and was then betrayed by one of his followers to the high priest's guards. He was tried in some fashion, and was then turned over to the Roman prefect, Pontius Pilate, with the recommendation that he be executed. After a hearing to consider the case, the prefect ordered the execution, and Jesus was put to death by crucifixion for treason against the government, along with two others.

He died after a relatively brief period of suffering on the cross. A few of his followers placed him in a tomb. According to reports that circulated among his early followers, some of the disciples returned to the tomb about two days following his burial to find an empty tomb. Then his followers saw him again in some fashion, and became convinced that Jesus was alive again, that God had acted in his death to bring salvation, and that he would return again in glory and power. The early community used titles to describe Jesus, such as "Anointed" ("Messiah" in Hebrew or "Christ" in

Greek), "Lord," and "Son of God." As the decades passed, the followers of Jesus became more and more distinct from Judaism at large, and finally emerged as a largely Gentile Christian church. Yet at the time the Gospels were written, this parting of the ways between Jewish and Gentile Christians, on the one hand, and all other Jews, on the other hand, was still occurring.

A number of uncertainties plague the chronology of Jesus' life — the sort of problems that plague almost all studies of ancient history.[6] Unable to appeal to any universally accepted calendar, and often unable to gain access to archives that provided a fixed chronological reference, ancient authors often provided dates that were indefinite. Matthew seems to place Jesus' birth late in Herod's reign (6-4 B.C.E.), while Luke links the birth to the census under Quirinius, who became legate of Syria after Herod's death. (Various proposals have been made to explain the apparent discrepancy.[7]) Yet the general time and place parameters of Jesus' birth are fairly clear. The Gospels mention Augustus Caesar (31 B.C.E.–14 C.E.) at the time of Jesus' birth and Tiberius (14-37 C.E.) later in his life. When Jesus was executed, Pontius Pilate was prefect of Judea (26-36 C.E.) and Caiaphas was high priest (18-36 C.E.). Thus the conclusion is that Jesus was killed between 26 and 36 — based on three "big names" in Palestine — Tiberius, Pilate, and Caiaphas.

Taking into account this broad information, and Luke's dating (Luke 3:1) of the beginning of John's ministry in the fifteenth year of Tiberius, together with additional information from the chronology of Paul's life, most scholars are content to say that Jesus was executed sometime between 29 and 33. The exact date of Jesus' birth is not known, since there is no information in the Gospels regarding the day and the month. Concerning Jesus' death, the synoptic Gospels agree in their presentation that Jesus died on 15 Nisan. The Gospel of John might place it one day earlier, on 14 Nisan, though there are theories to account for the apparent discrepancy.

It is hard to find categories from Jesus' own cultural context by which to describe Jesus and his ministry. What we learn from the Gospels regarding Jesus only partially fits prevailing ideas regarding a religious office or mission at that time. Messianic or christological titles, such as "Messiah"/ "Christ," "Son of David," "Son of God," "Son of Man," and "Lord," were applied to Jesus by the earliest Christians, but scholars debate whether Jesus applied any such title or titles to himself. The title "priest" or "high priest" is applied to Jesus relatively late, and only in very limited circles of early

Christianity (as in the Epistle to the Hebrews). Philosophical influences were present in Palestine beginning with the Hellenistic period, and yet Jesus was not in any sense a wandering philosopher or a school philosopher. Not until the time of the Christian apologists in the early second century was there an effort to combine Jesus' teachings with philosophical insights. Furthermore, Jesus does not fit the general profile of the apocalyptic seer or visionary. He did not present a specific timetable of future events, nor is there any tradition of Jesus taking a celestial journey, which are both common characteristics among ancient apocalyptic authors. There is no evidence that he ever used written communication — something very important within apocalypticism.

In many respects Jesus' words and actions reflected the earlier Israelite traditions of the prophets and wisdom teachers. Like the prophets of old, Jesus made clear and unequivocal declarations concerning God's will, rather than elaborate legal judgments regarding right and wrong in specific circumstances. Like the earlier wisdom teachers, he preferred simple sayings, proverbs, metaphors, and parables to the speculative and spiritualizing literature that had become more common in Judaism during the preceding centuries. Yet despite Jesus' recourse to prophetic and wisdom traditions that were centuries removed from his day, there is no artificial or archaic tendency in his teachings. Rather, his words and actions come across as a renewal of much earlier Israelite traditions.

At the same time, many of the typical signs of a prophet or wisdom teacher are absent from the reports about Jesus. There is no tradition recording Jesus' call to prophethood in the customary sense, nor are there reports of visions of God, voices from heaven, or other stories about his receiving a prophetic commission. (The story of Jesus' baptism bears only a partial analogy to the earlier Israelite stories of prophetic calling.) Jesus does not introduce his sayings with the common prophetic formula "Thus says the Lord." In Jesus' wisdom teaching there is no appeal to sayings given by earlier sages and teachers, or to their reliable transmission across generations. Consequently it is clear that Jesus' preaching is quite different from rabbinical instruction. As Helmut Koester notes, "The visible documentation of Jesus' authority thus remains an enigma. Whoever wants to understand Jesus' authority is referred absolutely to his words and to that which they say and announce."[8]

Piles of Books

A Short History of Jesus Research

On the vast subject of Jesus, one might think that nothing new could or would be said. Yet recently much has changed. Only two or three decades ago, many scholars approached the biblical texts with the assumption that very little could actually be known regarding Jesus. Rudolf Bultmann, representing this earlier viewpoint, made the famous assertion: "I do indeed think that we can now know almost nothing concerning the life and personality of Jesus, since the early Christian sources show no interest in either, are moreover fragmentary and often legendary; and other sources about Jesus do not exist."[1] As a spokesperson for the more recent school of thought, E. P. Sanders has declared, "The dominant view today seems to be that we can know pretty well what Jesus was out to accomplish, that we can know a lot about what he said, and that those two things make sense within the world of first-century Judaism."[2] The Jewish scholar Paul Winter makes a similar claim: "The last decade [of the 1970s] has seen an amazing transformation. Now, the Jesus of history seems more accessible than ever. Like archaeologists swarming over a prime location, the historians and theologians have turned with gusto to the original documents, parallel historical records, and the geographical sites, and at every turn have found a clearer and clearer picture emerging of Jesus of Nazareth."[3]

Sanders and Winter are not alone. A host of English-language scholars have blazed a new trail back to the first century, including such authors as Dale Allison, Craig Blomberg, Raymond E. Brown, Marcus Borg, James H. Charlesworth, Bruce Chilton, John Dominic Crossan, F. G. Downing, James Dunn, Bart Ehrman, Craig Evans, Harvey Falk, Paula Fredriksen, Sean Freyne, Robert Funk, A. E. Harvey, Richard Horsley, Luke Timothy Johnson, Burton L. Mack, Scot McKnight, John P. Meier, Ben F.

Meyer, Pheme Perkins, Jonathan L. Reed, John Riches, Ellis Rivkin, Morton Smith, Geza Vermès, David Wenham, Ben Witherington III, and N. T. Wright. All of these writers in varying ways have attempted what Bultmann thought impossible: a reconstruction of Jesus' life history, teachings, actions, and early following, based on a judicious reading of the ancient sources. Some today are convinced that we can know as much about Jesus as we can about any figure of the ancient world. While we do not have the fullness of biographical detail and the wealth of firsthand accounts that are available for recent public figures, such as Winston Churchill or Mother Teresa, we nonetheless have much more data on Jesus than we do for such ancient figures as Alexander the Great.[4]

An outsider to the academic guild is bound to wonder: Why the shift from severe skepticism to cautious confidence? Are professors of Bible as faddish as Parisian clothes designers, whose occupation requires them to invent new styles? Without denying the reality of academic fads, much of the current thinking on Jesus rests on new sources of information and new methods of interpreting the old sources. The last half-century has witnessed the deciphering and eventual publication of the Dead Sea Scrolls — a revolutionary event in the study of ancient Jewish culture. Archaeology in the ancient Near East has also become more closely intertwined with the study of ancient texts, often confirming or disproving the conjectures of textual scholars and pointing out promising new directions for inquiry.[5] Today's student of the Hebrew Bible, New Testament, or early Judaism can learn much from studies of the material culture of the ancients. The social sciences, too, have played a large part in encouraging new paths of interpretation. A cadre of capable scholars has applied social-scientific methods to the investigation of biblical texts, using such categories as social class, gender, kinship, patron-client relations, ethnocentrism, purity rules, urban-rural distinctions, and social marginalization to open up new perspectives on old texts.[6] The comparative study of millenarian movements throughout the world has also shed light on Judaic and New Testament apocalypticism.[7]

Last but by no means least among the factors, recent investigations into first-century Judaism have unveiled a rich and varied picture of religious life that defies the stereotypes regarding "the scribes and Pharisees" that prevailed in most of nineteenth- and early twentieth-century scholarship on Jesus. A number of major works have demonstrated that Jesus had more in common with Jewish religious leaders than previously imagined.[8]

Christian scholars have more than ever relied on work done by Jewish colleagues, while numerous Jewish writers have sought to reclaim Jesus as a major teacher within the Judaic tradition. According to one account, more was written about Jesus in Hebrew from about 1950 to 1975 than during the preceding eighteen hundred years![9] And this trend has continued up to the present. A spate of recent books all emphasize the *Jewishness* of Jesus.[10] This stress on the Judaic context is crucial to the major reconstructions of Jesus' life and activity by E. P. Sanders, John P. Meier, and N. T. Wright, though, as we will see in what follows, it is less prominent in the works on Jesus by such figures as Burton L. Mack and John Dominic Crossan.

Everyone who studies Jesus is stepping into a stream that has been flowing for generations.[11] It may be helpful therefore to survey the path that has already been traced in studies of the historical Jesus during the last two centuries. Prior to the late 1700s it is very difficult to find any attempts at a biography or a life of Christ. The apocryphal texts of early Christianity sought to fill in the missing years of Jesus' life, and the medieval period witnessed miracle plays and Gospel paraphrases based on episodes in the biblical texts. A life of Christ in the modern sense only arrives near the middle of the nineteenth century.[12] Yet when we consider the last 150 years, there is a great deal to be learned from earlier investigations. To a remarkable degree the issues, motifs, agendas, and dilemmas of earlier researchers continue to find expression in the more recent works.[13]

The book that did more than any other to sum up nineteenth-century scholarship on the life of Jesus, and to set the tone for twentieth-century research, was Albert Schweitzer's *Quest of the Historical Jesus,* published in German in 1906 and in English in 1910. Indeed, Schweitzer's work was so influential that it may have encouraged some misunderstandings regarding historical-Jesus research. Schweitzer gave the impression that scholarly research on Jesus was part of a unified "quest" and that this began with Hermann Samuel Reimarus (1694-1768). In fact, Reimarus drew extensively on the work of earlier writers and especially the English Deists.[14] As N. T. Wright points out, the general impression of a single overarching quest for the historical Jesus does not do justice to the diversity of methods and aims among the individual researchers of the nineteenth and twentieth centuries. While some were motivated by a desire to lay a firm historical foundation for the church's faith, others were in search of a more-or-less objective account of the first-century Jesus, and still others had the aim of discrediting Christianity. From the mid-1800s up to the present, there have been innumerable books on Jesus that, in the words of John Dominic Crossan, were theology disguised as history or autobiography in the form of biography.[15] Perhaps the only thing these authors had in common was that each produced a text on Jesus.

The phase of development from Reimarus to Schweitzer, sometimes designated the "first quest" for the historical Jesus, began during an Enlightenment and post-Enlightenment era in which Christian orthodoxy was under assault from rationalism. In differing ways the authors who wrote on the life of Jesus sought to respond to the charge that Christianity was a superstition grounded on an untenable belief in miracles and divine intervention in the world. H. S. Reimarus in essence argued that Jesus was a Jewish revolutionary whose disciples, after his failure and death, conceived the notion that he was divine. They stole his body and then promulgated a new idea regarding his life and significance, according to which the world would end with the arrival of a divine being upon the clouds of heaven. Thus Christianity originated in a kind of double mistake in which Jesus first failed as a revolutionary and then his followers mistakenly expected the immediate end of the world. Reimarus's hypotheses continue to hold significance for many later writers who see the delayed return of the Messiah as a key factor in the early development of Christianity, and for those few who have carried forward the interpretation of Jesus as a revolutionary.[16]

Like Reimarus, David Friedrich Strauss (1808-74) was preoccupied with the issues posed by the apparently supernatural or miraculous aspects of the New Testament. Yet for him a critical rereading of the biblical texts still allowed one to find truth in them. One had to realize that the Gospels are myth rather than history and must be read in accordance with their literary genre. Supernatural events did not and do not occur — here Strauss is at one with the later scholar Bultmann — and the mythical events contained in the New Testament are nonhistorical projections and inventions that reflect the faith of the early Christian community. While Strauss took steps to win the favor of the academic authorities, the publication of his *Life of Jesus* (1835) alienated the conservatives in Germany and brought a swift end to his university career. He entered politics, continued to publish, and influenced academic life through the challenging questions posed in his writings.[17]

While Strauss was finding myth in the Gospel texts, many other writers were in effect using the Gospels to create myth, that is, to fashion a mythicized Jesus that conformed closely to the cultural expectations of well-educated, late nineteenth-century western Europeans. Jesus was not in opposition to the culture of his day, or our own. Instead he was the flower of humanity, revealing the essential genius that lies in the heart of each man and woman. The kingdom of God was not an external realm of laws and regulations but a matter of pure hearts and proper intentions. Jesus' predictions of the world's judgment by God and ultimate demise were carefully omitted from these accounts of his life. For some, especially in North America, the kingdom of God was a program of human betterment that required Christians to devote themselves to the cause. The Jesus of the late nineteenth century was less a savior than a teacher, and his most important instructions were embodied in the "Sermon on the Mount" (Matt. 5–7) and other passages of ethical exhortation.[18] Yet unlike the cool, rational Jesus of the eighteenth-century Enlightenment, the Jesus of nineteenth-century romanticism embodied and encouraged a life of sentiment and feeling. In his *Life of Jesus* (1863), the Frenchman Ernest Renan referred to Jesus as a "sublime person" who "every day still presides over the destiny of the world," so that "his worship will constantly renew its youth, the tale of his life will cause endless tears, his sufferings will soften the best hearts." Given the popularity of books like Renan's — which sold 60,000 copies during its first six months — it is obvious that a sentimentalized Jesus was appealing in an era in which the traditional Christ of church and dogma seemed less compelling.[19]

While the popular biographies of Jesus were sprouting up like mushrooms after a warm summer storm, technical studies of the Gospel texts were also proliferating during the late nineteenth century. H. J. Holtzmann proposed the theory that Mark's Gospel was chronologically prior to Matthew and Luke and served as a source for the two later Gospels — a view still held by the great majority of New Testament scholars. Thus he laid the groundwork for many later studies of the sources of the Gospels. He showed that the ministry of Jesus fell into a series of clear-cut and comprehensible stages, with the decisive turning point in the episode at Caesarea Philippi (Mark 8:27–9:1). Holtzmann has continued to exert an influence through his portrayal of the ministry of Jesus and his belief that source criticism of the Gospels allows us to reconstruct the events that lay behind the birth of Christianity.[20]

A slender book by Johannes Weiss (1863-1914), published in German in 1892, provoked a rethinking of the meaning of "the kingdom of God" in

Jesus' teaching.[21] Together with Schweitzer's book on the quest, Weiss's work led to a rediscovery of the apocalyptic and eschatological elements in Jesus' teaching, which had been largely ignored in nineteenth-century scholarship. (Intellectual history has its ironies: Weiss was the son-in-law of Albrecht Ritschl, perhaps the foremost liberal Protestant thinker in Germany at the time, and Weiss's work propelled scholarship regarding the kingdom of God in a direction opposed to that of Ritschl.) Jesus, according to Weiss, announced the immediate or imminent ending of the world. Yet the great cataclysm did not materialize as predicted. Although various efforts have been made to address Weiss's arguments, the basic issues he posed remained dominant in twentieth-century scholarship, as seen in recent works by Dale Allison and Bart Ehrman.

Schweitzer's *Quest of the Historical Jesus* (1906),[22] which summarized and appraised earlier scholarship and anticipated many twentieth-century trends, is probably still the single most influential book on the historical Jesus. Its lively style and forceful arguments chiseled out a new image of Jesus. Schweitzer argued that Jesus chose to keep secret his messiahship, disclosing it only to the disciples at the transfiguration and then commanding them to tell no one of the experience. Judas then broke the silence by revealing the secret to the chief priests. At the beginning of his ministry, Jesus had expected the end of the age to come in short order, and when this hope was not realized, he went to his death in order to bring upon himself the "messianic woes" that had to be endured before the Jewish people could be delivered. "The Jesus of Nazareth who . . . preached the ethic of the Kingdom of God, who founded the Kingdom of Heaven upon earth," argues Schweitzer, "never had any existence." Yet Schweitzer coupled this negative assertion with the positive affirmation that "Jesus means something to our world because a mighty spiritual force streams forth from Him and flows through our time also." The eschatological sayings regarding the kingdom of God, despite or perhaps even because of their oddity for modern people, "raise the man who dares to meet their challenge . . . above his world and his time, making him inwardly free."[23]

One era of research ended and another began when Schweitzer forthrightly posed the question, in N. T. Wright's words, of "how such a strange and remote Jesus could be relevant in a different culture and time."[24] In many ways this issue of Jesus' relevance continues to dominate scholarship up to the present time. What Schweitzer did was to sharpen an awareness of the cultural distance between ancient and modern times.

When we scrutinize the paintings of biblical scenes done by medieval and early modern artists, we can usually spot any number of anachronisms: Adam is reclining in a garden scene that is obviously Flemish; Mary Magdalene wears a Florentine headdress; and Rembrandt's Jerusalem has the look of a seventeenth-century town. Yet when one reads prose descriptions of Jesus' inner thoughts and feelings, attitudes toward others, and ultimate purposes, it is not as easy to detect what is unhistorical. Schweitzer's significance is that he made it harder for scholars to inject their personal biases — consciously or not — into their interpretations of Jesus. Those who read Jesus as a man of the twentieth century had to do so in defiance of Schweitzer's image of Jesus as a first-century Palestinian Jewish apocalypticist.

During the first half of the twentieth century, the dominant trends in scholarship were not favorable toward an investigation of the historical Jesus. Some have referred to this as the era of "no quest." In part this was due to a failure of nerve subsequent to Schweitzer: How *could* a Jewish apocalyptic prophet speak to the people of the early twentieth century? The neglect of the topic was also due to theological movements, emanating in the German-language countries, which made the life of Jesus largely irrelevant for Christian faith. In the so-called dialectical theology of Karl Barth, Emil Brunner, and Friedrich Gogarten during the 1920s and 1930s, the earthly Jesus met his end on the cross, and at the cross God also rejected and passed judgment against human religiousness and piety. Jesus' earthly life is thus irrelevant, and preoccupation with it can in fact become an impediment to Christian faith and theological reflection. During this period the philosophy of existentialism highlighted the importance of human freedom and decision, but not the rational basis one might have for one's decision. Faith was a "leap" rather than an historical judgment. Existentialist and dialectical thinkers cited a verse from Paul's letters to make the point: "Even though we once knew Christ from a human point of view, we know him no longer in that way" (2 Cor. 5:16).

Rudolf Bultmann (1884-1976), one of the towering figures in twentieth-century New Testament studies, had a dampening effect on historical Jesus research. His literary analyses of the synoptic Gospels attempted to show that the sayings and stories attributed to Jesus actually took their origin in the circumstances of the early Christian movement. Contending parties in the church sought to buttress their positions by coining stories in which Jesus supported their point of view. This approach to the Gospels became known as "form criticism." Furthermore, Bultmann argued in a celebrated essay that the New Testament texts presuppose a prescientific outlook that is unacceptable to contemporary persons. "It is impossible," Bultmann quipped, "to use electric light and the wireless . . . and at the same time believe in the New Testament world of spirits and miracles."[25] In consequence he called for a "demythologization" of the New Testament that would strip away its miraculous elements and preserve its enduring meaning — which happened to coincide with the ideas of the existentialist philosopher Martin Heidegger (1889-1976). Both the form criticism of the Gospel texts and the program of demythologization represented an effort *not* to find Jesus. One of the personal factors driving Bultmann was an idiosyncratic interpretation of Lutheran theology: to find Jesus by historical inquiry would be a human "work," and we must be saved "by faith" and not "by works." In Bultmann's 1934 book *Jesus and the Word,* not much remains of the first-century Jesus except an ongoing challenge to live in existential authenticity. Little is said regarding his actions. Only his sayings remain, and these, filtered through the sieve of Bultmann's critical method, yield only a modicum of material that certainly goes back to Jesus. To reconstruct the life and personality of Jesus himself is neither desirable nor possible. Since Bultmann explained the rise of early Christianity largely in terms of Greek and Hellenistic culture, Jesus' Jewish context was tangential to his research.[26]

Following a common pattern in German academic life, Bultmann's school of thought spawned an opposition movement that revolted against the eminent scholar. A lecture delivered by Ernst Käsemann in 1953 announced the opening of a "new quest" for the historical Jesus. While Käsemann agreed with Bultmann that no one could write a "life of Jesus," he maintained nonetheless that Christianity should not be severed from its historic roots. The earthly Jesus is essential to the faith of the Christian church. Without the historical life of Jesus, faith in a heavenly Christ can easily become fanciful or unreal. In certain respects, though, the post-Bultmannians maintained much of Bultmann's tradition. The apple fell near the tree. Günther Bornkamm's *Jesus of Nazareth* (German 1956; English 1960) kept the miraculous out of the picture and portrayed a Jesus who did not use messianic titles for himself. Bornkamm's Jesus spoke of eschatological fulfillment in the present time rather than the future. All in all, it was the message of Jesus rather than his deeds that remained the primary focus. Nonetheless, Bornkamm parted company with Bultmann on the calling of the twelve apostles. According to the former, this was an actual occurrence during the lifetime of Jesus and not a later tradition deriving from the fact that there were twelve leaders during the time of the earliest church.

Beginning in the mid-1980s, the "Jesus Seminar," under the direction of the American scholars Robert Funk and John Dominic Crossan, has promoted research along the general lines of the post-Bultmannian "new quest." A principal concern has been to establish insofar as possible the actual words spoken by Jesus. Several dozen scholars have participated in the seminar.[27] At their regular meetings the individual Gospel sayings are discussed, debated, and then voted on according to a scale of probability ranging from a high likelihood of genuineness to a near certitude of spuriousness. Members of the Jesus Seminar use one of four different colored beads to indicate their judgment regarding each saying, according to the following formula: red — Jesus said this or something very much like it; pink — he probably said something like this; gray — he did not say this but the idea is close to being his own; black — he did not say this and it represents a later and differing perspective. One member suggested a more down-to-earth interpretation of the colors: red — "that's Jesus!"; pink — "sure sounds like Jesus"; gray — "well, maybe"; and black — "there's been some mistake."[28] The summary conclusion reached by the Jesus Seminar is that only about 18 percent of the sayings attributed to Jesus in the Gospels were actually spoken by him. If this assertion is disturbing to Christian believers, then Funk and the others stress that theological preconceptions should not stand in the way of an open and honest inquiry. The seminar's stated rule is, "Beware of finding a Jesus entirely congenial to you."[29]

The co-founder of the Jesus Seminar, Robert Funk, acknowledges that his work is motivated by a desire to overcome "the tyranny of . . . Schweitzer's eschatological Jesus."[30] As he noted in his opening statement to the seminar in 1985: "We are having increasing difficulty these days in accepting the biblical account of the creation and of the apocalyptic conclusion in anything like a literal sense. . . . What we need is a new fiction. . . . In sum, a new narrative of Jesus, a new Gospel, if you will, that places Jesus differently in the grand scheme, the epic story."[31] To be relevant today, Jesus has to be interpreted as non-eschatological. Some Jesus Seminar participants have an agenda underlying their scholarship, namely, to rescue Jesus from conservative Christianity and especially from fundamentalists and evangelicals.[32] They oppose a literal reading of the Gospels and belief in a literal return of Jesus. In general the seminar participants portray Jesus as a first-century iconoclast and antitraditionalist. He was, in Funk's words, "no goody two-shoes" but "a sort of flower child with an idealistic view of life that is virtually impossible to achieve."[33] The movie director Paul Verhoeven, whose credits include *RoboCop*, *Basic Instinct*, and *Showgirls*, has been in conversation with some members of the seminar about producing a film that would embody and publicize their point of view regarding Jesus.[34]

Connected with the Jesus Seminar and its portrayal of Jesus as a cultural iconoclast is an emphasis on the Hellenistic background of the Gospels and especially Cynic philosophy. Such a stress reverses the idea, generally accepted since Schweitzer, that the more we put Jesus into his historical context, the more Jewish he will turn out to be.[35] John Dominic Crossan and F. Gerald Downing both argue that the wandering ministry of Jesus can best be understood according to the model of the Cynic philosopher-sage.[36] The ancient Cynic was an individual who questioned the cultural values and civilized presuppositions of his society. He appeared everywhere ragged and dirty, carrying wallet, staff, and cloak, and always insuring that his right shoulder remained bare. He never wore shoes and allowed his hair and beard to be long and unkempt. His dress code dramatized his rejection of the material values of society. In a little bag like a rucksack the Cynic carried everything necessary for his vagabond life, and so the bag itself served as a symbol of self-sufficiency. The basic assumption, as Crossan notes, is that "the one who has nothing and wants nothing is totally free."[37] The most famous story regarding the Cynics comes from an earlier period, when the victorious general Alexander the Great encountered the Cynic philosopher Diogenes and asked him if there was anything that he might do for him. "Stand a bit away from the sun" was the answer he got, because Alexander was blocking his light.[38]

One of the most radical new interpretations of Jesus and the Gospels comes from Burton L. Mack, who argues that the Jewish strands in the Gospels are later accretions and that the more authentic traditions show Jesus as akin to the wandering Cynic preachers. Jesus, according to Mack, was in no sense an apocalyptic or eschatological prophet. Instead he was a popular sage, a wordsmith who uttered pithy aphorisms that shocked his hearers and forced them to reflect on themselves and their social and personal situations. His death by crucifixion was not directly related to his life and teachings, and might be called accidental. He may have been in the wrong place at the wrong time and so have gotten himself arrested by the Romans along with some Jewish insurrectionists.[39] The eschatological imagery in the New Testament texts originated subsequent to Jesus. In effect Mack has reversed the customary order of development. For him, the Hellenistic or sapiential (i.e., wisdom) traditions must have come earlier, while the Jewish and apocalyptic elements arose later. The Gospel of Mark served to create a "myth" of a cosmic Savior that in no sense corresponded to the earthly life of Jesus.[40]

A benefit of the studies by Crossan and Downing is that they have led to a closer examination of the non-Jewish background to the Gospels. In light of their arguments, it is not so easy to isolate Palestinian Judaism from the wider cultural influences and resonances of Greco-Roman antiquity. At the same time, Downing's argument is weakened by the lack of evidence for a Cynic presence in Galilee in Jesus' day and by the fact that his argument for parallels between Jesus' teaching and that of the Cynics relies on texts that come from different geographical regions and chronological periods. Crossan, too, in his argument for Jesus as a Palestinian Jewish Cynic, has to admit that there are discrepancies between the New Testament injunctions for the apostolic preachers and the basic ground rules that applied to Cynic preachers. Both sets of texts agree that one is to wear no sandals and waste no time in greetings and gossip along the way. Yet the Gospel texts forbid the use of staff and wallet, while the Cynics required it, and indeed, constantly harp on the importance of cloak, staff, and bag or wallet.[41] Another problem is that the Cynics were extremely individualistic and probably were never gathered together into any sort of social grouping — a decisive point of difference from the early movement around Jesus.[42] There is also a religious element in the Gospel instructions that is lacking in the Cynic texts. Jesus' disciples viewed themselves not as self-sufficient but as dependent on God to provide for their necessities. Material provision was to come through generous individuals who would provide food and lodging during the preaching expeditions, and this was a reflection of God's active care for those engaged in the task of proclaiming the kingdom of God.[43] Still another problem with the interpretation of Jesus as a Cynic sage is that it fails to provide a convincing rationale for Jesus' execution by the Roman authorities. His death by crucifixion — a well-attested fact, as shown below — implies that he was perceived as a threat to imperial power in a way that a typical Cynic philosopher was not.[44]

The Jesus Seminar and the Cynic interpretation of Jesus stand in a certain tension with a broader phenomenon of the 1980s and 1990s that has been dubbed "the third quest" for the historical Jesus (in distinction from the "old quest" prior to Schweitzer and the "new quest" of the post-Bultmannians). N. T. Wright stresses that this third quest is more diffuse than cohesive: "The current wave of books about Jesus offers a bewildering range of competing hypotheses. There is no unifying theological agenda; no final agreement about method; certainly no common set of results. But there are certain features which justify a unifying label."[45] Probably the most distinctive feature of the third quest is its reliance on our greatly expanded knowledge of Second Temple Judaism as a background for understanding Jesus. This stress on the Jewish context creates an affinity between third-quest authors and Schweitzer, and sets them against most nineteenth-century scholars, Bultmann, the post-Bultmannians, and the Cynic-Hellenistic interpretation of Jesus propounded by Crossan and others in the Jesus Seminar. To simplify somewhat, the fault line in contemporary Jesus studies runs between two tectonic plates, one representing Jesus as a Jewish apocalypticist and another as a Hellenistic Cynic. Much of the friction and fire of today's scholarship arises from the pressure between them.

The third-quest authors, such as E. P. Sanders, John Meier, Ben F. Meyer, N. T. Wright, and Marcus Borg (who also is a participant in the Jesus Seminar), are rereading first-century sources such as Josephus and situating Jesus in relation to the social, political, economic, and religious forces of his day. They pose a set of basic questions, such as: What was Jesus' intention in his life and ministry? What was his relationship to his contemporaries? Why did he die, and why did Christianity begin? The methods used by these authors are based less on theological considerations than on the ordinary canons of historical inquiry: hypothesis and verification, the testing of sources, the use of material culture to supplement textual data, and so forth. Ben Meyer has written a work on Jesus' aims and highlights the restoration of Israel as the theme that underlies his proclamation of the kingdom of God. He distinguishes Jesus' public and private messages and argues that he intended for his public actions (such as table fellowship with sinners) to allow the question of his role or identity to emerge. Jesus looked toward the emergence of a new community, involving a renewal of the covenant and the promise of the forgiveness of sins. Contrary to Bultmann and the Bultmannian school, Meyer affirms that the early Christian community in its interpretation of Jesus was simply deciphering the powerful clues and indications concerning his identity that he himself bequeathed to it.[46]

A. E. Harvey's Bampton Lectures at Oxford University, published in 1982, proceed from the assumption that Jesus must be understood in terms of the "historical constraints" that operated within the culture of his place and time. Regarding the religious law or Torah, Harvey notes that while Jesus started from the common assumption of the legitimacy and authority of the Jewish legal requirements, he "put his teaching in the form of instructions appropriate to exceptional circumstances."[47] This consideration leads Harvey to a further examination of Jesus' sense of time and eschatology and the significance of his miracles. He concludes that Jesus was known as Messiah, though without any divine overtones, during his own lifetime. Since the constraint of monotheism meant that no Jew would or could have thought of himself as God, we must think of Jesus as possessing a uniqueness in his actions rather than in his being per se.

Marcus Borg, in his many books and articles, may be regarded as a third-quest author who also embodies some of the emphases of the Jesus Seminar.[48] He argues that Jesus was non-eschatological and that his message set him at odds with the "politics of holiness" that characterized the religious leaders of his day. Jesus emerges as a cultural critic and iconoclast, and not an apocalyptic prophet. On the other hand, Borg is more attentive than Crossan to the Jewish background. Jesus did not intend to create a new religion, but rather wished to effect a "revitalization" of the Jewish tradition in which he had been reared. His actions and teaching took place in the Jewish context of Torah and Temple: "His challenge . . . was not a complete overthrowing or disregard of tradition. . . . He was a Jew who treasured his tradition. He quoted Scripture, explicitly affirmed the Ten Commandments, and so far as we know observed the Jewish law all his life."[49] At the same time, Jesus challenged the "conventional wisdom" that established clear-cut and insuperable boundaries between good people and bad, men and women, and Jews and Gentiles. Jesus spoke of a compassionate God and required his disciples to follow a "way of transformation" that involved a dying to their old way of thinking and being, the implanting of a new heart, and a practice of centering in God's Spirit. More than other recent authors on Jesus, Borg stresses Jesus' spirituality and his call for others to imitate his spirituality.

E. P. Sanders, in numerous works, has placed special emphasis on Jesus' relation to first-century Judaism.[50] He views Jesus with an historian's eye, and not through the lens of piety or theology. At the same time, Sanders believes that the Gospels contain a good deal of reliable historical information. With other third questers, Sanders is unsatisfied with an approach to Jesus that fixates on his words and speculates regarding the possible transmissional history of the reported sayings. Not all of our questions are answerable. "Our sources contain information about Jesus," says Sanders, "but we cannot get at it by dogmatically deciding that some sentences are completely accurate and some are fiction. The truth will usually lie somewhere in between."[51]

Sanders's general method is to start from the actions rather than the words of Jesus, and to construct an overall picture of Jesus by beginning first with the events in Jesus' life that may be regarded as indubitable: that he was baptized by John the Baptist, that he was a Galilean who preached and healed, that he was crucified by the Roman authorities, and so on. Sanders highlights Jesus' action in the Temple, which was less a "cleansing" of the Temple than a symbolic destruction of it. This one episode is an indication that Jesus' message fell within the general bounds of the first-century "Jewish restoration eschatology," according to which God would act in history to reestablish his kingdom and erect a new Temple in Jerusalem. The action in the Temple was probably the specific event that triggered Jesus' arrest and crucifixion by the Romans. Sanders leaves certain questions unresolved, such as the hotly debated issue of whether Jesus referred to himself as "the Son of Man." The reported disputes between Jesus and the Pharisees are for the most part a reflection of later church-synagogue controversies, according to Sanders. Yet there are reliably reported sayings of Jesus that indicate that he departed from at least some of the central Jewish teachings, such as the imperative of attending to the burial of one's parents.[52]

John Meier is currently completing a monumental study of the historical Jesus, *A Marginal Jew*, with three volumes already published and another forthcoming. Meier's work is probably the most meticulous and exhaustive of any of the third-quest authors. The endnotes to his chapters provide an encyclopedic survey of opinions on each topic he treats. The "historical Jesus," as Meier explains, is always a "scientific construct" or "theoretical abstraction" that prescinds from what the Christian faith or later church teaching says about Jesus. It neither affirms nor denies any theological claims. To explain his project, Meier whimsically imagines a discussion among a Catholic, a Protestant, a Jew, and an agnostic who are locked in the bowels of the Harvard Divinity School and must remain there on a spartan diet until they have hammered out a consensus document on who Jesus was and what he intended. *A Marginal Jew* is Meier's effort to anticipate the conclusions reached by such an "unpapal conclave."[53]

Meier regards Jesus as "marginal" in several senses. He was but a "blip" on the radar screen of ancient history. He forsook an honorable place in society and adopted an unusual way of life. He broke with the beliefs of his day in his teachings on voluntary celibacy and the impermissibility of divorce. He came from the periphery of society and had no upper-class claim to legitimate himself in the eyes of the aristocracy. Finally, by the end of his life "he had managed to make himself appear obnoxious, dangerous, or suspicious to everyone from pious Pharisees through political high priests to an ever vigilant Pilate," and so was pushed altogether out of society by his gruesome and embarrassing death.[54] Generally Meier's portrayal of Jesus, or what we have of it thus far, is in accord with other recent authors who stress Jesus' Jewish background. Meier is skeptical regarding the noncanonical *Gospel of Thomas*, holding that it does not add any significant new historical information to the picture of Jesus contained in the canonical Gospels.[55] Differing from E. P. Sanders, Meier maintains that the kingdom of God in the teaching of Jesus is not wholly futuristic but contains a present aspect as well. For him the kingdom is present and future, both experienced and anticipated.[56] In his wide-ranging treatment of Jesus and the miraculous in the second volume of *A Marginal Jew*, Meier argues that Jesus was known in the first instance as a doer of "startling deeds" rather than as a teacher or visionary.[57]

N. T. Wright's imposing book series on *Christian Origins and the Question of God* (1992-) situates Jesus in his Jewish context, and uses the idea of exile and return as a way of understanding the first-century Jewish hope. Wright is critical of the Jesus Seminar for ignoring the Jewishness of Jesus, and, like Meier, he judges that the *Gospel of Thomas* is dependent on the canonical Gospels. The eschatological language of the Bible, for Wright, does not imply "the end of the space-time universe," as many Christian believers have traditionally assumed. Instead eschatology points toward "the climax of Israel's history, involving events for which end-of-the-world language is the only set of metaphors adequate to express the significance of what will happen, but resulting in a new and quite different phase *within* space-time history." Wright's perspective thus lies somewhere between a naïve literalism in approaching the eschatological texts and an interpretation of them as unrelated to the material and historical realm. Perhaps Wright's most interesting suggestion is that Jesus saw "his final journey to Jerusalem . . . as the symbolic enacting of the great central kingdom-promise, that YHWH should at last return to Zion, to judge and to save." In enacting Yahweh's own plan of redemption, Jesus saw himself as the "Messiah," though Wright notes that this term did not carry divine or quasi-divine overtones in Jesus' era.[58]

Alongside of Wright's nuanced treatment of biblical eschatology, there has been a recent revival of the straightforward apocalyptic interpretation of Jesus. Bart Ehrman, in *Jesus: Apocalyptic Prophet of the New Millennium*, aligns himself with Albert Schweitzer, argues that Jesus is "best understood as a first-century Jewish apocalypticist," and that "Jesus expected that [the] cataclysmic end of history would come in his own generation, at least during the lifetime of his disciples." Hence Jesus got it wrong, and predicted a doomsday that never happened.[59] Dale C. Allison, in *Jesus of Nazareth: Millenarian Prophet*, construes Jesus' apocalypticism in a different way, insisting that his teaching embodies a form of "asceticism."[60] Like Ehrman and Allison, Paula Fredriksen concurs that Jesus "is a prophet who preached the coming apocalyptic Kingdom of God." Her book *Jesus of Nazareth, King of the Jews* represents Jesus much as E. P. Sanders does. He is steeped in a Jewish milieu, shares his fellow Jews' concern with ritual purity, and in fact did not actually engage in the rancorous disputes with the scribes and Pharisees depicted in the New Testament. The Gospel controversies are largely a projection into Jesus' lifetime of later disagreements between churches and synagogues. Fredriksen asks why Jesus was put to death, and concludes that Jewish messianic expectations had created an incendiary environment, and Jesus' prediction of the kingdom's coming was the spark that touched it off.[61] Bruce Chilton's *Rabbi Jesus: An Intimate Biography* stands apart from other scholarly works. In novelistic fashion, it supplies details where historical evidence is lacking. (Jesus was "shorter than the norm, overweight, and tending to baldness"!) Chilton's Jesus is deeply Jewish, and yet his religious practice is more mystical than rabbinical. He learned *merkabah* (i.e., chariot or throne) mysticism from John the Baptist, and his meditative practice and teaching were the basis for both his healings of the sick and the later visions of him that his disciples had after he died.[62]

The discussion thus far has treated only the scholarly works on Jesus. During the last several decades Jesus has continued to be a figure of immense importance for popular culture. Bruce Barton's best-seller *The Man Nobody Knows* (1925) portrayed Jesus as a successful leader and organizer and "the friendliest man who has ever lived . . . the type of man whom you would have chosen as a companion on a fishing trip."[63] Hugh Schonfield's *Passover Plot* (1965) viewed Jesus as a man sincerely convinced that he was the Messiah, who followed the "nightmarish conception" and "frightening logic of a sick mind" by planning his own arrest and crucifixion. Albert Cleage's *Black Messiah* (1968) presents the man from Galilee as "the non-white leader of a non-white people struggling for national liberation against the rule of a white nation, Rome."[64] Levi H. Dowling's *Aquarian Gospel of Jesus the Christ* (1911) and Elizabeth Clare Prophet's *Lost Years of Jesus* (1984) represent Jesus as a spiritual master propounding a mystical and esoteric religion. Writers such as D. H. Lawrence in *The Man Who Died* (1928) and Nikos Kazantzakis in *The Last Temptation of Christ* (1961) created imaginative renderings of Jesus' life in which he struggles to deny his sexual desire or else finds fulfillment through indulging it.

The British comedy troupe Monty Python produced *The Life of Brian* (1979), a movie about a first-century Jewish carpenter who bears a strong resemblance to you-know-who. As Brian runs to escape his eager followers and their impertinent questions, his shoe inadvertently falls off, and there ensues a dialogue among the disciples. *First Man:* "He has given us a sign!" *Second Man:* "He has given us a shoe!" *First Man:* "The shoe is the sign — let us follow his example." *Second Man:* "What?!" *First Man:* "Let us like him hold up one shoe and let the other be upon our foot. For this is his sign that all who follow him shall do likewise." *Third Man:* "No, no, no, the shoe is a sign that we must gather shoes together in abundance." *Woman:* "Cast off the shoe! Follow the gourd [touched by Brian]!" This tongue-in-cheek episode can be read as a Bultmannian gloss on Christian origins — the church's interpretation of Jesus originated in its independent interests and preoccupations. Adele Reinhartz notes that recent films on Jesus fall in line with broad scholarly trends. Director Francis Zeffirelli's *Jesus of Nazareth* (1977) stresses Jesus' Jewishness, Martin Scorsese's *The Last Temptation of Christ* (1988) inclines toward the Cynic sage interpretation, while Pier Paolo Pasolini's *The Gospel According to St. Matthew* (1995) is more Marxist or socialist and represents Jesus in solidarity with the downtrodden masses.[65]

Along with the scholarly and popular works, there is a good deal of pseudoscholarship on Jesus that finds its way into print. During the last two centuries, more than a hundred books and articles have denied the historical existence of Jesus. Today innumerable websites carry the same message.[66] The idea seems to have originated in the late 1700s, when some disciples of the skeptic Lord Bolingbroke began to spread the notion that Jesus never existed. Constantin-Francois Volney and Charles Francois Dupuis taught that Christianity was simply an updated amalgamation of Persian and Babylonian mythologies, with a mythical Christ at its center. Voltaire — no friend to traditional Christianity — rejected this conclusion, commenting that those who deny the existence of Jesus show themselves "more ingenious than learned."[67] During the nineteenth century, the most important denier of Jesus' existence was Bruno Bauer (1809-1882), who dismissed the historical reliability of the New Testament documents, viewed the references to Jesus in non-Christian sources as erroneous, and — like the earlier English and French skeptics — interpreted Christianity as a mythic religion with a nonhistorical Savior. Bauer had a major historical impact through his student, Karl Marx, who carried Bauer's teaching into the Communist movement, where it became a part of official Soviet and Maoist literature. Recently there has been only one major scholarly defender of the non-existence of Jesus, George A. Wells (1926-), a professor of German in London, and he has softened his earlier position somewhat by admitting that there may be some sort of historical personage behind the New Testament documents.[68] Most scholars regard the arguments for Jesus' non-existence as unworthy of any response — on a par with claims that the Jewish Holocaust never occurred or that the Apollo moon landing took place in a Hollywood studio.

One class of books claims that Jesus is fiction, while another turns Jesus into fiction. Consider for instance Barbara Thiering's *Jesus the Man* (1975), which makes the following remarkable claims: that Jesus was betrothed to Mary Magdalene at 10 p.m. on Tuesday, June 6, in the year 30; that the Last Supper took place on March 19, 33, between 6 and 10 p.m.; that Jesus swooned on the cross (after receiving poison to relieve his pain) and was revived by friends; that Mary Magdalene subsequently had a daughter by Jesus; that this daughter was named Tamar; that Jesus had another child by Mary Magdalene, named Jesus Justus, born in March 41; that Jesus thereafter separated from Mary Magdalene and was last heard of in Rome in 64; and that his manner of death is unknown.[69] No less fanciful in character is Faber-Kaiser's *Jesus Died in Kashmir* (1977), which is based in part on local legends in northern India. The author asserts that Jesus did not die on the cross but recovered from his crucifixion wounds, traveled eastward (accompanied by his mother and the apostle Thomas) in search of the ten lost tribes of Israel, settled down in Kashmir, begat children, and died of natural causes at a ripe old age. The living descendants of Jesus in Kashmir possess a genealogical table that traces their ancestry from Jesus.[70] Such books as *Jesus the Man* and *Jesus Died in Kashmir* do perhaps serve a purpose, in that they force a consideration of the foundational issues regarding the reliability of sources and the appropriate methods of historical inquiry.

Sources and Methods

What Can We Know? How Can We Know It?

In this chapter there are two questions to consider: What textual sources give us reliable information on the life and teachings of Jesus? And, after choosing our sources, what methods should be used to study them?

Recently scholars have shown a growing interest in noncanonical materials (i.e., texts not included in the Bible) in constructing a picture of Jesus' life. Helmut Koester claimed that noncanonical writings are "just as important" as the New Testament texts for the study of early Christianity and "contain many traditions which can be traced back to the time of the very origins of Christianity."[1] At the outset it is important to distinguish carefully the different kinds of writings that lie outside of the biblical canon and to weigh the historical value of each individually. They differ greatly in character and in their relationship to the contents of the New Testament Gospels. *First,* there are references to Jesus in non-Christian sources, such as Greco-Roman authors (Suetonius, Pliny the Younger, Tacitus, etc.), the Jewish Talmud, and the rabbinical writings. Josephus's famous paragraph on Jesus, in his *Antiquities of the Jews,* is an especially important, though debated, text. *Second,* there are the agrapha, a term that refers to sayings attributed to Jesus that are not contained in the four canonical Gospels. These sayings come from a wide variety of sources — from noncanonical gospels (such as the *Gospel of Thomas,* the *Gospel of the Nazoreans*), from early Christian authors (such as the author of 1 *Clement,* Justin, Clement of Alexandria, Origen, Tatian, Eusebius, and many others), and from ancient Greek texts (such as the Oxyrhynchus Papyri). *Third,* there are the noncanonical gospels taken as a whole, which include not only sayings of Jesus but also narratives about him and reflections or exhortations on his life and significance. It is impossible in this brief chapter to enumerate all the relevant noncanonical materials, let alone to summarize the complex debates about these texts and their significance for understanding the historical Jesus. The footnotes provide references for further study.[2]

The Talmud, though put into written form centuries after the life of Jesus, contains some ancient traditions and therefore might shed light on Jesus. A number of statements occur regarding a certain Jesus (or Yeshua), and yet the references are brief or oblique and there is often doubt as to whether they pertain to Jesus of Nazareth. A reference to Mary, the mother of Jesus, who "played the harlot with carpenters,"[3] is clearly an anti-Christian polemic that presupposes the Gospels of Matthew and Luke, and thus is not an independent source of information on Jesus. The same should probably be said with regard to the traditions about Jesus in Egypt,[4] Jesus' five disciples,[5] Jesus' practice of magic or sorcery,[6] and the various allusions to Jesus as a teacher or pupil figure.[7] One of the most important passages speaks of Jesus' death and the reason for it: "On the eve of the Passover Yeshu [the Nazarean] was hanged. For forty days before the execution took place, a herald went forth and cried, 'He is going forth to be stoned because he has practised sorcery and enticed Israel to apostasy. Any one who can say anything in his favour, let him come forward and plead on his behalf.' But since nothing was brought forward in his favour he was hanged on the eve of the Passover!"[8] The best conclusion seems to be that the rabbinical writings add nothing to the picture of Jesus derived from other sources that are more detailed and reliable.[9]

Suetonius is among the classical Roman authors who briefly allude to Jesus in their writings. In *The Lives of the Caesars* (ca. 120 c.e.), he refers to the expulsion of the Jews from Rome in 49 c.e. during the reign of Claudius: "[Claudius] expelled the Jews from Rome who, instigated by Chrestus, continually caused unrest."[10] The wording here may reflect an error arising from the confusion of "Chrestus" — a common slave name — with the title "Christus," a word that would not have been familiar to many of the Romans. In any case the passage indicates that by the early second century some knowledge of "Chrestus" had spread among the Romans. One of the more interesting passages in the Roman writers comes from Pliny the Younger, who was governor of Bithynia and in the year 110 wrote to the emperor Trajan requesting advice on how to deal with the Christians. He purports to tell the Caesar what the Christians had told him: "They [the Christians] declared that the sum of their guilt or error had amounted only to this, that on an appointed day they had been accustomed to meet before daybreak, and to recite a hymn antiphonally to Christ, as to a god." Pliny goes on to say that the Christians made it their practice "to bind themselves by an oath, not for the commission of any crime but to abstain from theft, robbery, adultery and breach of faith . . . [and] to depart and meet again to take food."[11] None of these Greco-Roman sources provide new information on Jesus per se. Yet they suggest that an exalted image of Jesus (singing "as to a god") was widespread among Christians at this early stage.[12]

One of the hostile witnesses to early Christianity in the second century was the philosopher Celsus, whose treatise *The True Doctrine* survives only in the fragments within the spirited rebuttal *Against Celsus,* written by Origen in the mid-third century. Celsus frequently refers to Jesus as a sorcerer who deceived the people with his magic.[13] These statements echo an earlier assertion of Justin Martyr regarding the Jewish rejection of Jesus: "But though they saw such works, they asserted it was a magical art. For they dared to call Him a magician, and a deceiver of the people."[14] This particular accusation is already found in the Gospel texts (e.g., Matt. 12:22-32) where Jesus is charged with casting out demons by the power of Satan. The statements by Celsus along with the parallel Jewish statements on "sorcery" corroborate the impression given by the New Testament that Jesus was widely known by Christians and non-Christians alike as the performer of supernatural deeds. Their disagreement was over the *source* of Jesus' spiritual power, whether from God or from Satan and the forces of darkness.[15]

The most important non-Christian reference to Jesus is found in a key paragraph in Josephus's *Antiquities,* probably written during the 90s c.e. The text as it has come down to us contains certain statements that almost certainly could not have been penned by Josephus himself, including an apparent confession of faith in Jesus as "the Messiah." While some scholars believe the entire paragraph is a Christian forgery or interpolation, inserted into the text to make Josephus more palatable for Christian readers, a more plausible theory is that much of the paragraph derives from Josephus while certain statements were later sandwiched in. The celebrated passage, sometimes known as the *Testimonium Flavianum,* is given below, with the likely Christian interpolations rendered in italics:

> About this time there lived Jesus, a wise man, *if indeed one ought to call him a man.* For he was one who wrought surprising feats and was a

teacher of such people as accept the truth gladly. He won over many Jews and many of the Greeks. *He was the Messiah.* When Pilate, upon hearing him accused by men of the highest standing amongst us, had condemned him to be crucified, those who had in the first place come to love him did not give up their affection for him. *On the third day he appeared to them restored to life, for the prophets of God had prophesied these and countless other marvellous things about him.* And the tribe of the Christians, so called after him, has still to this day not disappeared.[16]

As John Meier has argued, the three highlighted passages above are the only assertions that suggest a Christian point of view regarding Jesus. Their deletion, moreover, creates a compact and fluent set of statements that is fairly neutral in its tone. Thus the most economical and least complicated theory would seem to be that Josephus wrote a paragraph that lacked these three segments.[17]

One notes that Josephus's paragraph does not exaggerate the role played by the Jewish leaders in Jesus' arrest, trial, and crucifixion. If the entire passage were a later Christian invention, one might have expected the Jewish leaders to be portrayed as outright villains. Also the text lacks the animus toward Jesus that is conspicuous in the later rabbinical texts we have already considered. Thus the *Testimonium* reads as we might expect if it had been written (apart from its later interpolations) by a first-century Jew prior to the emergence of Jewish-Christian animosities. A later and passing reference in Josephus's *Antiquities* to Jesus, mentioned alongside of "James the brother of Jesus who was called the Christ,"[18] demands some prior mention of Jesus by Josephus, and the *Testimonium* seems to be the implied reference. Thus the later passage lends support to the authenticity of the former. Josephus has considerable significance for recent debates over Jesus. Some have questioned the Gospels' presentation of Jesus' death as the outcome of his public ministry and teaching. Burton Mack argues that the causes leading to Jesus' death are obscure, and that the bond created by the Gospel of Mark between Jesus' teachings or miracles and his death is fictional in character.[19] David Seeley claims that "Mark concocted the Jewish conspiracy against Jesus for his own, redactional reasons."[20] Yet the implication of the *Testimonium* is that Jesus' actions and teachings were linked with his arrest and accusation, and that the leaders or "first men" of the Jews played a role of some kind in his death.[21]

The agrapha, or noncanonical sayings attributed to Jesus, are probably less reliable than the non-Christian sources on the life of Jesus. Joachim Jeremias considered hundreds of different sayings attributed to Jesus in a wide variety of ancient texts, and isolated only eighteen that were worthy of serious consideration as possibly authentic.[22] More recent surveys of the agrapha, by O. Hofius and Robert E. Van Voorst, are even less optimistic.[23] To give the reader a feel for the agrapha, a few examples will be cited along with the respective sources. "Blessed is the man who has suffered; he has found the Life" *(Gospel of Thomas).* "Woe to the Pharisees, for they are like a dog sleeping in the oxen's manger, which neither eats nor allows the oxen to eat" *(Gospel of Thomas).* "He himself will give you your clothing" (Oxyrhynchus Papyri). "If you are in my bosom and do not the will of my Father in heaven, I will cast you out of my bosom" (Codex 1424 to Matt. 7:5). "As you prove yourselves kind, so you will experience kindness" *(1 Clement).* "Save yourself and your life" (Theodotus, as reported in Clement of Alexandria). "There will be schisms and heresies" (Justin Martyr). "I choose for myself the best, the best are they whom my Father in heaven gives me" *(Gospel of the Nazoreans).* "The one who has not forgiven seventy times seven times is not worthy of me" *(Liber Graduum).* "They who are with me have not understood me" *(Acts of Peter).* "Let your Holy Spirit come upon us and cleanse us" (Codex 700 to Luke 11:2). "It is more blessed to give than to receive" (Acts 20:35).[24]

The final agraphon above — considered such because it is not from the canonical Gospels, though it is in the New Testament — is the most likely of the group to be authentic.[25] In many cases the agrapha are simply embellishments or variations of sayings that are already attested in the synoptic Gospels or elsewhere in the New Testament. Furthermore, even if the eighteen or so agrapha that Jeremias considered were added to the "database" on Jesus, this would not appreciably alter the canonical Gospels' picture of Jesus' life and teachings.[26] Hofius finds little evidence to suggest that extrabiblical sources provide additional sayings or a new picture of Jesus' teaching. Quoting Jeremias with approval, Hofius declares that the "four canonical Gospels embrace with great completeness almost all the early Church knew of the sayings and deeds of Jesus in the second half of the first century." Van Voorst finds the agrapha "disappointingly meager" in augmenting our understanding of Jesus.[27] Nonetheless, the agrapha have importance for the study of early Christianity. If a saying proves to be inauthentic, then one can imaginatively reconstruct the historical setting and social group that might have been responsible for creating such a saying and attributing it to Jesus. The agrapha, like the apocryphal gospels generally, enrich our understanding of the variants of Christianity (or Christianities) that flourished during the early centuries.

Many of the noncanonical or apocryphal gospels have been well known among scholars for decades or centuries, and yet it is only within the last generation that many scholars have argued that they should be taken seriously as sources for the life of Jesus. Bultmann considered the apocryphal texts to be nothing more than "legendary adaptations and expansions"[28] of the material already contained within the canonical Gospels. Certain features of the apocryphal gospels seem plainly legendary. In the *Gospel of Philip*, for instance, Jesus goes into the dye works of Levi, takes seventy-two different colors, throws them into the vat, and they all come out white. Stranger still, Joseph the carpenter grows a tree from which he makes the cross on which Jesus is later hanged.[29] The *Gospel of Peter* also features a talking cross and angels whose heads reach into heaven.[30] Yet today some scholars accept certain apocryphal texts as bona fide historical sources. Particularly important for current study is the *Gospel of Thomas*, written in the Coptic language and included in the Nag Hammadi library unearthed in Egypt in the late 1940s.[31] (This *Gospel of Thomas* is not to be confused with the so-called *Infancy Gospel of Thomas*, a different text that was known prior to the discovery of the Nag Hammadi writings.) A group of contemporary scholars, led by professors and graduates of Harvard University and Claremont Graduate School, asserts that the *Gospel of Thomas* is nothing less than a "fifth Gospel" that embodies traditions as early and as reliable as those contained in the synoptic Gospels.

A key claim is that *Thomas* is independent of the canonical texts, and the sayings it records may be set over against those of the synoptic Gospels as a test of their genuineness and authenticity.[32] Obviously if *Thomas* is just a reworking of themes contained in the synoptics, was written several decades later, and was inspired and influenced by the canonical texts, then this makes it unlikely to shed new light on Jesus. If, however, *Thomas* is as early or almost as early as the synoptics, and is literarily independent of them (i.e., composed without knowledge of the written synoptic Gospels), then it might tell us a good deal regarding Jesus not already known from canonical texts. In particular, it could address the issue of Jesus' teaching. A distinctive of *Thomas*, as compared with all four New Testament Gospels, is the absence of a narrative framework or recounting of Jesus' actions. *Thomas* is basically a compilation of 114 sayings attributed to Jesus.[33]

A number of features in the *Gospel of Thomas* weigh against regarding it as independent of the synoptic Gospels. It appears to quote or allude to some sixteen different New Testament books — all four canonical Gospels, Acts, many of the epistles, and Revelation — and could be seen simply as a collage of canonical and noncanonical materials, often interpreted allegorically, assembled to advance second- and third-century gnostic ideas. To circumvent the problem of *Thomas*'s allusions to the canonical texts, Crossan and some other scholars have attempted to extract a hypothetical earlier version of *Thomas* from the Coptic and Greek texts now extant. Yet the problems besetting an early dating of the *Gospel of Thomas* run deep. *Thomas* not only contains *sayings* that are distinctive to Matthew, Luke, and John, but even *redactional* elements as well. That is, the sayings in *Thomas* are arranged in ways that suggest the unmistakable influence of the canonical Gospels. The Gospel of Matthew, for instance, links together the three themes of almsgiving, prayer, and fasting (Matt. 6:1-18), and *Thomas* echoes this. And since *Thomas* views almsgiving, prayer, and fasting in a negative light, this probably links *Thomas* with a later gnostic antipathy toward Jewish piety and once again shows it to be secondary to Matthew. These and other considerations have led a number of leading scholars to view the *Gospel of Thomas* as subsequent to the synoptic Gospels and derivative from them.[34]

After reviewing the complex arguments regarding the various possible sources for the life of Jesus, John Meier makes the following remarks:

> For all practical purposes, then, our early, independent sources for the historical Jesus boil down to the Four Gospels, a few scattered data elsewhere in the NT, and Josephus. Contrary to some scholars, I do not think that the rabbinic material, the *agrapha*, the apocryphal gospels, and the Nag Hammadi codices (in particular the *Gospel of Thomas*) offer us reliable new information or authentic sayings that are independent of the NT. What we see in these later documents is rather the reaction to or reworking of NT writings by Jewish rabbis engaged in polemics, imaginative Christians reflecting popular piety and legend, and gnostic Christians developing a mystic speculative system. . . . We are left alone — some would say forlorn — with the Four Gospels, plus scattered tidbits. It is only natural for scholars — to say nothing of

popularizers — to want more, to want other access roads to the historical Jesus. This understandable but not always critical desire is, I think, what has recently led to the high evaluation, in some quarters, of the apocryphal gospels and the Nag Hammadi codices as sources for the quest. It is a case of the wish being father to the thought.[35]

If the canonical Gospels are the only substantive sources that we presently possess for an investigation of Jesus, then it is important to consider carefully the nature of the canonical texts and the possible methods of inquiry to be used in studying them. To this topic we will turn briefly in this chapter before launching into a consideration of Jesus' life, sayings, actions, and influence in later chapters.

The question of the authenticity or inauthenticity of the synoptic Gospels is one of the neuralgic points of modern scholarship. The issues have been debated for decades, no consensus has emerged, and nothing that I write here could be satisfactory to all interested parties. You cannot please all the people all the time, and sometimes it seems that you cannot please even some of them some of the time! Traditional or orthodox Christians of varying types may be inclined to dismiss the whole question of authenticity in the canonical Gospels, affirming that these texts are the word of God in written form and are therefore incapable of containing errors or distortions regarding Jesus. Here we encounter a difference between the characteristic attitude of the believer — accepting, trusting, and doubtful of self — and that of the historian — cautious, questioning, and doubtful of the sources. The tension between these two ways of approaching the biblical texts is a fundamental issue in modern Christianity and in other religions that purport to be based on a written revelation of God's will (particularly Judaism and Islam).[36] The issue of faith and history is like an underground stream beneath the literature on the Bible. It bubbles to the surface, hurtles into whitewater, levels off and submerges, only to reappear again — a flow that varies from placid to tempestuous and yet never ceases.

One need not be a skeptic to perceive that issues of historical reliability crop up in the synoptic Gospels. All one has to do is read *closely*. As Crossan observes, if one approaches the Gospels "vertically," that is, reading straight through one before moving on to the next, the dominant impression one gains is that of coherence and harmony. Yet if one approaches them "horizontally," pausing to consider each saying or episode in the life of

Jesus and comparing it with the accounts given in the other Gospels, one sees many differences between the passages.[37] The small divergences in each passage add up, and patterns become visible in each Gospel. This has given rise to a field of research known as redaction criticism, which examines the ways in which the material concerning Jesus is transmitted and shaped in each respective Gospel. Thus, to give one of many possible examples, the Gospel of Matthew replaces Jesus' references to the "kingdom of God" with the phrase the "kingdom of heaven" — probably a reflection of the Jewish veneration for the name of God and desire to avoid putting it into print.

Little has been said regarding the Gospel of John. The observant reader may have noted already in this chapter that I have sometimes used the expression "synoptic Gospels" where one might have expected "canonical Gospels." Few scholars would put the Gospel of John on a par with Matthew, Mark, and Luke as an historical source for the life of Jesus. John's Gospel omits many of the key episodes and themes in Jesus' life as presented by the synoptic Gospels: extended teaching on the kingdom of God, the parables, Jesus' baptism, the calling of the Twelve, the casting out of demons, the Transfiguration, and the institution of the Lord's Supper. The Christ of John speaks in a different way than the Jesus of the synoptics — not in parables, not in pithy phrases that show the coloring of first-century Palestine, and only rarely in talk about "the kingdom of God." Instead the Christ of John engages in extended soliloquies that revolve around himself and his unique identity. Only in John do we find the remarkable assertions: "I am the bread of life" (6:35), "I am the light of the world" (8:12), "I am the true vine" (15:1), and so on. The nearest we come to this in the synoptic Gospels is probably in the "Son of Man" sayings, whose authenticity is disputed by scholars. Yet John goes much further than the other canonical Gospels in bringing Jesus himself and his identity into the foreground. Having said this, a number of scholars have demonstrated that the author of the Gospel of John exhibits a knowledge of Palestinian geography and Jewish custom that is unrivalled by the authors of the synoptic Gospels.[38] This militates against reading John as a very late first-century or early second-century text composed in a Gentile and Hellenistic environment.[39] Craig Blomberg argues that John is literarily independent of the synoptic Gospels and the material in John that parallels the synoptic Gospels is thus likely to be authentic.[40] Nonetheless, because of the unique character of the Fourth Gospel and the many unresolved debates concerning it, the picture of Jesus presented in subsequent chapters will be based primarily on the synoptic Gospels.[41]

This brings us to some questions that are critical for everything that follows in this book: Exactly what *kinds* of texts are the synoptic Gospels of the New Testament? What are their distinctive literary *features?* What, if anything, can we learn from the present form of the texts about the compositional *process* that led to the Gospels in their present form? And, finally, how should the answers to the above questions influence our judgment regarding the historical *reliability* of the picture of Jesus presented in the synoptic Gospels? Seas of ink have been spilled over mountains of paper in answering each of these questions. Only a brief and cursory account is possible here. As in the earlier discussion of the non-Christian sources on Jesus and the noncanonical Gospels, the reader is referred to the notes containing references for further study.[42]

A number of foundational principles should be kept in mind regarding the synoptic Gospels and their portrayal of Jesus. First, the earliest Christians probably did not write out a full narrative of Jesus' life, but preserved individual units of tradition (called pericopes or pericopae — literally "cut around") about his life and deeds. These units were later moved and arranged by editors and authors. This means that we cannot be completely certain regarding the immediate context of Jesus' sayings and actions. Second, much of the material included in the Gospels has been significantly shaped by the concerns of the early Christians who gathered together the traditions concerning Jesus. Third, the inscriptions of authorship for the Gospels may have been added after the works were written. Fourth, as we have mentioned already, the Gospel of John is quite different from the other three Gospels, and it is primarily in the latter that we must seek information about Jesus. Fifth, the Gospels lack many of the characteristics of biography, and we should especially distinguish them from modern biographies.

To understand the Gospels it may be helpful to envision the immediate aftermath of the crucifixion. After Jesus' death his followers fled or hid, but their hopes were renewed when they had a vision of him alive again. Convinced that the kingdom Jesus predicted would soon arrive in full force, they waited in Jerusalem and sought to convince others that Jesus was the promised Messiah. Given their situation, it is unlikely that they sat down together at this early stage, collectively ransacked their memories, and in this deliberate fashion composed a biography of Jesus. Since they expected that he would soon return and be among them, the question of how best to preserve the knowledge of his life for future generations was probably not in their minds. Yet, even at this earliest stage, while trying to communicate their convictions regarding Jesus to others, they must have often told stories of Jesus' actions and words. These stories may have circulated for some time in oral form prior to being written down. Alternatively, there may have been written records of at least a fragmentary sort relatively soon after Jesus' death.[43] Thus the sayings and doings of Jesus were preserved, though in different context than that of Jesus' own life, namely, in the teaching and practice of the earliest Christian communities. As time passed, and as Jesus' expected return did not occur, the traditions about Jesus were put into written form.

The process that resulted in the New Testament Gospels is not fully known to us. We can only draw inferences from the finished product, like an architect inspecting a completed house from the front lawn and making conjectures regarding its foundation and frame. While it is plausible to think that the material regarding Jesus was organized into pericopes, there is an important and far-reaching question regarding the redaction or editing of these pericopes. In other words: How did the authors of the Gospels make decisions to include or exclude, to abridge or amplify, the units of tradition that were passed down to them? How did they decide on the order of presentation? It is clear that they shifted these units around. This is obvious when we see that the same saying or act of Jesus is presented in different contexts in different Gospels. The authors of the Gospels may not have known the immediate context and circumstances of the individual stories and sayings of Jesus. This was not a part of the tradition that was passed down to them. Thus they organized the pericopes according to principles of their own devising.

It is possible that there were proto-gospels that preceded the present synoptic Gospels of Matthew, Mark, and Luke. Most scholars believe that Mark was the first of the New Testament Gospels to be written. Scholars refer to this as the theory of "Markan priority." A few believe that Matthew was written earlier than Mark, and this is known as "Matthean priority" or the Griesbach hypothesis.[44] A likely basis for many of the sayings attributed to Jesus in the Gospels was a source called "Q" (from *Quelle*, the German word for source). Thus Mark (if it did come first) and Q (if it really existed) were two major sources for the Gospel of Matthew and the Gospel of Luke. Some material is unique to Matthew and some to Luke, however, and so scholars have hypothesized the existence of "M" (a Matthean source) and "L" (a Lukan source) to account for this fact. The final texts of the Gospels as we have them today were probably composed sometime between the years 55 and 90, with some scholars favoring the earlier decades (50-70 C.E.), others leaning toward the later period (70-90 C.E.), and still others in the middle (60-80 C.E.).[45]

The authorship of the Gospels is a matter of debate. Although the Gospels presently have headings — "according to Matthew," etc. — it is possible that the canonical Gospels remained untitled until the second half of the second century. Though the Gospels were quoted often in the surviving Christian literature of the second century, they are quoted anonymously rather than by a writer's name. This changes during the late second century. By this time there were any number of gospels, and not merely the four that were ultimately accepted by Christians as canonical. So it became necessary to specify which gospels were to be accepted, and the naming of the canonical Gospels was a way to deal with the issue. E. P. Sanders argues that it would be unlikely for second-century Christian writers to have known the names of the Gospel authors and yet not mention these names when citing the Gospels. Another line of argument, presented by Martin Hengel, is that the titles of the Gospels must have been firmly attached to them from the very beginning of their dissemination in the expanding Christian movement. Otherwise there would never have been any agreement later on about which author wrote which Gospel.[46] Whoever may be right on this debated issue, one thing is clear. The authors of the Gospels wanted to diminish interest in the question of *who* wrote them and focus attention on *what* was written.

One of the fundamental questions to be posed is the following: Did Jesus really utter the sayings attributed to him in the Gospels? Are these Jesus' own words (translated from Aramaic into Greek)? Or are the sayings to be understood as early Christian modifications and adaptations of things that Jesus said at various times and places? Or should some of the sayings attributed to Jesus be regarded as plain and simple inventions of the early church? As one can infer from the questions themselves, there is a spectrum of possible opinions on this topic. To address the issue, scholars have proposed various "criteria of authenticity" to determine which Gospel sayings are most likely to go back to Jesus himself.[47] Prior to the rise of modern critical studies of the Bible, the only criterion for authenticity was the presence of a particular saying in the canonical Gospels. What was in the Gospels was assumed to be genuine; what was not was thereby suspect. Once this assumption was shaken during the 1700s and early 1800s, other tests had to be used. In the earlier phase of the quest for the historical Jesus there were few if any carefully formulated criteria for determining the presence of authentic tradition within the Gospels. Miracle stories were often assumed to be unhistorical or legendary in character, and at times this seems to have been the only functioning criterion. Thomas Jefferson used such a criterion for his "Life and Morals of Jesus of Nazareth." In 1804, while President of the United States, Jefferson ordered two copies of the King James Version of the Bible and used scissors to separate Jesus' teachings from the miraculous reports concerning him. The resulting text was not published until the twentieth century.[48]

It is important to distinguish authenticity in the historical sense from relevance in an interpretive or theological sense. The criteria of authenticity are a part of the attempt to determine what material in the attributed sayings actually derives from Jesus and what aspects of the narratives accurately describe the events of Jesus' life. The relevance or authority of the material judged as authentic is another question, not directly addressed by the criteria of authenticity.[49] Among the proposed criteria that have received widespread attention are those of multiple attestation, dissimilarity, embarrassment, Semitic or Palestinian background, and coherence. Each of these will be briefly described and critiqued in turn.

The criterion of multiple attestation arose in connection with source criticism, and essentially it asserts that the claim of any saying to authenticity is strengthened when it is attested in more than one source (Mark and the hypothetic sources — see above — Q, M, and L). A liability is that this criterion relies on the "two-source theory" (i.e., Mark and Q as sources for Matthew and Luke), and the theory is not universally accepted. Furthermore, the criterion of multiple attestation can prove only that a multiply attested tradition is early and widespread, and not necessarily that it is authentic.

A criterion widely touted in the mid-twentieth century was the so-called criterion of dissimilarity. Norman Perrin went so far as to refer to it as "the fundamental criterion for authenticity upon which all reconstructions of the life of Jesus must be built."[50] A basic description comes from Rudolf Bultmann: "We can only count on possessing a genuine similitude of Jesus where, on the one hand, expression is given to the contrast between Jewish morality and piety and the distinctive eschatological temper which characterized the preaching of Jesus; and where on the other hand we find no specifically Christian features."[51] Note that this criterion rests on a double dissimilarity: Jesus' teaching is assumed to be unlike that of both first-century Judaism and emergent Christianity.

Bultmann's statement rests on a number of debatable assumptions. It presupposes that "Jewish morality and piety" in the first century were noneschatological in character, in contradistinction to the "eschatological temper" of Jesus' message. Yet in light of the newer studies of first-century Judaism, it is no longer possible to uphold a dichotomy between "piety" and "eschatology." Only a misleading stereotype regarding Judaism — as a religion of literalistic and picayune adherence to law — could sustain such a dichotomy between Jesus and Judaism. Bultmann also assumes that the voice of the authentic Jesus stands against that of the earliest Christians. Yet this too is unwarranted as a methodological principle. Only with independent evidence that the earliest Christians diverged from Jesus' teaching can we assume that the reported sayings of Jesus, to be judged authentic, must differ from the characteristic thoughts and symbols used by Jesus' first followers. In other words, a rift between Jesus and his followers cannot be built in as a methodological principle before one has done the necessary investigation of the sources. It may be a conclusion but cannot serve as a presupposition.

There are further reasons to doubt the utility of the criterion of dissimilarity. It isolates Jesus from his immediate environment, and tends to portray Jesus as a non-Jew and as a leader without followers.[52] Just as crucially, the criterion runs into the objection that we simply do not know enough to apply it effectively. Our present knowledge of first-century Judaism is very imperfect, and in many cases our only attestation for important Jewish ideas and practices lies in texts that date from the 200s, 300s, 400s, or even later. So in these cases our general picture of Judaism in the first century has to be created by extrapolating backward from the later texts. Often we are uncertain as to when certain practices began — for example, the water baptism of proselytes (Gentile converts to Judaism). Likewise we run into the same problem in trying to distinguish Jesus from his first followers. There is not enough evidence to allow us to reconstruct the founder and his first followers in independence of one another.[53]

The criterion of embarrassment focuses on sayings or actions that would have embarrassed or created difficulty for the earliest Christians. The point of the criterion is that the earliest church would hardly have gone out of its way to create material that brought embarrassment or else weakened its position. On the contrary, one might expect that embarrassing material that came from Jesus would be suppressed or at least softened in the later stages of the Gospel tradition. Perhaps the classic instance is the baptism of Jesus by John the Baptist, an act that would seem to make Jesus a disciple of John and perhaps even imply that Jesus needed a baptism for the "remission of sins" — an idea clearly in contradiction to the early Christian teaching on the sinlessness of Jesus. It is virtually unthinkable that anyone in the first or second generation of the Christian church would have invented a story of Jesus' baptism by John. The criterion of embarrassment can function as a strong positive test for certain conspicuously embarrassing episodes and sayings. For this reason it can provide foundation stones on which to build — e.g., Jesus was certainly baptized by John. Yet the absence of embarrassment connected with a text does not prove that text to be inauthentic.

The Gospels contain many passages that would have been embarrassing to early Christian leaders such as Peter, the Twelve, Mary, and the brothers of Jesus. These include the following: the disciples' failure to understand Jesus and their sharp rebuke by Jesus (Mark 8:14-21); Jesus telling Peter that he was acting on Satan's behalf (Mark 8:31-33); Jesus' apparently dismissive statements about his immediate family members (Matt. 12:46-50); James and John's request to sit on thrones at either side of Jesus (Mark 10:35-45); Judas's inclusion as one of the Twelve (Mark 3:13-19); Peter's denials of Jesus (Mark 14:66-72); the rejection of Jesus by his own family members (Mark 3:21; John 7:1-9); the disciples' timid behavior after Jesus' death (John 20:19); and the refusal of the apostles to believe the first reports of Jesus' resurrection (Mark 16:14, longer ending; Luke 24:9-11; John 20:26-29). In each of these cases it is highly implausible to think that the episode was invented during the period of the early church. The application of the criterion of embarrassment suggests that each of these passages reflects an actual event during the life of Jesus.

The criterion of Semitic or Palestinian background rests on the idea that any saying is likely to be genuine if it shows traces of the Aramaic language (e.g., the word *Abba*, "Father," for God), characteristic Semitic thought forms (e.g., antithetical parallelism), or elements of the first-century Palestinian culture (e.g., references to customs connected with farming, taxation, etc.). Yet this criterion too may be criticized. Since the earliest Christian community was itself Semitic and Palestinian, the presence of these features does not guarantee that the tradition in question goes back to Jesus. Furthermore, this criterion cannot be used in the other direction, to argue that sayings that lack Semitic or Palestinian elements should be treated as inauthentic. The absence of Semitic features might simply be an indication that the original teaching of Jesus had been fully translated into Hellenistic language or culture forms, which is not enough to allow one to claim that it is inauthentic.

Subordinate to the other criteria of authenticity is the criterion of consistency (or coherence). Norman Perrin sums it up in this way: "Material which is consistent with or coheres with material established as authentic by other means may also be accepted."[54] This criterion assumes the others, since it begins from the presumption that some body of tradition has already been determined to be authentic. A possible problem here is circular reasoning, since the scholar starts from what is assumed to be characteristic of Jesus and then uses this to filter the data for reconstructing the historical Jesus. It is easy to use the criterion of consistency to dismiss material that might serve as evidence against one's pet theories. This would be a case of theory controlling data, not data controlling theory. Another problem with the criterion of consistency is that it seems to assume that Jesus himself was perfectly self-consistent in his public statements. Great teachers are commonly known for adapting themselves to changing audiences, and so authentic material that derives from Jesus himself could easily carry the appearance of inconsistency and contradiction. Meier comments that "Jesus would hardly be unique among the great thinkers or leaders of world history if his sayings and actions did not always seem totally consistent to us."[55]

When all is said and done, an application of the various authenticity criteria does not provide a watertight argument for or against the authenticity of the individual sayings attributed to Jesus. Some decades ago Ernst Käsemann acknowledged that "we possess absolutely no kind of formal criteria by which we can identify the authentic Jesus material."[56] E. P. Sanders is on the right track, in my view, when he says that "our sources contain information about Jesus, but we cannot get at it by dogmatically deciding that some sentences are completely accurate and some are fiction."[57] Sanders further notes that "there are no hard and fast laws of the development of the Synoptic tradition. On all counts the tradition developed in opposite directions. It became both longer and shorter, both more and less detailed, and both more and less Semitic."[58] This means that no one can construct a trajectory of the early literary development that is complete and detailed enough to allow definitive judgments regarding what in the Gospels does or does not go back to Jesus. At best the criteria of authenticity can help to ascertain the varying degrees of historical plausibility or implausibility that attach to particular sayings or events in the Gospels.[59]

For the reasons just indicated, the elaborate scheme that John Dominic Crossan uses for authenticating Gospel traditions is open to question.[60] The validity of his method depends on his stratigraphy of Jesus traditions, which are sorted into four time periods: 30-60, 60-80, 80-120, 120-150 C.E. Many scholars will not attempt to identify which century the *Gospel of Thomas* was written in, let alone what portion of the first or second century. "One wonders," writes Dale Allison, "how he dares to be so confident about such uncertain things."[61] Crossan's system of dating and classification also seems arbitrary. Why, after all, should a text written in 81 be classified with one written in 119, rather than with one written in 79? Another basic problem with Crossan's approach is that it seems to tie each tradition's authenticity to the date at which it found its way into writing. Yet there is no necessary connection between the date at which an oral tradition is first written down and the antiquity or authenticity of the tradition that is preserved in that written version. Some very early traditions related to Jesus may have circulated in oral form for decades prior to being written, while other traditions could have been coined long after Jesus but then put immediately into written form. In such a case, the date that a written text began to circulate would not serve as a reliable indicator of its degree of authenticity. Crossan has said that his "methodology does not claim a spurious objectivity,"[62] yet his discussion of authenticity does not lay enough emphasis on the uncertainty of the many judgments that have to be made and the element of subjectivity that enters into all such discussions.

The completed New Testament Gospels can be compared to jigsaw puzzles. While one can use various methods to piece them together — for example, starting with the pieces of a single color, building inward from the edge pieces, and so on — once the puzzle has come together, no one can tell what method was used to assemble it. Allison observes: "We cannot separate chemical compounds with a knife. Nor can we tell at the end of a river what came from the fountainhead and what from later tributaries." The complex tradition histories that scholars have proposed for particular sayings of Jesus cannot be falsified or disproven, and this should lead us to wonder to what extent the alleged tradition histories are just educated guesses or imaginative exercises.[63] The truth is that *everyone* makes some kind of conjecture regarding the nature of Jesus and his teaching prior to examining the individual sayings. This is a point that Crossan himself expresses: "Nobody initiates historical Jesus research without any ideas about Jesus. It is therefore a little ingenuous [*sic*] to start from certain texts and act as if one discovered the historical Jesus at the other end of one's analysis. There is and should be always an initial hypothesis that one tests against the data."[64] The upshot is that a general picture of Jesus is not assembled piecemeal from the tidbits of authenticated tradition. Instead there is a larger paradigm or gestalt that comes prior to the examination of the various traditions. The mark of a good paradigm is its explanatory power. Over time it proves itself more capable than other possible paradigms of accounting for the existing data and assimilating any new data that come along.

To enunciate my own paradigm of interpretation, I would generally agree with E. P. Sanders that "enough evidence points toward Jewish eschatology as the general framework of Jesus' ministry that we may examine the particulars in the light of that framework."[65] At the same time, in what follows I hope to show that Jesus was sapiential as well as eschatological (see "Wisdom, Apocalypse, and the Identity of Jesus" below). These two aspects of the life and teaching of Jesus, so often set against one another in recent interpretations, should rather be related and coordinated. Jesus was an eschatological sage. That is, his wisdom teaching must be interpreted against the backdrop of eschatology, and vice versa. Furthermore, I concur with James Charlesworth that there is substantial continuity between Jesus and his first followers: "The dreams, ideas, symbols, and terms of his earliest followers were inherited directly from Jesus."[66] Certainly the Gospel accounts as we read them have been shaped by the interests and concerns of the earliest Christians. They chose what to transmit and how to transmit it. Yet there is a difference between authoring or inventing sayings or stories and editing or otherwise modifying existing traditions. E. P. Sanders notes: "The gospel writers did not wildly invent material. They developed it, shaped it, and directed it in the ways they wished."[67] Since many elements in the Gospel narratives (for example, the "embarrassing" episodes) pertain to actual events during Jesus' lifetime, the persons responsible for editing and transmitting the Gospels demonstrated a concern for historical authenticity. They were not creators of the tradition but custodians.

The Palestinian Context

Geography, Politics, Economy, and Religion

Like all human beings, Jesus lived in a particular time, place, culture, and society, and the interpretation of his life requires an understanding of that context. The following is a concise portrait of first-century Jewish Palestine that emphasizes what is most pertinent for interpreting the life of Jesus.

In terms of its natural features, the land of Israel/Palestine consists of four regions.[1] These are the Mediterranean coastal plain, the hilly territory of northern and central Israel, the Great Rift Valley, and the Negev Desert. The coastal plain is about 115 miles in length — a narrow strip in the north that gradually widens to a breadth of about 20 miles in the south. The mountains of Galilee in the north are the highest portion of the land, rising to the peak of Har Meron (or, in Arabic, Jebel Jarmaq), which is 3,963 feet in elevation. Toward the east these mountains grade off into an escarpment that overlooks the rift valley. The mountains of Galilee are separated from the hills of Samaria and Judea to the south by the Plain of Esdraelon ('Emeq Yizre'el), which, running from the northwest to the southeast, connects the coastal plains with the rift valley. The hills of Samaria and Judea culminate in the spur of Mount Carmel (1,791 feet), and reach almost to the coast at Haifa.

The Great Rift Valley is part of a massive fissure in the earth's crust that runs beyond the northern border of Israel along the length of the country to the Gulf of Aqaba in the south, and then down the Red Sea and East Africa. The Jordan River flows southward through this rift, from the region of Israel's northern border, where the river is 500 feet above sea level, into the Sea of Galilee (also known as Lake Tiberias or Yam Kinneret; 696 feet below sea level), and then into the Dead Sea, which is 1,302 feet below sea level and the lowest point on the earth's surface. As the principal drainage system in the region, the Jordan flows into both the freshwater Sea of Galilee and the intensely saline Dead Sea. The Negev Desert, in the southern part of Israel, forms an arrow-shaped wedge of land that comes to a point at the port of Elat on the Gulf of Aqaba.

The land of Israel, situated between the subtropical and arid zone prevailing in Egypt to the south, and the subtropical and wet zone in Lebanon to the north, experiences great climatic contrasts. Rainfall is light in the south, amounting to only an inch per year in the territory south of the Dead Sea, yet plentiful in the north, with up to forty-four inches per year fall in the region of Upper Galilee. The most readily cultivated regions have a rainfall of a dozen or more inches per year. The annual rainfall occurs over a period of some forty to sixty days, spread over a season of about seven months between October and April. Dry and hot weather prevails during the summer months, though in the coastal regions the sea breezes diminish the heat. In the summer the sun ascends high in the sky (over eighty degrees above the horizon), and the temperature depends on the elevation and the distance from the sea. The mean annual temperature in the coastal areas is from 68 to 70 degrees Fahrenheit, while at Elat in the far south the temperatures are around 59 degrees in January and may rise to 120 degrees in August. The relative humidity is highest near the coast and higher in summer than in winter. The Jordan Valley is hotter and drier than the coast, and the hilly regions experience occasional snows in winter. In attempting to visualize the life of Jesus, one should bear in mind this varied landscape. Within a few short verses the Gospel of Mark begins with Jesus' sojourn in the "wilderness" (1:12) — a barren and uninhabitable moonscape of white rock and blazing sun — and shifts to the lush region surrounding the Sea of Galilee where Jesus announces the kingdom of God and calls his first followers (1:14-20).

Along with variation in climate, there is variation in plant and animal life. The original evergreen forests disappeared long ago because of the centuries of cultivation and the depredations of goats.[2] The hills are mostly covered with wild shrub vegetation. Only desert scrub grows in the Negev and on the sand dunes of the coastal plains. Yet north of Beersheba, most of the land may be cultivated or used for hill grazing. The animal life is diverse. Mammals indigenous to the region include wild cats, wild boars, gazelles, ibex, jackals, hyenas, hares, coneys, badgers, and tiger weasels. Among the reptiles are the agama and gecko lizards, the viper, and the carpet viper. The partridge, tropical cuckoo, bustard, sand grouse, and desert lark are native birds. Many kinds of fish and insects may be found, and invasions of desert locusts sometimes occur. This background information gives some local coloring to the statement of Mark's Gospel that Jesus "was in the wilderness . . . [and] was with the wild beasts" (1:13).

Three non-Jewish writers of ancient times — Strabo, Pliny the Elder, and Tacitus — refer to ancient Palestine in their writings.[3] Strabo (ca. 64 B.C.E.–20 C.E.) speaks of various regions in Judea, and claims that the land is inhabited by a mixture of Egyptian, Arabian, and Phoenician tribes. He mentions a lake known to produce excellent fish, but seems to have confused the Sea of Galilee with the Dead Sea (or Lake Meron) when he states that the same lake also produces aromatic rush, reeds, and balsam. From this it is clear that Strabo had no firsthand acquaintance of Palestine, and the same is true of Pliny (23-79 C.E.) and Tacitus (ca. 55 C.E.–ca. 117 C.E.). By contrast, the New Testament Gospels show marks of eyewitness acquaintance with the land. The Gospel authors are familiar with the threefold division of Jewish territory — Galilee, Perea, and Judea. John and Luke are aware of Samaria as intervening between Galilee and Judea (John 4:1-4; Luke 9:51-52).[4] In addition, Idumea is known to Mark as being adjacent to Jewish territory (Mark 3:8). These divisions were established in the early Roman period and were maintained under Herod, though they date back to the Hasmonean wars of conquest. Differences occur, however, in the ways the synoptic Gospels and the Gospel of John present Jerusalem. The synoptic Gospels concentrate their attention on Galilee, except for Jesus' brief and final visit to Jerusalem, while John treats Jerusalem and Judea as the center of Jesus' ministry, with Galilee as a place of retreat for Jesus and his disciples.

All four Gospels mention Nazareth as the place of Jesus' upbringing, even though Matthew and Luke locate the birth of Jesus in Bethlehem. Capernaum stands out as the real center of Jesus' ministry in the synoptic Gospels, emphasized by the special woe pronounced against it for rejecting Jesus (Matt. 11:23) and Matthew's reference to it as Jesus' own city (9:1). The Gospel of John, in distinction, has a predilection for Cana (John 2:1-2; 4:46), though John also mentions Capernaum (2:12). As often noted, the Fourth Gospel, despite its high theological tones, shows a much better acquaintance with the geography of Palestine and the topography of Jerusalem than do the synoptic Gospels. There are references to Aenon near Salim (3:23) and Sychar, a city of Samaria (4:5). The Gospel of John shows knowledge of such places as the pool of Bethesda with its five porticoes, Solomon's portico in the Temple district, and the exact location of Golgotha. On this basis some have conjectured that the author of the Fourth Gospel may have been a native of Jerusalem.

Despite the numerous place references, the New Testament Gospels provide no specific description of land and water in Palestine, and this sets them apart from the writings of Josephus. The rabbinical authors were keenly aware of the boundaries of the land, since many aspects of Jewish law (e.g., tithing) applied only within the borders of Israel. The Gospel authors had different interests. Still, a puzzling feature in the Gospels is the absence of reference to Sepphoris and Tiberias, the former refurbished and the latter founded during the lifetime of Jesus. Both were major commercial and administrative centers in Lower Galilee. This point is important for interpreting Jesus' teaching, for if he had visited Sepphoris and Tiberias, then it is more likely that he would have gained some firsthand acquaintance with Greek culture and philosophy. Those who view Jesus as a kind of Jewish Cynic have sometimes asserted that he was exposed to Greek thought while on business in Sepphoris, though the city is unnamed in the Gospels.[5]

Throughout the Gospels, and especially in Mark, Jesus seems to move with ease between different regions of Palestine, apparently indifferent to the tensions between these areas. According to Josephus, Jewish and Gentile relations deteriorated in the period after Jesus' life and hostilities broke out in the Greek cities of Palestine in the years immediately prior to the general Jewish revolt in the 60s.[6] Sean Freyne notes that interregional travel would have been easier in the late 20s — the period of Jesus' ministry — than subsequently. Palestine, like other parts of the Mediterranean world, enjoyed relative peace during the reign of Tiberius. In Galilee Herod Antipas had political quarrels only with the Nabateans. The Phoenician cities, the territory of Herod Philip, and the Decapolis would all have been accessible to Jewish traders and craftsmen, and the Herodian cities of Lower Galilee would have been more friendly to Gentiles than they were some decades later.

The archaeological data lend support to the picture of interregional movement and trade, for an analysis of pottery during the period shows a thriving export industry of Galilean wares to the surrounding cities, including those in the Golan as well as Ptolemais and Caesarea Philippi. The discovery of Tyrian coinage in the sites of Upper Galilee also points to commercial movement between the regions. In sum, the political realities and the material remains make free movement between Jews and Gentiles in the north quite plausible for the period of Jesus' life. These movements are more plausible for the period of Jesus' life than the period in which the Gospel of Mark was written. Hence the Gospel of Mark seems to reflect the circumstances that were likely to have prevailed during Jesus' own lifetime, rather than those that existed during the 60s and later decades.

The Gospel of Matthew portrays Jesus' ministry as largely confined to the Jewish population. Jesus declares that he did not intend to go "among the Gentiles" but rather "to the lost sheep of the house of Israel" (Matt. 10:5-6; 15:24). The Gospel of Mark presents Jesus as going to the countryside and villages of mostly Gentile population. Mark also indicates that Jesus, despite his healing powers, was not welcome to the people of Gerasa, who on hearing of his successful exorcism of the "legion" of demons asked him to depart from their territory (Mark 5:17). Thus Mark's narrative does not efface the cultural divide of Jew and Gentile. In light of Jesus' mission to the Jews, the silence regarding Sepphoris and Tiberias remains puzzling. If the reason for the omission is Jesus' lack of success after preaching and healing in these areas, then one might have expected a series of woes against these cities like those spoken against Chorazin, Bethsaida, and Capernaum. If Jesus' stated mission was to go to the dispersed Jews, and if he was generally willing to go into Gentile regions, then it is not clear why the two great Herodian cities of Sepphoris and Tiberias were not included in his mission.

Regarding the political life of Galilee in Jesus' day, the key questions concern the distribution and exercise of power: Who exercised political power in Galilee on behalf of Herod Antipas, and toward whom was this power exercised? That is, what were the demands on and benefits to different segments of society, and what sanctions did the ruling class use to enforce its will? Josephus, the main authority for the period, states that Herod Antipas was allowed 200 talents in personal income from his territories.[7] Presumably this was collected as a land tax or poll tax, as was customary throughout the Roman world. Paid in kind, this would have amounted to 440,000 bushels of wheat each year. In addition to this, tribute had to be paid to Rome, though we do not know the exact amount. Beyond these fixed taxes, it is likely that Herod Antipas could impose special levies for building projects or other public works. He could also force peasants to live in his new city — a form of compulsory labor that was prevalent throughout the empire and against which there was little redress. In addition to this, there were also customs, tolls, and sales taxes on goods transported from one district to another. The burdens borne by the people and their daily hardships are seen in the appeals of the Jerusalem populace to the ruler Archelaus, and in the complaints of the Jewish delegation to Rome about Herod's misrule.[8]

Herod the Great raised an extra 100 talents in Galilee during his early years as governor of the region, and was rewarded by Rome.[9] On another occasion he sent part of his army to be billeted (i.e., housed by civilians) for the winter in Galilee — one of the impositions most dreaded by the people.[10] Although there is no direct evidence for either of these practices during the reign of Herod Antipas, the threat loomed over the peasants of the region. It is surprising that Josephus does not specifically mention taxation as an issue in Galilee as well as Judea. In Jerusalem the peasants sought to destroy the debt records. Josephus speaks of the serious complaints made in Rome against the Herodian tax system and the bribery and corruption connected with it.[11] No such incidents are recorded for Antipas's reign, and this makes it likely that he had learned a thing or two from his father's mistakes.

An episode revealing something of the economic situation was the threatened agricultural strike at Tiberias over the proposal to place Emperor Caligula's statue in the Jerusalem Temple.[12] Crops had not been sown during the period of political turmoil, and the *Antiquities* notes that the Jewish leaders feared an outbreak of banditry because the peasants could not pay the tribute. This shows that the farming during that period was basically of a subsistence character and did not provide for surpluses from year to year. The payment of the tribute was not in dispute between the leaders and the peasants, but only the latter's inability to pay and the resulting threat of social upheaval.

Under foreign rule the Jews of Palestine were saddled with a double burden — Roman taxes and the Jewish tithe. While Christians have generally regarded the tithe as a voluntary or optional contribution, among the Jews it was a matter of divine law and so was regarded as compulsory. The combined level of Jewish and Roman taxes may have reached as high as 35 percent, which would have been a crushing burden within a subsistence economy.[13] Since the collection of revenue was left to tax farmers who often extorted and pocketed more than the stipulated amount, the actual tax levies could have gone even higher. The impact on the Jewish people was severe, because they were in no position to change either of the two systems of taxation. One was dictated by Rome, the other by divine law. The difference between them was that the Roman taxes were enforced by police power, while the Jewish taxes were not. If one simply could not get by while paying both taxes, then one seemingly had to disobey God's law. Thus it may not have been the appeal of Gentile or Hellenistic ways of life but the stark realities of economic life that drove many Jews away from strict observance of the Jewish law. The double tax burden helped to swell the ranks of nonobservant Jews.[14]

The benefits that operated within the patronage system were distributed very unevenly. This gives added significance to the saying of Jesus reported in Matthew: "'What do you think, Simon? From whom do kings of the earth take toll or tribute? From their children or from others?' When Peter said, 'From others,' Jesus said to him, 'Then the children are free'" (Matt. 17:25-26). During the reign of Herod Antipas, and that of his father, Herod the Great, a considerable amount of land was in the form of royal estates exempt from taxation. The money or produce paid by the tenants on the land came to the owners as tax-free income. Jesus' cryptic comment regarding the execution of John the Baptist, "Elijah has come, and they did to him whatever they pleased" (Mark 9:13), is, in the words of Sean Freyne, "a typical 'view from the bottom' of how such power was seen to operate."[15] Josephus noted the popular belief that the defeat of Herod Antipas by the Nabateans was divine retribution against him for having John killed.

Richard Horsley, on the basis of studies by Eric Hobsbawm, has argued that the phenomenon of "social banditry" was endemic to the whole Palestinian region under Roman rule, and that it reached epidemic levels just before the revolt of 66 c.e.[16] This social banditry could be described as a spontaneous outburst of resentment against the ruling class. It was revolutionary only when large numbers of the peasantry became involved and it exhibited an apocalyptic or millennial worldview suggesting an alternate social order — as in the case of the 66 revolt.[17] Sean Freyne questions whether the episodes in question properly fall under the heading of "social banditry." Freyne notes that the threatened agricultural strike would seem to indicate that banditry was the direct outcome of scarcity in production and an inability to pay tribute. In Horsley's presentation, by contrast, banditry was symptomatic of more permanent social changes that were occurring.[18]

The first century c.e. in Palestine witnessed the rise of a monetary economy rather than one based primarily on subsistence and barter. This new market worked to the advantage of the few rather than the many. Status became a primary concern of those who controlled the land and its resources. Their aim was to obtain from their property the life of luxury that they regarded as their right. They had no incentive or motivation whatever for improving the lot of the peasants or lower classes. The market economy, far from improving the situation, increased the rift between the ruling elite and the rest of the population. Thus there is a historical context for Jesus' critique of Herod's court style: "Look, those who wear soft robes are in royal palaces" (Matt. 11:8). As the peasantry came under increased pressure to maintain the opulence of the rulers, hostility increased toward economic centers such as Sepphoris and Tiberias. Even though these cities provided markets for agricultural produce and manufactured goods, they could not disguise their exploitative character.[19]

Jesus' immediate environment was more culturally diverse and cosmopolitan than has generally been recognized.[20] It is probable, and perhaps likely, that Jesus had enough competence in Greek to converse in that language during his itinerant ministry.[21] Nonetheless Jesus' primary language was Aramaic, as indicated by the presence of some twenty-six Aramaic words in the New Testament Gospels. Some argue that a sizable group in the population used Hebrew as their daily spoken language during this period. Mishnaic Hebrew is a probable language of first-century Palestine, and hence a possible language of Jesus. According to Luke 4:16-20, Jesus knew enough Hebrew to locate a passage from Isaiah in a Hebrew scroll and then read it aloud. While virtually no contemporary scholars have argued that Jesus spoke *only* Greek, a number of writers have concluded that Jews in first-century Palestine used Greek extensively. Perhaps a majority of them spoke Greek. Many Jews even chose Greek for memorializing the dead in their burial inscriptions. That even rabbis and their families phrased their epitaphs in Greek strongly indicates that Greek was the language of their daily life.

Without question, Greek was the lingua franca or common language of the Roman Empire as a whole. Stanley Porter writes: "Galilee was completely surrounded by Hellenistic culture, with Acco-Ptolemais, Tyre and Sidon in the west and north-west, Panias-Caesarea Philippi, Hippos and Gadara in the north-east, east and south-east, and Scythopolis and Gaba in the south. Besides being connected by a number of waterways, there was a road system that utilized a series of valleys to interconnect the Galilean region. . . . As a result, Galilee was a center for import and export as well as general trade, resulting in a genuinely cosmopolitan flavor."[22] Jesus was from Nazareth, and spent a good part of his career in Lower Galilee around the cities of Nazareth, Nain, Cana, and Capernaum. Although Nazareth was a village of some 1,600 to 2,000 in population and relied heavily on agriculture as its economic base, it is not accurate to think that Jesus grew up in cultural and geographical isolation. Nazareth was situated alongside of, and overlooking, one of the busiest trade routes in ancient Palestine, the Via Maris, which stretched all the way from Damascus to the Mediterranean. Capernaum, a town of 12,000 to 15,000, was yet more culturally diverse than Nazareth. Matthew (perhaps also known as Levi), the tax collector in Capernaum, would probably have had to use Greek to converse with the local taxpayers and the officials of Herod Antipas. The fishermen disciples would also probably have needed to speak Greek in order to carry on their business of selling fish.

Jewish religion in first-century Palestine is an unusually rich topic that has become even more complex and colorful in the recent academic literature. Only an outline of major trends can be offered here.[23] Contemporary scholars recognize the enormous diversity within Judaism during the period from the Roman conquest of Palestine (63 B.C.E.) to the destruction of the Jewish Temple at the conclusion of the war against Rome (70 C.E.). In this era it is probably best to speak and think of "Judaism" in the plural. That is, there were competing "Judaisms" that shared certain common preoccupations — with Temple, with Torah, with ceremonial law and purity, and so forth — but held to diverse and even diametrically opposed opinions on all these topics. Some decades ago George Foot Moore published a classic study of Judaism in the first centuries of this era which presented rabbinical teaching as "normative Judaism."[24] While this may accurately describe the period from about the seventh to the nineteenth centuries, it does not do justice to the complexities of the first century. Jacob Neusner, in his many important books, has portrayed a "first age of diversity" in Judaism that is unrivaled for its breadth of outlook and variety of practice until the developments of the last two centuries.[25] Even a basic rite such as circumcision was understood quite differently in the Hebrew Bible, 1 Maccabees, Philo, the writings of Paul, and Josephus.[26] Similarly, the concept of "Messiah," often thought to be essential to all forms of Judaism, is in fact used in only some of the texts of this period, and even then with different meanings.[27]

The question arises: What, if anything, tied together the various "Judaisms" that flourished during the first century? A number of broad and overarching concerns connected the differing groups: the Temple, the Torah or scripture, the role of nonscriptural or extrascriptural tradition, and apocalypticism. Not all groups shared these interests to an equal degree. Each concern, if taken singly and separately, had the capacity to absorb or nullify all the others. Thus an apocalyptic Judaism could, and sometimes did, negate the importance of the Temple and of priestly ritual, while a Judaism based on Levitical tradition and ritual purity would often rely on noncanonical texts as a basis for its claims and practices. In some versions of Judaism the Temple in Jerusalem was a concrete physical reality with spiritual meaning. Others spiritualized the Temple, so that it became a metaphor or an idealization. To survey the various points of view, I will first treat the general Judaic concerns of Temple and Torah, and then move on to the specific groups such as the Pharisees, the Sadducees, and the Essenes or Qumran community.

The overriding importance of the Temple in first-century Judaism becomes apparent in the persistence of the Jewish people in rebuilding and maintaining the Temple and in the large place given to it in ancient literature. Bruce Chilton notes that the Jewish Temple was renowned throughout the Roman world and was perhaps "the largest religious structure in the world at the time."[28] It was certainly the most prominent institution in Judea that was under Jewish control. As such, it had unmistakable symbolic meaning: "As the center of the cult of Yahweh, and the seat of native Jewish, as opposed to Roman, rule, it represented both the forgiveness of sins and the hope for national sovereignty."[29] The desecrations of the Temple by Antiochus Epiphanes (165 B.C.E.) and the Roman general Pompey (63 B.C.E.) are recorded in the canonical book of Daniel and the noncanonical *Psalms of Solomon*. Offenses against the Temple contributed to the Jewish revolts against foreign domination in the Maccabean period (165 B.C.E.), the first revolt against Rome (66 C.E.), and the Bar Kokhba rebellion (133 C.E.). The Temple plays a central role even in the Mishnah, the first collection of rabbinical writings, put into writing about 130 years (ca. 200 C.E.) after the destruction of the Temple and the cessation of the sacrifices there. The opening paragraph of the Mishnah asks when the evening prayer (i.e., Shema) may be recited, and formulates an answer in terms of the activities of the priests in the Temple. This might be compared to Americans today debating the hour at which Abraham Lincoln delivered the Gettysburg Address! It indicates how central the Temple and its rituals had become to the religious life of the Jewish people during the preceding centuries.

The fierce controversies surrounding the Temple underscore its importance. People fight over issues that they care about, and concerning the Jerusalem Temple there were both profound concern and passionate argument. The Qumran community, which produced the Dead Sea Scrolls, may have come into existence in the second century B.C.E. in response to a change in the priestly succession that rendered the existing Temple leadership illegitimate in the eyes of these sectarians. In their organization and ritual practices they presented themselves as a *true* priesthood awaiting the unveiling of a purified and restored Temple. Yet the Qumran community was not the only group critical of the Temple leadership. The mid-first century B.C.E. *Psalms of Solomon* attack the priests as "sinners" and "lawless" persons who have stolen from the Temple's sanctuary and have no regard for the distinction between clean and unclean. Two other texts from the so-called Pseudepigrapha, the *Testament of Levi* and *The Lives of the Prophets*, make similar claims.[30]

The early movement surrounding Jesus seems also to have been critical of the Temple. In Mark's Gospel Jesus responded negatively to a statement praising the grandeur of the Temple: "Do you see these great buildings? Not one stone will be left here upon another; all will be thrown down" (Mark 13:2). When Jesus died, the Gospels report that the veil of the Temple was torn in two (Mark 15:38) — an event that might signify a devaluing of the Temple. Likewise the speech attributed to Stephen in the Acts of the Apostles includes a sharp critique of Temple-centered piety (7:48-53; cf. 6:13-14). The writings of Paul refer to the Temple, yet only as an image representing the spiritual community in Christ. The earthly structure fades from view. Likewise the Epistle to the Hebrews in the New Testament, in a fashion reminiscent of Philo (ca. 30 B.C.E.–45 C.E.), teaches that the earthly Temple is "a mere copy of the true one" which is in "heaven itself" (Heb. 9:24; cf. 8:2, 5). To sum up, the various forms of first-century Judaism were alike in valuing the Temple, and yet they criticized the existing priesthood and sacrificial service in a variety of ways. Some called for a replacement of the current priests with more qualified persons, others awaited a divine intervention to overthrow the Temple leadership and establish a new Temple with new priests, and still others viewed the earthly edifice as secondary to a spiritual Temple not made with hands.[31]

A telling phenomenon of Greco-Roman Judaism was the appearance of documents that retold the stories and history of the Hebrew Bible. Sometimes these documents copied a genre contained within the canonical writings (e.g., psalms, apocalypses, histories), while at other times they were a hybrid of biblical styles and the conventions of ancient romance. J. Andrew Overman and William Scott Green note that these new writings, supplementing the Hebrew Bible, underscore "the need on the part of Jews both at home and in the diaspora to clarify who they were, whose they were, and what the future held for them."[32] By seizing hold of the past, they sought to orient themselves in the present. The interpretation of the past was a way for the Jewish people to redefine and redirect themselves in an age of uncertainty.

With regard to sacred scripture or Torah, no single text was used by all Jews during this period. Greek-speaking Jews rarely resorted to the Hebrew original, but instead used the Greek translation known as the Septuagint (also identified as the LXX). Some even thought this translation (or a part of it) had been directly inspired by God and possessed as much authority as the Hebrew original, an idea that became apparent as early as the *Letter of Aristeas* (ca. 150-100 B.C.E.). (English-speaking Christians have sometimes had a comparable veneration for the Authorized or King James Version of 1611.)[33] Rabbinical Judaism had its Targums — renderings of the Hebrew Bible into the Aramaic language — but always regarded these as interpretations of sacred scripture and not as original or authoritative texts. In point of fact, the Septuagint translation was not completed all at once (notwithstanding the legends regarding its origin) and so there were many different manuscripts. The Greek version of Isaiah, for instance, may be 100 to 150 years later than that of the Pentateuch.

Of all the Jewish groups of the first century C.E., the Pharisees (probably from Heb. *perushim,* "separated ones") are perhaps the best known because of the role they play as Jesus' chief opponents in many Gospel stories. While Josephus and early rabbinical literature provide information on the Pharisees, all of the existing sources on them have to be used with caution and none presents a very complete picture. The aim of the Gospel writers was to present Jesus and not a detailed and accurate picture of the Pharisees and other Jewish groups. Josephus wrote with a view to commending the Pharisees to his Roman patrons and a Gentile reading audience, and so his presentation may be slanted in certain respects. The rabbinical writings appeared many generations after the pre–70 C.E. Pharisees, the crisis of the war against Rome, the destruction of the Temple, and other profound changes in Jewish life. The rabbis' presentation of the first-century Pharisees is often colored by a desire to promote their own later agendas. In fact, we have writings from only two persons who actually claim to be Pharisees — Saul of Tarsus or Paul the apostle, and Josephus — and neither can be considered representative of the Pharisees in general.[34]

Josephus lists the Pharisees as one of three different sects or philosophical groups (Gk. *hairesis*) that existed among the Jews, along with the Sadducees and the Essenes.[35] Josephus describes these groups in terms of their beliefs on fate or free will, the immortality of the soul, and rewards and punishments after death. The Pharisees, he says, affirm both fate and free will, believe that the soul is imperishable, that the dead will be raised again, and that the wicked are punished eternally. They eschew a life of luxury, show respect for elders, and follow the guidance of reason. It is clear that Josephus's description attempts to commend the Pharisees to Gentile readers who would likely have looked with favor on a group said to be mildly ascetic and reasonable in its outlook. Throughout Josephus's narrative, the Pharisees appear as a kind of political interest group, currying favor with rulers. They belong to a retainer class that has no political power of its own but cultivates good relations with the ruling group. In time they gained and then lost the support of John Hyrcanus (ruler from 134 to 104 B.C.E.), and then again won over Queen Alexandra (76-67 B.C.E.). Unfortunately, it is not really possible from Josephus's narrative to reconstruct a clear picture of the Pharisees' agenda or what program they might have sought to implement.[36]

In the Gospel texts the Pharisees and Jesus contend over issues of purity, Sabbath observance, fasting, and tithing. A dispute over eating with unwashed hands becomes the occasion for Jesus to set forth a contrast between the Pharisees' "traditions of the elders" and the "commandments of God" (Mark 7:1-23; Matt. 15:1-20). In general the notion of Jesus disputing with the Pharisees over matters of ritual and purity is consistent with the later evidence of the Mishnah and Tosephta, where the Pharisees and the Sadducees have seven different disputes with one another that are largely concerned with purity. The Pharisees' agenda for the renewal of Judaism almost certainly centered on such matters as strict tithing, the observance of ritual purity by non-priests, careful attention to the Sabbath and other holidays, and rules regarding the practice of sharing meals with others. Later rabbinic writings, such as *Tractate Demai* in *The Mishnah* (ca. 200

C.E.), make reference to a custom of "association" (Hebrew *habura*) and to people known as "associates" *(haberim).*[37] While these references do not imply the existence of a unified group of *haberim,* they do attest to a practice among some Jews of sharing meals only with those who practiced strict tithing and insured that the food met the other standards for ritual purity. It is therefore likely that the Pharisees of the first century C.E., in striving for purity, limited their food consumption to meals that they had prepared themselves or that were offered to them by a handful of like-minded individuals.

Concerning the Sadducees, we are in an even weaker position than with the Pharisees in terms of historical documentation. John Meier comments that we have "only a very fragmentary picture" of this group.[38] The term itself may be derived from the name Zadok, high priest at the time of David (2 Sam. 8:17; 15:24). Yet no surviving sources are written from the Sadducees' point of view, no Jewish movement from a later period claims descent from the Sadducees, and the sources that do mention the Sadducees tend to couple them with the Pharisees and rarely mention them separately. When Josephus wrote his major works, the Pharisees may have been gaining in influence, and his comments on the Sadducees could be biased against them. In the rabbinic literature the Sadducees are treated almost as outsiders.[39] The various sources all agree that they denied the resurrection of the dead.[40] Josephus adds that they do not believe in fate, accept no observance apart from the laws of the Torah, and reject the traditions of the Pharisees. In the New Testament the Sadducees are associated with the high priests and rulers of the Jews (Acts 23:6-8). These scant references do not justify the fuller picture of the Sadducees that is sometimes offered, namely, as a group of biblical literalists who had no oral traditions of their own in addition to the written Torah. This portrayal may or may not be accurate. Moreover, while the Sadducees played a role in the ruling elite, they should not simply be identified with it.[41]

Prior to the discovery of the Dead Sea Scrolls in the caves at Qumran in the 1940s, the Essenes were known largely through the references in Josephus, along with some additional information in Philo and Pliny the Elder. Although there is still debate on the issue, the Dead Sea Scrolls are today almost universally accepted as documents from an Essene community that shared a kind of monastic life in the isolation of the desert.[42] Thus the Dead Sea Scrolls give a much more detailed picture of the first-century sect than was possible before the discovery and decipherment of the scrolls. The texts span a period running from the middle of the second century B.C.E. to the destruction of the community by the Romans (ca. 68 C.E.). Some of the distinctive practices of the Qumran community included a sharing of material possessions, a disparaging attitude toward marriage, and a habit of adopting children into the community. Some members were celibate — a rarity within Judaism. For such infractions as speaking against the group or violating its purity rules the community inflicted severe penalties (for example, imprisonment for several years, permanent expulsion, and mulcting or diminishing food and water rations). The sensational claims that New Testament figures such as John the Baptist, James the brother of Jesus, or Jesus himself are referred to in the Dead Sea Scrolls have not won support within the international scholarly community.[43]

The documents show that the Qumran community was alienated from the Temple leadership in Jerusalem. The group may have withdrawn into the desert because its members rejected the Hasmoneans' claim to the high priesthood. The scrolls include an extensive discussion of a certain "Wicked Priest," whose identity is still in dispute. Among the texts in the Dead Sea collection, the Damascus Document and Thanksgiving Hymns condemn the false priests who fail to observe the distinction between clean and unclean as "teachers of lies and seers of falsehood" who lead the people "to exchange the Law engraved on [the] heart . . . for the smooth things (which they speak)."[44] The War Scroll describes a final battle between the sons of light and the sons of darkness, and indicates that the community believed that the holy war would be followed by a new and purified Temple. Those at Qumran followed Levitical regulations that normally applied only to the Temple priests. They held a rank or order (Hebrew *serek*) among themselves according to levels of purity or holiness approximating those of the Jerusalem Temple. Thus Qumran in its internal organization understood itself as the *true* Temple and ordered its life to accord with its tradition of how the Temple ought to be managed. The present corrupt leadership of the Temple would be overthrown and the true priests — the Qumran community itself — would take its place. There is not much evidence, however, that the Qumran community had a significant influence on the rest of Jewish society.[45]

In addition to the three schools of thought described by Josephus, there were other first-century Jewish groups that might be described as popular movements: the so-called Fourth Philosophy, the Zealots, the *Sicarii* (or "dagger men"), various prophetic and messianic groups, as well as social bandits. All of these groups played some role in the rebellion against Rome, which is their common trait in Josephus's description of them. Many of these movements justified their actions in religious terms, as expressions of loyalty or obedience to the God of Israel. The Fourth Philosophy was basically a tax-resistance movement, as typified by a Galilean named Judas who urged his countrymen to resist paying the tax assessment and upbraided those who would go on "tolerating mortal masters, after having God for their Lord."[46] Judas, together with Zaddok the Pharisee, filled the nation with unrest and thus paved the way, in Josephus's view, for the catastrophe of the war against Rome. Josephus also describes groups of bandits or brigands, especially prevalent in Upper Galilee.[47] The social unrest produced a series of popular or charismatic leaders, some referred to as "king" and others as "prophet" or "messiah." In the Galilean city of Sepphoris, Judas, son of Ezekias, a well-known brigand, led a raid and revolt at the death of Herod (ca. 4 B.C.E.). A servant of Herod named Simon was proclaimed king and led a popular uprising, plundering royal residences throughout the land until he was captured and beheaded.[48]

Other popular leaders described by Josephus were prophetic rather than opportunistic in character. They reiterated the message of the earlier prophets that Israel had strayed from obedience to God, had fallen under divine judgment, and needed to repent in order to be free from foreign domination. A certain Theudas persuaded a multitude to follow him to the Jordan River, where he said he would miraculously divide the river.[49] His movement ended speedily with his capture and execution. Another figure, known simply as "the Egyptian," managed to draw some 30,000 followers, whom he incited to storm the city of Jerusalem. Many were killed and captured, although the Egyptian escaped.[50] John the Baptist is also mentioned by Josephus as a figure who stood in the prophetic tradition of Isaiah or Elijah. The Zealots, as a distinct political movement, probably did not coalesce until the 60s when war with Rome was imminent.[51]

Standing above the political interest groups and the movements of popular insurgence was the Sanhedrin, or chief council of the Jews in Jerusalem. The term itself comes from the Greek *synedrion* (lit. "a sitting down with"), a common term for a meeting or assembly. There is considerable debate over the nature and function of the Sanhedrin, which has been variously understood as a political council of the high priests, a legislative body in Jewish Palestine, a judicial supreme court, a grand jury for important legal cases, the council of the Pharisaic school, and a final court of appeals in deciding questions of Jewish law. There is even debate over whether there was one or more than one group known under the title of Sanhedrin. In all likelihood, there were many assemblies and councils attached to the various Jewish groups, but only one supreme council in Jerusalem, composed of the most powerful and influential leaders at a given time. In the New Testament the term *synedrion* refers sometimes to local courts or councils that keep order and administer punishments (Matt. 5:22; 10:17; Mark 13:9). More often it denotes a supreme council in Jerusalem that acts as a judicial court, a political link to the Roman governor, and the guardian of public order. The high priest is said to preside over it, and its members include the chief priests, elders, scribes, and other leading citizens (Mark 15:1).

In Mark and Matthew the Sanhedrin condemns Jesus to death (Mark 14:64; Matt. 26:66), but then must approach the Roman governor to have him executed. In Luke no formal condemnation of Jesus is made until after the governor has been approached (Luke 22:71). The Gospel of John attributes a political motivation to the Sanhedrin, led by Caiaphas, which feared that Jesus might precipitate social unrest and provoke the Romans to destroy the nation (John 11:47-53). The Sanhedrin's function in the Acts of the Apostles is consistent with the picture presented in the Gospels. It upholds public order, guards the sanctity of the Temple, and metes out punishment to offenders (Acts 4-6; 23). It represents the nation to the Roman authorities (Acts 22:30), is composed of Sadducees and Pharisees, and is led by the high priest (Acts 5:21, 34). Under its direction are Temple officials, guards, and a prison, and so it resembles a typical Hellenistic-Roman regional or city council.[52]

Debates over the character of the Sanhedrin, its procedures, and its authority vis-à-vis the Roman governor have been driven by a desire to explain Jesus' arrest, trial, condemnation, and execution. Yet the Sanhedrin should be understood in terms of the general responsibilities assigned to ancient councils in cities and territories. A nation under Roman domination had to keep order among the populace, and this would have been a fairly routine matter in ancient Palestine. Governmental authority at that time did not follow the neat divisions of executive, legislative, and judicial powers that are familiar to those living in modern nation-states. Certainly there was no demarcation between the religious and the political spheres, as Anthony Saldarini notes: "The theory of two sanhedrins, one political and one religious, during this period is improbable in the extreme because political and religious life were one."[53] The Pharisees, Sadducees, and other groups may have had their own private assemblies, yet this does not mean there was more than one Sanhedrin. Ellis Rivkin may be correct in his argument that the Sanhedrin was an ad hoc group dependent on the will of the current ruler. He suggests further that it was not really a standing council, but one convoked from time to time under the firm hand of the Jewish high priest and his immediate associates.[54]

The preceding discussion has shown the remarkable vitality and diversity of first-century Judaism. This diversity has considerable significance for interpreting the life of Jesus, because it suggests that he lived in an era when the basic concepts of Judaism were hotly contested and few practices or teachings were a matter of general agreement. Consequently one should not think of Jesus and his first followers as a tiny minority set over and against a unified Judaism or the Jewish people as a whole. Such a portrayal of "Jesus vs. Judaism," though reinforced by traditional interpretations of certain New Testament texts, mistakenly presumes a degree of religious consensus that did not exist among the Jewish people in this era. Just as importantly, it fails to account for the Jewishness of Jesus and Jesus' followers. J. Andrew Overman and William Scott Green speak of the earliest Christians as constituting a "Jesus-centered Judaism," and they observe: "It is anachronistic, though still commonplace, to identify the Jesus movement of 1st century Palestine as 'Christianity.' In its historical and religious context and in its varied forms, the Jesus movement was a type of *Judaism* and was viewed as such by non-Jews." The same authors note that there were significant internal differences within the Jesus movement: "Jesus-centered Judaism was not monolithic. The internal differences within this Judaism parallel those that distinguished other Judaisms from one another. Some variants of this Judaism stressed scripture, tradition, and aspects of Levitical piety, while others were dominated by apocalypticism."[55]

Having now portrayed, with broad brush strokes, the complex, contentious, passionate, and ultimately revolutionary context of first-century Palestine, we are now in a position to examine the particulars of Jesus' life, beginning with the appearance of Jesus' kinsman and predecessor, John the Baptist.

The Forerunner

John the Baptist

❧

The story of Jesus' adult life begins with John the Baptist.[1] John is named no fewer than eighty times in the canonical Gospels and nine times in Acts. Though each of the Gospels portrays John somewhat differently, they all proceed from the assumption that the beginning of Jesus' ministry and the beginning of the gospel message lie in John and his preaching. John the Baptist is thus a part of Jesus' identity. "Some key elements of John's preaching and praxis," writes Meier, "flowed into Jesus' ministry like so much baptismal water."[2] A scrutiny of the Gospels shows, however, that John's role is more ambiguous than at first appears. He did not oppose Jesus as did Herod Antipas and Pilate, and yet he is said to have posed to Jesus the skeptical question: "Are you the one who is to come, or are we to wait for another?" (Matt. 11:3; cf. Luke 7:19). The Gospel of John suggests that there was some measure of competition between the followers of John and those of Jesus, and that for a period these two figures were developing their ministries and followings alongside of one another (John 3:22–4:2). In light of the criterion of embarrassment, discussed above, it seems quite certain that John the Baptist and his movement were originally independent of Jesus and his followers. At the same time, Jesus was baptized by John, and this indicates that at least for some period of time the two had a close affinity. Between John and Jesus there was an intricate and intriguing relationship that can be interpreted in a number of different ways.[3]

John was the leader of a sectarian baptizing movement centered in the wilderness of Judea — a place with eschatological as well as ascetic associations. Like earlier prophetic and apocalyptic figures, John announced the imminent end of the world and the time of divine judgment. John also spoke of a "Coming One" who would carry out the judgment. He summoned people to repentance because the remaining time was short, and the end was drawing near.[4] The accounts of his preaching given in the Gospels carry a tone of urgency: "Even now the ax is lying at the root of the trees; every tree therefore that does not bear good fruit is cut down and thrown into the fire" (Matt. 3:10). While John's baptism shows resemblances to the water lustrations and ritual cleansings at Qumran in the desert, there is a decisive difference. This water ritual does not seem to have been administered more than once, and so it does not fit into the pattern of the Levitical laws that specified that ritual washing was to occur whenever a person became ceremonially unclean.[5] Instead John's baptism marks a once-for-all transition into a new religious identity. Baptism in the Jordan River might also have carried a symbolic meaning, indicating that the people of Israel were in a spiritual state of exile, and that the act of passing through the waters of the Jordan was a way of reentering the promised land. In the later Hebrew prophets, one finds the return from exile presented as a kind of new exodus for the people of Israel, and connected with the promise of a new covenant with God (Isa. 59–66; Jer. 31; Ezek. 36).

The Gospels agree in connecting John's baptism with repentance and forgiveness, calling it a "baptism of repentance for the forgiveness of sins" (Mark 1:4). The exact relationship between the water ritual and forgiveness is not, however, spelled out. Robert Webb suggests that the water ritual symbolized a person's repentance and God's forgiveness, and that the forgiveness itself would be conferred at the final judgment rather than at baptism itself.[6] Baptism was thus an expression of hope. Josephus seems to support this interpretation when he states that John's baptism was not "to gain pardon for whatever sins they committed, but as a consecration of the body implying that the soul was already thoroughly cleansed by right behavior."[7] On the other hand, since John required baptism of his followers, they may have regarded the act of baptism (or even John himself) as a means of forgiveness and spiritual cleansing. This would have put John into competition with the Temple priests and their sacrifices, and may help to account for the controversy surrounding him.

The origins of John's mission are not spelled out in any detail in either the New Testament Gospels or Josephus. Yet Luke indicates that John was the only son of a Jerusalem priest who had served in the Temple (Luke 1:5-80), and this would suggest that John's decision to preach in the wilderness represented a decisive break with family and tradition. Meier notes that John would have had "a solemn duty to follow his father in his function and to make sure that the priestly line was continued by marriage and children." Instead John seems to have "scandalously rejected his obligation" and "struck out into the desert to embrace the role of an Israelite prophet of judgment."[8] More than this cannot be asserted with confidence, although it is tempting to take a stab at composing a kind of first-century screenplay about the events that may have led John to take up his solitary calling. Another unanswered question regards the custom of baptizing itself. As already noted, the cleansing rites associated with the Jerusalem Temple and with Qumran afford only a partial analogy to John's baptism. Furthermore, the Jewish custom of proselyte baptism (that is, for Gentiles who wished to become Jews) is not clearly attested in the sources that might be expected to mention it during this period, and so the custom may have originated after the time of John the Baptist. If proselyte baptism came later than John, then obviously John's baptism cannot be considered as a modified version of it. The likely conclusion is that John's baptism derived from his own eschatological vision and message, and represented something new arising from the hallowed custom of water rituals. The distinctive practice made an impression on John's audience and resulted in the designation by which he became forever known — the Baptist.[9]

While John spoke of a "Coming One," the identity of this figure has been disputed. He could have been thinking of a heavenly or apocalyptic "Son of Man," a human Messiah of some kind, or simply God himself coming in judgment at the end of the age. John in several passages says the "Coming One" was "more powerful" than he, and that he himself was "unworthy" — statements that would have been unnecessary if John had been comparing himself to God. Also John speaks of untying "the thong of his sandals," and this too suggests that the "Coming One" was a human figure (Matt. 3:11-12; Mark 1:7-8; Luke 3:15-17; John 1:25-27). If the "Coming One" cannot be God, then whom did John have in mind? Perhaps John himself did not know. As Meier notes, the references to the "Coming One" in the Gospels are really too vague to have been coined by early Christians. They do not have the specificity one might expect if they were invented ad hoc to connect John with Jesus. The hazy statements about a "Coming One" are, after all, a rather odd way to herald a person if the identity of that person is definitely established.[10] The question posed by John to Jesus, "Are you the Coming One?" (cf. Matt. 11:3), is another argument in favor of the theory that John himself was uncertain regarding the successor he himself predicted.

John may not have intended to form a sect or gather followers around himself, and yet his message and the baptism he offered initiated people into a new group that sought to prepare itself for the eschaton or end of the world. It is possible that although John offered his message to all Jews, the baptism he offered was in effect an initiation into "true Israel," a people prepared for the "Coming One" and for the impending judgment by God. After their baptism, most of John's followers were likely to have returned to their ordinary lives and occupations (cf. Luke 3:10-14), but a few became John's disciples and remained with him in the desert. The Fourth Gospel indicates that some of Jesus' closest disciples, including the apostles Simon and Andrew, were followers of John before they became followers of Jesus (John 1:35-42), and there is little reason to think that this kind of tradition would have been invented after the fact.

Yet the Gospels stress not only a connection between John and Jesus, but differences too.[11] John was ascetic and self-denying, while Jesus was not (Matt. 3:4; 9:14-17; 11:18-19; Mark 1:6; 2:18; Luke 5:33-35; 7:33-34). John is portrayed in camel's hair garments and a leather belt, eating locusts and wild honey (Matt. 3:4), while Jesus is known for partaking in food and drink and is even accused of being "a glutton and a drunkard" (Matt. 11:18-19). John's disciples fasted, but Jesus' followers did not (at least during his lifetime; Matt. 9:14; Mark 2:18; Luke 5:33). Associated with John's fasting was prayer, and John had taught his disciples to pray during a period when Jesus had not (Luke 11:1). John's activities were concentrated in the wilderness, while Jesus focused on towns and villages (Matt. 4:23; Mark 1:38-39; Luke 4:43-44). John did no miracles (John 10:41), while Jesus' entire ministry was characterized by miracle working (Matt. 8:16; Mark 1:32-34; Luke 4:40-41). Thus the differences between John and Jesus are just as striking as the similarities.

What then is the significance of John the Baptist for understanding the life of Jesus? Jesus began his public ministry within John's movement, and at first may have shared in John's general attitude and outlook. Yet Jesus moved beyond that initial ministry with John and came to differ from John. The outward differences in John's and Jesus' respective forms of life — ascetic denial versus moderate enjoyment, and social withdrawal versus social engagement — are important in assessing the two figures. The two forms of life represented two different notions of public ministry and two different conceptions of the kingdom of God. Jesus' withdrawal from John may have been associated with his work of healing and exorcism — activities that are never attributed to John.[12] Still more basically, Jesus' departure from John is seen in his teaching on the coming of God's kingdom: "But if it is by the finger of God that I cast out the demons, then the kingdom of God has come to you" (Luke 11:20). These words bear witness to the *presence* of the kingdom in connection with Jesus and his activity. Jesus' table celebrations with despised and marginalized persons were also an indication of the kingdom's presence. What for John had been a hope and expectation that loomed in the future, for Jesus became a present reality to be enacted and acknowledged here and now. It was not just that John's future had become Jesus' present, for the *character* of the kingdom had shifted as well.[13]

John is important for understanding Jesus because the Gospel accounts consistently portray Jesus' baptism as a major transition. "As far as our meager sources allow us to know," writes John Meier, "before his baptism by John, Jesus was a respectable, unexceptional, and unnoticed woodworker in Nazareth." Family and friends alike were offended by Jesus once he undertook his ministry, and not without reason. In all probability there was little if anything in his previous life that foreshadowed his later mission to Israel. Consequently "his baptism by John is so important because it is the only external, historically verifiable marker of this pivotal 'turning around' in Jesus' life — his 'conversion' in the root sense of the word."[14] The accounts of the baptism by John and temptation in the synoptic Gospels (Matt. 3:13–4:11; Mark 1:9-13; Luke 3:21-22; 4:1-13) indicate that Jesus had a new set of spiritual experiences. These narratives attest to Jesus' experience of a call by God and to his wrestling with the significance of this call.[15] John the Baptist played a central role in the story of Jesus' call by God and the beginnings of Jesus' public ministry.

Once he had been baptized by John, Jesus began to announce that "the kingdom of God has come near" (Mark 1:15).

The Central Message

The Kingdom of God

Jesus proclaimed "the kingdom of God." Of this there is no doubt. Scholars across the entire spectrum of opinion concur that, in the words of Joachim Jeremias, "the central theme of the public proclamation of Jesus was the kingly reign of God."[1] This is a rare area of virtually unanimous consensus in contemporary biblical studies. One might go further and assert that Jesus' proclamation of the kingdom of God was not only central to his teaching but is pivotal for understanding the various aspects of his life and ministry. Thus Perrin claims: "Jesus appeared as one who proclaimed the Kingdom; all else in his message and ministry serves a function in relation to that proclamation and derives its meaning from it."[2] The theme of God's kingdom or reign leads directly into all the enduring issues concerning Jesus — his understanding of God, the significance of his miracles, the parables and other sayings, his call to repentance and gathering together of followers, his fellowship with "sinners," the opposition he faced, the death he endured, the claim that he rose from the dead, and the way he understood himself. Because of its crucial character, the kingdom of God in Jesus' teaching has generated a rich literature of discussion and debate.[3] Every presentation of the life and ministry of Jesus may be judged by the way in which the kingdom of God is understood. Some of the recent debates over the kingdom were mentioned in the earlier chapter on Jesus research, yet more background is necessary before delving into the issues posed by the biblical texts.

While discussions of the kingdom of God make frequent use of the terms "eschatology" and "apocalyptic," these terms are not used in any consistent fashion, and therefore the participants in debates over the kingdom of God have often misunderstood and spoken past one another. As

G. B. Caird has pointed out, some authors have resorted to "tactical definitions" of their terms and "in this way they built the conclusion of their argument into the meaning of the word 'eschatology.'"[4] Albert Schweitzer would seem to be an example of this trend when he writes that "the term eschatology ought only to be applied when reference is made to the end of the world as expected in the near future."[5] This way of defining words tends to obscure the evidence in the Gospels concerning the kingdom of God as a present reality and as unconnected with the end of the world. Confusion arises also in Marcus Borg's call for a "non-eschatological Jesus" where an "eschatological prophet" is understood as one "who proclaimed the end of the world *in his own time.*"[6] But what if Jesus had proclaimed a kingdom of God that was not tied to the immediate ending of the world? Would such a kingdom then not be "eschatological"? Crossan too fosters misunderstanding when he broadens the term "eschatology" to refer to "world-negation" in all its variety — "mystical, utopian, ascetic, libertarian, or anarchistic" — and concludes that "Jesus was not an apocalyptic prophet like John the Baptist, but he was an eschatological or world-negating figure."[7] Surely the term "eschatology" has to be understood more narrowly than "world-negation," or else everyone in religious history from first-century Jewish Zealots to medieval Catholic nuns and modern Hindu *saddhus* will turn out be "eschatological"!

The term "eschatology" was introduced in the early nineteenth century to refer to that part of theology that deals with Christian beliefs concerning death, the afterlife, judgment, and the resurrection of the dead.[8] Today this term is almost always used more broadly "to refer to the whole constellation of beliefs and conceptions about the end of history and the transformation of the world which particularly characterized early Judaism, and early Christianity, and Islam, i.e., *cosmic* eschatology."[9] Central to eschatology are the twin notions of the salvation of the righteous and the punishment of the wicked. Eschatology is a way of understanding the complete realization of salvation as a future event or series of future events that are nonetheless linked with the present moment. It presupposes that there is a relation between the present and the future, and also a tension between them. The present time could be a point of departure for the unfolding of the eschatological drama, or alternatively the time of fulfillment might be further deferred. The future may also be anticipated in the present through a partial and incomplete fulfillment.

A fundamental issue in eschatology is the relation between material and spiritual realities. As we will see in what follows, the language of eschatology can be understood in a more literal fashion as referring to tangible, this-worldly objects and persons, or else in a more symbolic way as pertaining to intangible realities or ineffable experiences. Early Christianity, as compared with Judaism, tended to spiritualize the conceptions of the land, the holy city, and the Temple. The earthly blessing, multiplied descendants, and possession of land that God promised in his covenant with Abraham and his descendants (Gen. 12:1-3) became for early Christians a set of symbols for a spiritual homeland not to be identified with ancient Palestine (Heb. 11:8-16). Hope centered on the new heavens and new earth that God would create at the end of the age. On the other hand, some strands of early Christianity were strongly influenced by Judaism's emphasis on the renewal (not replacement) of this present earth and the exaltation of Jerusalem among the nations.[10] This was particularly true of the "Jesus-centered Judaism" or "Jewish Christianity" of the late first and early second centuries C.E.[11]

In recent literature, many authors distinguish eschatology from apocalypticism.[12] The definition of these terms is directly related to the debates regarding Jesus' kingdom of God and whether it was eschatological, apocalyptic, both eschatological and apocalyptic, or neither of the two. Those who distinguish eschatology from apocalypticism typically view the former in a positive light and the latter negatively. The earlier Hebrew prophets anchored their hope for the future in the certainty that God had acted in past historical events, was still acting, and would continue to act. Where the people of Israel faced catastrophe, this was because God was acting in judgment and called upon the people to repent. Even in the darkest moments, hope was still possible because God could and would come to deliver his people from their suffering and travail. In the writings that reflect an apocalyptic understanding of history, written between about 200 B.C.E. and 70 C.E., the understanding of history and God's action in it changes significantly. Rather than considering each historical event and epoch separately and seeking to understand the work of God in that occasion, the apocalyptic authors conceived of history as a total series of events that, from the perspective of the final consummation, is already unified, sequential, and complete, stretching from the creation of the universe to the final conflict and consummation.

In apocalypticism the important thing about history is that it is running its foreordained course to a predetermined climax in accordance with the divine plan. Earthly life is overshadowed by supernatural forces of good and evil — angels and demons — that battle in the heavenly realms (cf. Rev. 12:7-12). Such a viewpoint makes human beings spectators rather than participants in the drama of history and its consummation. The interest of apocalypticism is directed almost entirely toward the conclusion of all things, and apocalyptic seers are preoccupied with the calculation of the time of the end and the delineation of the signs of its coming.[13] Apocalyptic writings are rife with visions of God, angels, demons, journeys into celestial regions, heavenly books that disclose the secrets of the future, and the recording of these esoteric visions in written form. Given these characteristics of apocalypticism, it is appropriate to follow the distinction observed by most Hebrew Bible scholars between "prophetic eschatology" and "apocalyptic eschatology." Where concepts differ, so should terminology. At the same time, one finds overlap between prophetic and apocalyptic eschatology, and so a watertight division is not really desirable or possible.[14]

James Charlesworth, with many others, sees apocalypticism as resulting from a collapse in the world of meaning. The apocalyptic texts are a lament over the failure of ordinary historical processes to resolve human problems. They are a eulogy over an exhausted, worn-out earth and the present age of suffering, and they culminate in a vision of a new age in which "the wolf shall live with the lamb" (Isa. 11:6) and peace will prevail throughout the world. One side of Hebraic apocalypticism is irenic and conciliatory — the nations will finally be at peace with one another — while the other side is warlike and vengeful — the enemies of God's people (either all Gentiles, or some of them) will suffer ultimate defeat and receive punishment for their sins. Reactions to apocalypticism have varied, but a common modern response is to see it as escapist.[15] It tells us that though the present world is filled with ineradicable evil, there is a realm beyond where God triumphs, the righteous flourish, and the wicked suffer. Furthermore, this other domain will soon overtake and replace the present world of evil. Once again, the lines are somewhat blurry inasmuch as the classical Hebrew prophets all announced that ultimate salvation was God's work and not a human accomplishment. Apocalypticism is in effect an intensification of the sense of human powerlessness in the face of evil.

Having thus distinguished prophetic eschatology from apocalyptic eschatology, one may assert that Jesus was not an apocalypticist in the usual sense. The apocalyptic authors were constantly exhorted to write down what they had seen in their visions (Rev. 1:11; 10:4), and we have no evidence that Jesus ever wrote anything. The apocalypticists were often scribes, preoccupied with the minutiae of encyclopedic and technical details (e.g., the exact appearance of the angels, calendrical calculations, etc.), while Jesus was a wandering teacher whose message emphasized such generalities as the approaching kingdom and the need for repentance. The apocalypticists tended to be vengeful, calling on God to destroy the forces of evil and especially the Jews' enemies, yet Jesus sought to cultivate an attitude of compassion and outgoing love. "Love your enemies" (Matt. 5:44) was one of his most distinctive teachings — although he spoke of a God who came in judgment as well as in grace. The apocalypticists denigrated the earth, insisting that God would bring a purified or even a wholly new world. Jesus, by contrast, celebrated God's creation in many of his sayings, such as that about the lilies of the field that bloom so gloriously and yet so briefly (Matt. 6:28-30). While the apocalypticists tended to situate God further and further away from the living world of humanity, Jesus stressed the nearness of the compassionate Father, who should be addressed in an almost childlike way as *Abba* (meaning "dear father"). Finally, Jesus spoke of the kingdom of God not as a separate reality that was coming nearer, but as somehow already present in and through his own miracles and preaching.[16]

Though not apocalyptic, Jesus' teaching on the kingdom of God shows many characteristics of prophetic eschatology. This means that it is in line with the major features of the earlier Hebrew prophets, canonical scriptures, and postbiblical Jewish texts. This will become clear if we examine just a few of the many relevant passages from the Hebrew Bible. According to the later part of the book of Isaiah (chapters 40–66), God will restore "Jacob" or the "tribes of Israel" through a figure known as the "Servant" (Isa. 49:5-6). "The outcasts of Israel" will be gathered together, along with the foreigners who keep the Sabbath and the covenant. These righteous Gentiles will make sacrifices on the altar, "for my house shall be called a house of prayer for all peoples" (Isa. 56:1-8). Nations (Hebrew *goyim*) will come to Israel's light, and her sons and daughters will come before God with "the wealth of the nations." The Temple will be glorified, foreigners will rebuild the walls of Jerusalem, and God announces that "I will glorify my glorious house." The Gentiles who do not submit will be destroyed (Isa. 60:3-14). God will gather "all nations and tongues," and he will send out messengers to declare his glory "among the nations." The Jews who are dispersed among the nations will be brought as "an offering to the Lord," and some will become priests and Levites. In the book of Jeremiah, God promises to establish a "new covenant" with the house of Israel and the house of Judah, in which he says he will "put my law within them . . . on their hearts" and "forgive their iniquity, and remember their sin no more" (Jer. 31:31-34). In Ezekiel we read of God's intention to bring his people back from exile and to restore and transform them: "I will take you from the nations, and gather you from all the countries, and bring you into your own land. I will sprinkle clean water on you . . . and from all your idols I will cleanse you. A new heart I will give you, and a new spirit I will put within you; and I will remove from your body the heart of stone and give you a heart of flesh. I will put my spirit within you, and make you follow my statutes and be careful to observe my ordinances" (Ezek. 36:24-27). God promises to establish a new heaven and a new earth (Isa. 66:18-24). In the latter days the mountain of the house of the Lord will be established as the highest mountain, where many nations will come to learn the law, the word of the Lord. Israel will defeat opposing nations and shall devote their gain to "the Lord of the whole earth" (Mic. 4). The Temple will be rebuilt (Isa. 44:28; Ezek. 40-43), the Gentiles will be subservient to Israel (Isa. 54:3; 60:16; 61:6), and dispersed Israel will be restored, sometimes, it is said, under the leadership of "David" (Ezek. 34; 37; 47:13–48:29).[17]

The Jewish postbiblical literature repeats many of the eschatological themes of the Hebrew Bible. While God has chastised Israel by giving the nation into the hands of her enemies, what lies ahead is the punishment or subjugation of the nations. Israel will be regathered "from east and west" (Bar. 4:37; 5:5). The book of Ben Sira calls on God to crush and destroy Israel's enemies, to "gather all the tribes of Jacob," and to "give them their inheritance, as at the beginning" (Sir. 36:11). Elijah is ready to act, "to restore the tribes of Jacob" (Sir. 48:10). In 2 Maccabees Jonathan prays to God to "gather our scattered people," to "set free those who are slaves among the Gentiles," to "look upon those who are rejected and despised," and to "afflict those who oppress and are insolent" (2 Macc. 1:27ff.). The text expresses a "hope in God that he will soon gather us from everywhere under heaven into his holy place" (2 Macc. 2:18). The *Psalms of Solomon* speak of the gathering of Israel from east, west, and north, as well as "from the isles afar off." This shows that God takes pity on Israel (*Pss. Sol.* 11). God will gather "a holy people" and "divide them according to their tribes upon the land" (17:28-31; cf. 8:34). A benediction is pronounced upon those who see what God does for his people: "Blessed be they that shall be in those days, in that they shall see the good fortune of Israel which God shall bring to pass in the gathering of the tribes" (17:50). The *Testament of Moses* speaks of the twelve tribes (*T. Mos.* 3:4; 4:9), as well as the punishment of the Gentiles and happiness of Israel (10:7).

In the text of the War Scroll from Qumran, the twelve tribes will be represented in the Temple service (1QM 2.2ff.), all the tribes will supply troops for battle (2.7ff.), and the army will march forth by tribes (3.13; 5.1). The conquering Israelites are known as "the poor" (11.13; 13.13f.). In the Temple Scroll the twelve heads of tribes offer twelve loaves (11QTemple 18.14-16). A thousand come from each tribe, making a total of twelve thousand (57.5f.). An expectation of the reassembling of the twelve tribes continues even after the destruction of the Temple in 70 C.E., as shown in the book of Revelation (Rev. 21:12) and in rabbinical writings (*t. Sanh.* 13:10; R. Eliezer).[18]

If one broadly compares the Hebrew Bible with postbiblical literature, one finds some differences in emphasis. While a prediction of and a hope for the salvation of Gentiles do not disappear, the postbiblical writings have a stronger and sterner stress on the punishment to be inflicted on Gentiles. The same trend continues into the rabbinical period, where there is debate as to whether Gentiles can be saved and, if so, which ones have a "portion in the world to come."[19] There is also a change in the way the Jewish restoration is conceived. The canonical authors typically focus their attention on the "remnant" that is saved, and this suggests that many of the Jews are not included in the restoration. The later texts tend to speak of a restoration of Israel as such, and not on its reduction to a "remnant." At the same time, the texts at Qumran have hard-line passages where the final war is against both the Gentiles and the "wicked of the covenant" (1QM 1.2). The general thrust of the Commentary on Habakkuk seems to be that the "breakers of the covenant" will be destroyed (1QpHab 2.6). Yet even in the Dead Sea Scrolls the hard line is sometimes softened, as for example in the passage which seems to teach that the suffering of the wicked Israelites, if they begin to obey the commandments, will atone for their misdeeds (1QpHab 5.3-6).[20]

In light of the texts just summarized, it should be clear that Second Temple Judaism, in its varied expressions, held to the expectation of a coming restoration by God. It was to involve a regathering of the twelve tribes, return from exile, renewal of the covenant, rebuilding of the Temple, and perhaps repentance on the part of Gentiles. This Jewish context is germane to the interpretation of the Gospels, where Jesus preached "the kingdom of God," gathered together a group of followers that became known as the Twelve, and near the end of his life took decisive and controversial action at the site of the Temple. This brings us to the first and fundamental question regarding Jesus' eschatology, namely: What exactly did Jesus mean by "the kingdom of God"?

The exact phrase "the kingdom of God" is extremely rare prior to Jesus. This is rather surprising, given that the general concept of God as king over creation is a very familiar idea in the Hebrew Bible and other ancient Jewish writings. Yet the precise phrase used in the synoptic Gospels to capture this general concept, "the kingdom of God," almost never occurs elsewhere. It does not occur even once in the Hebrew Bible, and there are only a few instances in Jewish Apocrypha and Pseudepigrapha, the Dead Sea Scrolls, Philo, Josephus, and the Targums. In the book of Psalms one finds instead many affirmations that "Yahweh reigns," as shown especially in the so-called enthronement psalms (e.g., Pss. 93, 96, 99). Even in the New Testament exclusive of the synoptic Gospels, there are relatively few occurrences of the phrase "kingdom of God." In the letters of Paul, there are only eight instances, and even here it seems often to be a summary of traditional sayings that preceded Paul. One may conclude then that its prevalence in the synoptic Gospels does not derive either from pre-Christian Judaism or from first-century Christianity.[21] Hence the phrase "kingdom of God" easily satisfies the (rather too stringent) criterion of dissimilarity as well as the criterion of multiple attestation. It occurs all through the Gospels — in individual sayings, as well as parables and narrative passages. Unquestionably, then, the "kingdom of God" was central to Jesus' teaching.

One of the distinctive features of Jesus' kingdom of God is its range of meaning. It does not seem to have a single, unified, easily identifiable definition. In a general sense the phrase is "meant to conjure up the dynamic notion of God powerfully ruling over his creation, over his people, and over the history of both . . . the kingdom of God means God ruling as king. Hence his action upon and his dynamic relationship to those ruled, rather than any delimited territory, is what is primary."[22] John Meier here is expounding a commonly accepted viewpoint among recent scholars that "kingdom" is not to be conceived in a static or substantive fashion, as a thing-in-itself or fixed locality. Instead it is dynamic and fluid, like God's relationship to the world in general and his people in particular. Hence the phrase "God's reign" might capture the original meaning better than the time-hallowed English words "kingdom of God."

Many of the parables in the Gospels explain differing aspects of the kingdom of God. Moreover, the sheer variety and detail shown in these parables suggest that Jesus' perspective on the kingdom of God was not widely shared by others, and so had to be carefully explained.[23] Among these are the following parables: the sower and the soils (Matt. 13:3-23), the wheat and the tares (Matt. 13:24-50), the unforgiving servant (Matt. 18:23-35), the workers in the field (Matt. 20:1-16), the slighted wedding invitation (Matt. 22:1-14), the wise and foolish maidens (Matt. 25:1-13), the seed growing secretly (Mark 4:26-29), the mustard seed (Mark 4:30-34), and the yeast and the dough (Luke 13:20-21).

Some of the parables lay emphasis on Jesus' immediate context, and so seem to teach the *presence* of the kingdom. The "strong man" (i.e., Satan) has already been bound (Mark 3:27). The disciples of Jesus are like a person who has found a "treasure hidden in a field" and promptly purchases that land (Matt. 13:44), or like a merchant who sells all his possessions to purchase "one pearl of great value" (Matt. 13:45-46). Jesus requires the disciples of the kingdom to practice forgiveness here and now toward one another (Matt. 18:23-35). The marriage feast is prepared and ready, but most of the invited guests would not come (Matt. 22:3). The kingdom of God is like scattered seed that secretly grows while the one who sowed it sleeps (Mark 4:26-27), or like yeast that is causing a lump of dough to rise (Luke 13:21). In addition to the parables, some of the individual sayings of Jesus that are most distinctive make reference to the presence of God's kingdom. "But if it is by the Spirit of God that I cast out demons, then the kingdom of God has come to you" (Matt. 12:28). "The kingdom of God is not coming with things that can be observed; nor will they say, 'Look, here it is!' or 'There it is!' For, in fact, the kingdom of God is among you" (Luke 17:20-21). Other sayings do not use the word "kingdom," yet emphasize Jesus' coming as the fulfillment of God's purposes, and so indirectly bear witness to the *presence* of the kingdom. "Go and tell John what you hear and see: the blind receive their sight, the lame walk, the lepers are cleansed, the deaf hear, the dead are raised, and the poor have good news brought to them" (Matt. 11:4-5). "Blessed are your eyes, for they see, and your ears, for they hear. Truly I tell you, many prophets and righteous people longed to see what you see, but did not see it, and to hear what you hear, but did not hear it" (Matt. 13:16-17). "Today this scripture has been fulfilled in your hearing" (Luke 4:21).

It is also evident that other Gospel texts stress the *future* arrival of the kingdom of God. The so-called Lord's Prayer is a key piece of evidence that the kingdom was in some sense yet to come: "[May] Your kingdom come. [May] Your will be done, on earth as it is in heaven" (Matt. 6:10).[24] Likewise, the Beatitudes stress the blessings that are yet to come to Jesus' followers. Those who mourn "will be comforted," the meek "will inherit the earth," those who hunger for righteousness "will be filled," the merciful "will receive mercy," and the pure in heart "will see God" (Matt. 5:4-8). Jesus speaks of the kingdom of heaven as a banquet in which "many will come from east and west and will eat with Abraham and Isaac and Jacob," while others "will be thrown into the outer darkness, where there will be weeping and gnashing of teeth" (Matt. 8:11-12). Another saying regarding the coming of the kingdom implies that it is yet to come: "Truly I tell you, there are some standing here who will not taste death until they see that the kingdom of God has come with power" (Mark 9:1). One of the more intriguing sayings relates to drinking wine in the kingdom of God: "Truly I tell you, I will never again drink of the fruit of the vine until that day when I drink it new in the kingdom of God" (Mark 14:25). The pièce de résistance of Schweitzer's argument in *The Quest of the Historical Jesus* was a verse in Matthew that seemed to predict the end of the world before the apostles had even finished their initial preaching tour: "Truly I tell you, you will not have gone through all the towns of Israel before the Son of Man comes" (Matt. 10:23).[25]

Numerous sayings and parables attributed to Jesus convey a situation of immediate crisis or impending judgment. "Those eighteen who were killed when the tower of Siloam fell on them — do you think that they were worse offenders than all the others living in Jerusalem? No, I tell you; but unless you repent, you will all perish just as they did" (Luke 13:4-5). "Do not weep for me, but weep for yourselves and for your children. For the days are surely coming when they will say, 'Blessed are the barren, and the wombs that never bore, and the breasts that never nursed'" (Luke 23:28-29). The sayings that refer to "entering" the kingdom of heaven must also be understood in terms of futurity: the kingdom is not yet (Matt. 5:20; 7:21; Mark 9:43-48; 10:15; 10:23). Last but not least in possible importance are the "Son of Man" sayings that refer to the future coming (or parousia) of this figure (Matt. 19:28; 24:27, 37; Mark 8:38; 13:26; 14:62; Luke 12:8-9; 17:24, 26).[26] Scholars have called into question the authenticity of some of the sayings and parables cited above. The "Son of Man" sayings in particular are fiercely contested.[27] Yet the remarkable volume and variety of the teachings concerning the kingdom of God give it a central place in interpreting Jesus.

The scholarship of the past century has generated divergent interpretations of Jesus' teaching on the kingdom of God. The so-called "consistent eschatology" of Johannes Weiss and Albert Schweitzer stressed the kingdom's imminence, or its future and impending character. Thus Weiss's and Schweitzer's viewpoint "made an end of the modern [i.e., nineteenth-century] view that Jesus founded the Kingdom. It did away with all activity, as exercised upon the Kingdom of God, and made the part of Jesus purely a waiting one."[28] E. P. Sanders agrees with Schweitzer, at least to the extent that the kingdom of God for Jesus primarily referred to a future event.[29] Yet, as if in counterpoise to Weiss and Schweitzer, the "realized eschatology" of C. H. Dodd stressed a completely different aspect of the kingdom of God in the Gospels.[30] While recognizing that Jesus sometimes referred to the kingdom as future, Dodd argued that Jesus' emphasis on the presence of the kingdom was the truly distinctive feature of his teaching. The "kingdom of God" was not apocalyptic, but rather "the manifest and effective assertion of the divine sovereignty against all the evil of the world." In Jesus' teaching, "history had become the vehicle of the eternal."[31] For Dodd the problem posed by the early Jesus movement was not the delay of Christ's second coming or parousia, as for Weiss and Schweitzer, but rather how the imminent return of Christ ever became an expectation within early Christianity. For Dodd the Fourth Gospel and the Epistle to the Hebrews retained the original emphasis on realized eschatology as taught by Jesus.[32] Problems overshadowed both Schweitzer's and Dodd's proposals, to wit: If Jesus had erred so monumentally by predicting the end of the world in his own day, then why should the early Christians or anyone else have taken him seriously? Alternatively, what sense is there in speaking of an eschaton or end of the world that is already present or realized? Is not "realized eschatology" a contradiction in terms?

A number of scholars, dissatisfied with the antithetical alternatives provided by Schweitzer on the one hand and Dodd on the other, proposed a model of "proleptic" or "inaugurated eschatology." Included in this school of thought are Joachim Jeremias, Oscar Cullmann, W. G. Kümmel, G. E. Ladd, Herman Ridderbos, and Scot McKnight. These authors acknowledge a certain tension or paradox in a kingdom that was "already but not yet." Not all sought to resolve the tension in the same way, but they were agreed that neither the present nor the future aspect of the kingdom could be subsumed or dissolved into the other.[33] Generally they appealed to a preponderance of evidence in the Gospels which, in the words of David Aune, "strongly suggests that Jesus himself understood the kingdom as provisionally present in his own person and message but that complete arrival of the kingdom of God was the object of imminent expectation."[34]

The debate among the three viewpoints mentioned — "consistent (i.e., imminent) eschatology," "realized eschatology," and "proleptic" or "inaugurated eschatology" — occurred on the basis of a shared assumption that the kingdom of God has had or will have fulfillment at a particular point in time. Yet some recent authors suggest that Jesus' teaching on the kingdom should not at all be understood with reference to time. An influential presentation of this perspective was Norman Perrin's *Jesus and the Language of the Kingdom* (1976), which modified the author's earlier position. Here he questions whether it is "legitimate to think of Jesus' use of Kingdom of God in terms of 'present' and 'future' at all."[35] The kingdom of God was not a concept or idea but a symbol that pointed Jesus' hearers toward "the manifestation of the reality of which it speaks in the concrete actuality of their experience."[36] Perrin distinguished two kinds of symbols. The kingdom of God was not a "steno-symbol" that has a simple one-to-one relationship with its referent, but rather a "tensive symbol" that conveys a reality without exhausting it.[37]

In certain respects Perrin continued many of the emphases of Bultmann's existentialist interpretation of the New Testament. Eschatology translates into anthropology — statements not about the cosmos, or society, but about the individual and his or her experience. Marcus Borg too, at least in some of his statements, interprets the terminology of kingdom in terms of religious experience or what he calls "eschatological mysticism," according to which the promised new age is the realm of religious experience and "the phrase Kingdom of God is thus a symbol for the presence and power of God as known in mystical experience." On this account, the kingdom exists in a fashion that somehow transcends time.[38] Borg's conclusions regarding the kingdom of God, like those of Perrin, are grounded in an understanding of the symbolic or mythic function of eschatological language. "Language about 'the other world,'" writes Borg, "is necessarily metaphorical and analogical, simply because we must use language drawn from the visible world to try to speak of another world constituted by very different realities and energies."[39]

Crossan's approach to the kingdom of God, like that of Borg and the later Perrin, does not fit comfortably into any of the three categories of imminent, realized, or proleptic eschatology. At points Crossan moves away from the notion of temporal reference, as for instance in his mind-teasing words regarding the village of Emmaus, where the Gospel of Luke (24:13-35) situates one of Jesus' postresurrection appearances: "Emmaus never happened. Emmaus always happens."[40] Resurrection language for Crossan symbolizes something that cannot be tied down to the events of a certain morning in first-century Palestine. Like Dodd, though, Crossan sees the kingdom of God as already embodied or fulfilled in some sense in Jesus' own time. The kingdom comes not in individual and mystical experience, as in Borg, but rather in the new *social* experience of Jesus' followers, a "kingdom of nuisances and nobodies." Perhaps the most distinctive thing about Jesus' ministry in Crossan's presentation is his practice of "open commensality" in which different social groups — rich and poor, male and female, observant Jew and nonobservant — shared their meals in common. This was truly revolutionary, a ritual enactment of an inclusive kingdom that challenged the existing social hierarchy. Crossan distinguishes the apocalyptic conception of the kingdom from his understanding of it as "sapiential" (from the Latin *sapientia,* "wisdom"). "One enters that kingdom," he writes, "by wisdom or goodness, by virtue, justice, or freedom."[41]

On any hotly contested topic, the participants are often more likely to be correct in their affirmations than in their denials. This would seem to be the case in the recent discussions of the kingdom of God. Each of the major authors offers something worth considering, some partial insight into the whole, or some new angle of vision on the complex topic of Jesus' preaching of the kingdom of God. After reviewing the biblical texts related to the topic, it should be clear that the inaugurated or proleptic eschatology model provides a firmer grasp on a wider range of texts than either the imminent or realized eschatology theories. Both the so-called consistent theory and the realized eschatology theory require one to ignore a great many relevant texts. By far the simpler explanation is that Jesus himself spoke of the kingdom of God in both these ways, and today this is probably the viewpoint accepted by a majority of New Testament scholars. This conclusion does not, however, negate either Schweitzer's or Dodd's insights. It merely suggests the need to coordinate or synthesize them in some fashion.

Regarding the conception of the kingdom of God as somehow transcending time or temporal reference, one must acknowledge Borg's point that the language of the kingdom has a metaphorical or analogical character. While all language has its metaphorical aspect,[42] this seems to be especially true of language about transcendent or spiritual realities — God, heaven, spirits, and angels. Of the various Gospel statements on the kingdom of God, those that present the kingdom as already present — e.g., "the kingdom of God is among you" (Luke 17:21) — are most easily interpreted in a symbolic or nontemporal fashion. Yet the statements regarding the coming kingdom are not so easily interpreted in this way. Perrin's nontemporal kingdom is closer to Dodd's realized kingdom than to Schweitzer's imminent kingdom. In response to Perrin, Meier comments: "It does not follow that the kingdom of God, simply because it is a multifaceted tensive symbol, does not or cannot, in individual instances, convey a reference to the time of the kingdom's arrival. A time frame, however vague . . . was part of the underlying story of the kingdom evoked by the tensive symbol."[43] God's reign, in the Jewish background of Jesus, was a richly textured story of a good and ordered universe, the rebellion of creatures against the Creator, God's choice of Israel to be his people, the Exodus from Egypt, the kingdom as established under David and Solomon, and so forth. It is reasonable to think that Jesus' references to the kingdom of God invoked, in the first instance, not an individual's private experience, or a mystical state of consciousness, or some ineffable reality beyond the space-time universe, but this cosmic narrative in which the creation of the world, the call of Israel, the coming of Messiah, and the consummation all unfold in chronological sequence.

Crossan is correct in insisting that Jesus' "open commensality" with the marginalized people of his society was a distinctive feature of his life and teaching — a point to which we will later return. Yet this does not in itself imply that Jesus saw God's reign as fully actualized in his own ministry. Scholars have referred to this way of viewing the kingdom as "immanentizing the eschaton," and it is one of the problematic features in Crossan's presentation of Jesus. He seems to have resolved the tension of the kingdom that is present and still to come by eliminating the kingdom's future aspect. Furthermore, Crossan's assertion that one enters the kingdom "by wisdom or goodness" is misleading. The Gospel texts present the kingdom of God as a divine gift and not a human achievement. It is God's announcement of the kingdom that elicits the human response, which begins as repentance rather than as wisdom or goodness.

In a summary statement on the kingdom of God, Bruce Chilton draws together a number of key assertions that have been treated above:

> Jesus' preaching of the kingdom is in the first place an announcement of God's dynamic rule. Human response, which might generally be described under the category of repentance, is performed as response, not initiating cause. The fact that the kingdom is normally a challenge of the future removes the possibility of understanding it within immanental terms of reference alone. The kingdom is immanent insofar as God's rule impinges upon, and elicits a response from, those who live in the present. At the same time, the kingdom cannot be reduced to human expectations of the future, any more than it can be reduced to human activities in the present.[44]

The kingdom of God as announced by Jesus had a future aspect. It was not simply present, but was still to come. At the same time it was present insofar as it elicited a response from Jesus' contemporaries. This kingdom involved human activity, and yet as a response to the prior initiative of God. Much of this is concentrated and encapsulated in the simple prayer of Matthew 6:10: "[May] Your kingdom come! [May] Your will be done, on earth as it is in heaven!" Jesus sought to announce and exhibit the kingdom of God in actions as well as words, as should become clear in the ensuing discussion of miracles.

The Man of Power

Healings, Exorcisms, and Other Works of Wonder

The topic of miracles draws one immediately into the contrasting attitudes of those who believe that miracles can and do happen and those who deny this. The entire historical-critical approach to the life of Jesus in the late 1700s and early 1800s began in large part as a reaction against or reinterpretation of the alleged miracles of Jesus. Reimarus understood the miracle accounts in the Gospels to be the result of perceptual errors: Jesus was not really walking on the water, but a fog on the water led the disciples to see it in this way. David Strauss took a yet more radical approach when he treated the Gospel narratives as essentially "mythic." Properly understood, these texts were not attesting to extraordinary events, but extraordinary insights that had been clothed in the form of miraculous narratives. Among twentieth-century authors one sometimes found blanket assertions of the impossibility of miracles, or at least the impossibility for contemporary persons to affirm them. In the 1940s Bultmann declared that "it is impossible to use electric light and the wireless . . . and at the same time believe in the New Testament world of spirits and miracles."[1] Similarly Gerd Theissen wrote: "Today we can no longer regard miracle stories as evidence of divine intervention in the normal course of things."[2]

One wonders about Theissen's "we." Is he including himself and all his contemporaries? He and his German university colleagues? A recent cross-cultural study indicated that about 75 percent of the world's population believes in the existence of demons and the reality of demonic possession.[3] Perhaps as many accept the idea of spiritual healing in some form. These people do not all fall into any simple, easily identifiable category, but are rich and poor, non-Western and Western, Ph.D. recipients and illiterates. So what Bultmann said is impossible — to use electricity and believe in spirits or miracles — is evidently not impossible.[4] Billions of people prove otherwise. So if miracles cannot be ruled out of bounds at the very outset by some kind of scholarly fiat, then there remains an important question of historical method. How is an historian to approach the sources when these record astonishing events that find no parallel in ordinary experience? What is to be said regarding such reported phenomena as sudden healings, exorcisms of demons, predictions of future events, or mind reading?

Perhaps the best general principle is to have no general principle. Individual cases must be treated individually. The German philosopher Ernst Troeltsch argued that historical inquiry is based on a "principle of analogy," according to which each event in history bears some resemblance to all other events in history.[5] While this concept has a measure of usefulness for the historical investigator, if applied too strictly it can become a kind of straitjacket. After all, there are plenty of surprises in human experience. It is said that the king of Siam, after meeting some travelers from far-away Holland, was at first inclined to trust these men. Yet when they told him that in their homeland it sometimes got so cold that the rivers became hard as stone, and one could even ride horses on top of them, he knew that the men were liars. Because new and unparalleled occurrences are possible, it is better not to prejudge claims regarding extraordinary or reputedly miraculous events. An historian must assess the evidence that pertains to the case at hand and then deliver some judgment as to what has transpired. The "mad monk" Rasputin is said to have prayed for the son of the Russian czar, and at the moment he prayed the bleeding of the hemophiliac child ceased. This was confirmed by the Russian court physician himself — a rather credible witness — and the phenomenon happened repeatedly.[6] In a case like this, the historian may avoid playing the theologian by discussing the religious claims of Rasputin, but he or she is entitled to assert that something extraordinary occurred — something that no doubt changed the conduct and policies of the royal family, and thus, the course of Russian history. With regard to the alleged miracles of Jesus, it is historically credible to make the same sort of claim: something extraordinary occurred. The multitudes that flocked around Jesus were drawn not only by his teaching, but also by what Josephus referred to as Jesus' "surprising feats."[7] Jesus' opponents confirm the point no less than his followers. The early attacks on Jesus as a "magician" or "sorcerer" in both pagan and Jewish sources establish that he was known for his remarkable powers.[8]

To gain a clearer understanding of the miracle stories related to Jesus, it is helpful first to consider the ancient context. In Jesus' era, just as today, those who suffered from serious illnesses often hoped for some kind of sudden recovery. Sometimes they sought healing from medical professionals or physicians, and yet in ancient times their reputation was not very high. As he approached his end, Alexander the Great is said to have remarked: "I am dying with the help of too many physicians!"[9] The Gospel of Mark (5:26) describes a woman who had suffered for twelve years with a hemorrhage and "had endured much under many physicians, and had spent all that she had; and she was no better, but rather grew worse." Those who needed help often turned to healing specialists other than physicians. Specially gifted persons, thought to have supernatural powers, were available to help. If the ailing wished to stay out of the hands of the physicians, then they (or their family and friends) could ask God or the gods for healing.[10]

Miraculous healings were reported in the Greco-Roman era among Jews and Gentiles alike. Hanina ben Dosa lived about a generation after Jesus, and the best-known cure attributed to him parallels that of the centurion's servant by Jesus (Matt. 8:5-13). The son of the great Pharisee Gamaliel was sick, and so he sent two of his disciples from Jerusalem to Hanina in Galilee to ask him to come and heal the boy. Instead Hanina went upstairs and prayed, and told the visitors to return, for the boy was well. Upon their return they found that he had returned to health at the exact hour of Hanina's prayer.[11] Among the Greco-Romans, the god Asclepius was well known as a healer.[12] The city of Epidaurus might be described as the Lourdes of the ancient Hellenistic world. Six pillars there contained inscriptions describing a variety of miracles alleged to have occurred. Some are rather fantastic, such as one about a woman who after five years of pregnancy gave birth to a four-year-old child. Others are more down-to-earth, such as the story of a certain Demosthenes who was lame in the legs and came to the shrine on a stretcher. As he lay down to sleep, he had a vision of God instructing him to spend four months in the shrine so that he might be healed. He remained on, and toward the end of his stay was able to dispense with his two canes and walk without any aid.[13]

In the ancient Greco-Roman world, erratic behavior was commonly attributed to demonic possession. Demons, conceived as independent spiritual forces of evil, were thought to take up residence inside a human body and dominate that person's thoughts, feelings, utterances, and actions. The only remedy for this miserable condition was the expulsion of the demon, or exorcism. In an age in which the spiritually or mentally disturbed typically lived with their family members, it is not surprising that exorcists were among the healing specialists most frequently sought out. The Jews were especially well known as exorcists. Josephus records the story of an exorcism performed by a Jew named Eleazar in the presence of the Roman general (and later emperor) Vespasian, in which he used a ring with special roots inside it and uttered the name and incantations of Solomon.[14] It is worth noting that the Gospels attribute the practice of exorcism to persons other than Jesus (Matt. 7:22; 10:1, 8; 12:27; Mark 3:15; 6:7, 13; 9:38; Luke 9:1, 49; 10:17; 11:19). In Mark certain unnamed exorcists are using Jesus' name to cast out demons, and the disciples at first are inclined to discourage this kind of copycat exorcising (Mark 9:38-40). Also in the Acts of the Apostles there is a story about a botched attempt at exorcism by some Jews who addressed the spirits "by the Jesus whom Paul proclaims" (Acts 19:13-17). The recently translated Greek magical papyri, containing various spells and incantations, include one passage indicating that Hellenistic exorcists invoked the name of Jesus: "I conjure you by the god of the Hebrews, Jesus."[15]

A remarkable case of demonic possession and exorcism is described in a Greco-Roman narrative, Philostratus's *Life of Apollonius,* which recounts the career of one of the most famous wonder-workers of the ancient world. In one episode a youth breaks out into such loud and coarse laughter that it drowns out the voice of Apollonius, and this elicits the following explanation: "And in fact the youth was, without knowing it, possessed by a devil; for he would laugh at things that no one else laughed at, and then he would fall to weeping for no reason at all, and he would talk and sing to himself. Now most people thought that it was the boisterous humor of youth which led him into such excesses; but he was really the mouthpiece of a devil, though it only seemed a drunken frolic in which on that occasion he was indulging." The story goes on to describe how Apollonius addressed the demon in the youth as a master does a servant, ordered it to come out, and after that the youth returned to his senses, and even took up a life of philosophical sobriety, modeled after Apollonius himself.[16] In partial analogy to this, the Gospel of Mark includes the following description of a demoniac: "They came to the other side of the sea, to the country of the Gerasenes. And when he had stepped out of the boat, immediately a man out of the tombs with an unclean spirit met him. He lived among the tombs; and no one could restrain him any more, even with a chain; for he had often been restrained with shackles and chains, but the chains he wrenched apart, and the shackles he broke in pieces; and no one had the strength to subdue him. Night and day among the tombs and on the mountains he was always howling and bruising himself with stones" (Mark 5:1-5). Like the young man in the tale of Apollonius, the possessed individual here is isolated, antisocial, disruptive, and seemingly unable to control his own behavior. Mark goes on to recount how Jesus directed the demons to leave the possessed man, and they entered into the swine. In the conclusion to the story, the man is "clothed and in his right mind" (5:15), and then goes out "to proclaim in the Decapolis how much Jesus had done for him" (5:20). The demons depart, and the disruptive person is calmed, brought out of isolation, and given a useful function in society.

The four New Testament Gospels narrate some thirty-three specific miracles performed by Jesus. This does not include parallels among the Gospels, summary statements of miracle-working activity, and the events connected with Jesus' conception and birth, baptism, transfiguration, resurrection, and ascension.[17] The summary statements regarding healing occur frequently, and these suggest that healing was quite prominent in Jesus' public ministry (see Matt. 4:23-24; 8:16-17; 14:14, 35-36; 15:30-31; 21:14; Mark 1:32-34, 39; 3:10-12; 6:5, 55-56; Luke 4:40-41; 6:18-19; 7:21; 9:11; John 2:23). The Gospels distinguish healings from exorcisms. Not all healings were conceived of as exorcisms, and not all maladies were thought to be caused by evil spirits.[18] The synoptic Gospels record about a dozen healings of specific conditions: fever (Mark 1:29-31), leprosy (Mark 1:40-45; Luke 17:11-19), paralysis (Matt. 8:5-13; Mark 2:1-12), a withered hand (Mark 3:1-6), bent back (Luke 13:10-17), hemorrhage (Mark 5:24-34), deafness and dumbness (Mark 7:31-37), blindness (Mark 8:22-26; 10:46-52), dropsy or edema (Luke 14:1-6), a severed ear (Luke 22:50-51), and a sickness near death (Luke 7:1-10).[19]

There are many Gospel passages that speak of demons and of exorcism. Jesus is said to have cast out a demon from a man in a synagogue (Mark 1:23-28; Luke 4:31-37), from a man possessed by a whole legion of demons (Matt. 8:28-34; Mark 5:1-20; Luke 8:26-39), from the daughter of a Syro-Phoenician woman (Matt. 15:21-28; Mark 7:24-30), from an epileptic child (Matt. 17:18; Mark 9:25; Luke 9:42), from his own follower Mary Magdalene (Luke 8:2), and from many other persons (Matt. 4:24; 8:16; 9:32-34; Mark 1:32-34, 39; 3:11; Luke 4:41; 6:18; 13:32). He engaged in controversy with some of the Jewish leaders over the source of his exorcistic power, after he had been accused of casting out demons on behalf of Beelzebul or Satan (Mark 3:20-30; Matt. 12:22-37; Luke 11:14-23). Jesus refers to the accusation that John the Baptist was demon-possessed (Matt. 11:18; Luke 7:33), and another saying describes how unclean spirits in leaving the body of their host search for another place to dwell (Matt. 12:43; Luke 11:24). It is notable that demonic possession and exorcism are not themes in the Hebrew Bible, and thus their presence in the New Testament did not derive from its influence.[20] Furthermore, John the Baptist is not said to have cast out demons. In the generation after Jesus, Theudas and "the Egyptian" promised miracles, but Josephus does not say that either of them exorcised. Honi and Hanina, the Jewish holy men of this period, were also not known as exorcists. A comparison of Jesus with these contemporaries makes it clear that his practice of exorcism was distinctive.[21]

In addition to the healings and exorcisms, the Gospels record miracles of revivification — the raising of Jairus's daughter (Mark 5:21-24, 35-43), the raising of the son of the widow (Luke 7:11-17), and the raising of Lazarus (John 11:1-44). Another category of action by Jesus is the so-called nature miracle, which includes the following: the calming of the sea storm (Mark 4:35-41), the feeding of the five thousand (Mark 6:30-44), Jesus walking on the water (Mark 6:45-52), the feeding of the four thousand (Mark 8:1-10), the cursing of the fig tree (Mark 11:12-14, 20-21), the coin in the fish's mouth (Matt. 17:24-27), and the miracle of water into wine at Cana (John 2:1-11). John Meier has questioned whether "nature miracle" is a helpful or appropriate category, given that these stories have no common elements that link them together.[22] In fact the term may be a kind of miscellany that includes all the extraordinary actions of Jesus that are not healings, exorcisms, or revivifications.

Often scholars have treated the nature miracles differently from the healings and exorcisms, in part because the latter can be explained as psychosomatic cures while the former cannot be accounted for in terms of any ordinary causes.[23] Another point of distinction is that the nature miracles, unlike the healings and exorcisms, are said to have occurred only in the presence of the disciples. They were for their eyes only, and, as private events, were akin to the postresurrection appearances of Jesus. Thus the nature miracles were not known to have played any role in Jesus' public ministry. Often the nature miracles show affinities to Hebrew Bible themes. Jesus' revivification and feeding miracles are paralleled in the lives of Elijah and Elisha (1 Kings 17:17-24; 2 Kings 4:8-44). The stilling of the storm depicts Jesus in a role reserved only for God in the Hebrew Bible (Job 38:8-11; Pss. 65:7; 89:9; 107:23-32; etc.).[24]

The Gospel texts presuppose a relationship between Jesus' miracles and the crowds. The crowds are never really explained — they are just assumed to be there, surrounding Jesus. Though Jesus may have drawn multitudes by his teaching, it seems more likely that his public appeal in the first instance was based on his reputation as a wonder-worker. The career of Jesus follows a clear progression: miracles-crowds-teaching-tumult-death.[25] The early part of Mark's Gospel especially stresses Jesus' miracles. About two-thirds of Mark, prior to the story of Jesus' final week in Jerusalem, concerns the miraculous.[26] While Mark regularly mentions that Jesus was teaching, he gives relatively little information on what Jesus taught. Matthew and Luke for their part offer large blocks of sayings and parables, and this may give the reader the idea that Jesus made his mark chiefly as a teacher. Yet the impression made by the Gospel of Mark may be closer to the viewpoint of Jesus' first audience, which knew him first and foremost as a worker of miracles.[27] After noting that no miracles were attributed to John the Baptist, John Meier comments: "To be blunt, without miracles, one wonders how much popularity this particular Jewish preacher and teacher [i.e., Jesus] would have enjoyed. Without miracles, many Palestinian Jews might have seen Jesus merely as a more 'upbeat' version of John the Baptist."[28]

A characteristic feature of Jesus' miracles is the way that he connects them with his teaching on the kingdom of God. In controversy with the Jewish leaders, they accuse him of exorcising demons by the power of Satan, and he retorts: "But if it is by the finger of God that I cast out the demons, then the kingdom of God has come to you" (Luke 11:20; cf. Matt. 12:28). Bultmann regarded this utterance as claiming "the highest degree of authenticity which we can make for any saying of Jesus,"[29] because of the unusual way it combines the kingdom of God with the activity of exorcism. Gerd Theissen agrees with this: "Jesus is unique in religious history. He combines two conceptual worlds which had never been combined in this way before, the apocalyptic expectation of universal salvation in the future and the episodic realization of salvation in the present through miracles."[30] This link between miracles and the kingdom of God is a point of distinction between Jesus and other ancient figures to whom wonderful deeds were attributed.[31]

The stories of Jesus' healing usually stress the faith of those seeking the healing. The miracles were granted to those with "faith," which might refer to persons who accepted Jesus' proclamation of the kingdom or, at the least, believed that he had received the power to bring healing. In Mark Jesus declared to the woman with the hemorrhage, "Daughter, your faith has made you well" (Mark 5:34). This statement is repeated in other episodes. Yet in the Gospel accounts it is not always a "faith healing" by virtue of the faith of the sick person. Sometimes it is the faith of those surrounding the sick person that is decisive. In the healing of the paralytic (Mark 2:1-12), Jesus healed when he "saw their faith" (v. 5), that is, the faith of those who brought the man to be healed. On the other hand, Jesus rebuffed those who demanded a miraculous sign for him to legitimate himself (Mark 8:11-13), and he performed only a few miracles in Nazareth because of the villagers' unbelief (Mark 6:5). The Gospel statement regarding Jesus' inability to perform miracles at Nazareth — "he could do no deed of power there" — would have been jarring to early Christian sensibilities, and so the saying easily meets the criterion of embarrassment as discussed above. In conclusion then, neither the curious nor the hostile could expect miraculous aid from him. The implication of the Gospel texts is that Jesus did not perform miracles as proofs of the truthfulness of his message or as a way of vindicating his own authority.

In response to Morton Smith's book *Jesus the Magician* (1978), scholars have debated the terms "miracle" and "magic," whether the two are synonymous, and, if not, which might be better applied to Jesus' actions. Smith argued that Jesus belonged to the social type that encompassed such figures as Apollonius of Tyana and the nameless persons who used the formulas that appear in the Greek magical papyri. He bases this in part on certain details in the Gospels, such as curing by touch, sighing, the use of foreign language formulas, and exorcistic techniques (e.g., Jesus' asking for the name of the demon; Mark 5:9). Crossan supported Smith's claim in suggesting that "magic" is simply a pejorative label applied to miracles that occur among groups considered marginal, disreputable, or déclassé. "*We* have religion while *they* have magic," writes Crossan. "Magic is especially a term that upper-class religion uses to denigrate its lower-class counterpart."[32] The point is that the very same phenomenon can be described appreciatively or disparagingly. (During wartime one hears of the "noble heroism of our troops" and the "savage fanaticism of the enemy," and yet the behavior may be almost identical.)

From an anthropological perspective, however, it is possible to classify different sorts of wonder-working along a continuum with magic at one end and miracle at the other. Characteristically the magician is someone who possesses a more-or-less automatic power by virtue of secret formulas and rituals. In magic there is a resultant coercion of divine or spiritual powers by human beings, who in turn receive a tangible solution to some practical problem. Usually magic involves individualism or a kind of spiritual entrepreneurship, rather than a stable and enduring community of faith.[33] Religiously speaking, magic has an ad hoc character. Miracle, by contrast, suggests faith in a personal deity to whom an individual submits his or her own will in prayer. It is associated with an enduring religious community and a divine presence that is independent of set rituals and formulas. Along these lines, Howard Clark Kee observed that preternatural phenomena take on a different significance depending on whether the context is Jewish monotheism or Greco-Roman polytheism. The framework of meaning is different in the two cases. When the focus lies on the communication of human beings with higher powers, the phenomenon is religious in character and the extraordinary event in question may be termed a miracle. When the focus lies on the functioning of forces that have been placed at the disposal of human beings, we find ourselves in the realm of magic.[34]

Magic and miracle, defined and distinguished in this way, represent ideal types that rarely occur in isolation from one another. Within the Greek magical papyri, which contain spells and incantations from the Hellenistic period, there are also prayers and humble supplications offered to the gods, and so these texts exhibit the characteristics of both magic and miracle as they have been defined here. Likewise, in the Gospels the actions attributed to Jesus sometimes have magical characteristics, as for instance when Jesus heals by spitting on the ground and forming clay to apply to the eyes of a blind man (John 9:6-7; cf. Mark 7:31-37). Saliva and other substances often play a role in facilitating the healings performed by magicians. Also when a woman receives healing by simply touching the fringe of Jesus' garment, this is in accord with popular Hellenistic conceptions.[35] Yet generally the miracles attributed to Jesus are marked by simplicity and a lack of spoken verbal formulas or other elaborate ritual processes. They fit the overall pattern of miracle better than that of magic.[36] Furthermore, it is clear that Jesus understood his works of power to be directly related to the kingdom of God that he announced (Matt. 12:28), and the notion of magic has essentially nothing to do with the coming of God's reign. Perhaps Jesus could appropriately be called a wonder-worker, a term that acknowledges both his similarity to, and difference from, the magicians of the Hellenistic age.[37]

Many of the miracles attributed to Jesus are rich in symbolic significance. That is, in addition to the historical value of the Gospel narratives, the events as described carry a surplus of meaning. The most detailed exorcistic account of all, in Mark 5, has a good deal of encoded information and carries both spiritual and political significance. The name of the demon, or rather horde of demons, is "Legion" — a title that signifies Roman dominance. The demons are consigned to the swine, which were regarded as the most impure of all the impure animals. The swine are then cast into the sea — surely the dream of every Jewish resister of the Romans.[38] On another level the story speaks of deliverance from impurity or uncleanness. The details in the narrative all contribute to a sense of the man's defilement. His home is in the Gentile region. The spirits in him are "unclean." He lives "among the tombs," where contact with corpses would have made him ceremonially impure. Swine are feeding nearby. Even the comment that he was "gashing" or "bruising himself with stones" (v. 5) suggests a flow of blood on his skin that would have rendered him yet more impure. Everything in his environment bespeaks uncleanness. Yet Jesus exercises authority over this manifold impurity, frees him from the demons, and completes his cleansing when he tells him to "go home to your friends" (v. 19).[39]

In the eyes of his contemporaries, what would Jesus' miracles have signified? Modern people have commonly misunderstood the ancient outlook on miracles. Defenders of Christianity have adduced the miracles as proof that Jesus was more than merely human, and was none other than the incarnate Son of God. With the rise of Deism in the eighteenth century, others viewed the miracles as obviously fictional and concluded therefore that the Christian faith is based on a fraud. "Both of these extreme views," writes E. P. Sanders, "miss the ancient perspective, which saw miracles as striking and significant, but not as indicating that the miracle-worker was anything other than fully human."[40] Blackburn notes that there is almost no evidence in the synoptic Gospels that Jesus ever performed his miracles to establish his status as God's spokesperson. While it is true that the Acts of the Apostles speaks of the miracles as showing that Jesus was "attested . . . by God" (Acts 2:22), this statement is in the context of the early Christian proclamation of Jesus and not in the context of Jesus' own life. To reiterate an earlier point, the truly distinctive thing about Jesus' miracle working is its link with the coming reign of God. The saying in Luke 11:20 (Matt. 12:28) is unparalleled in either Jewish or early Christian literature: "But if it is by the finger of God that I cast out the demons, then the kingdom of God has come to you." Jesus viewed his own "startling deeds" (to use Josephus's words) as signs of the kingdom and its coming.[41]

The Teacher

Sayings and Parables

As a teacher Jesus was unconventional both in the style and the content of his message. At the same time, his teachings contain frequent references to and reflections on the Hebrew scriptures, and this suggests that he did not reject the traditions that he inherited as a Jew, but built upon them in his own teaching. Some have questioned whether there is any specific element of Jesus' teaching that is completely unparalleled among the Jewish sages of his day or the centuries immediately following.[1] The task here is to unravel what was distinctive in Jesus as a teacher and set him apart from others and, conversely, what connected him to the traditions of his time and place. To anticipate the conclusion, if there is something unique about Jesus, it is probably the particular *combination* of elements in his teachings and actions. Other teachers, like the great Jewish sage Hillel, insisted on the need to love one's neighbor, and the first century had its exorcists, healers, and prophets announcing that God would soon intervene to deliver the people of Israel. Yet these elements all combine in a characteristic way in Jesus, and enter into some relationship with his teaching on God's reign or kingdom.[2]

Jesus' contemporaries understood a teacher as someone who offered instruction in a school. In the first century there were schools, especially in urban areas, where young people in their earlier years would spend their mornings learning the basics of reading and writing. After about age twelve, only the boys of wealthier families could continue their education, and it would have been customary for them to learn the classic texts and to seek to imitate famous orators of the past. Jesus, by contrast, did not establish a school with a philosophical doctrine or a special method of interpreting the Torah. His followers learned by observing what he said and did

93

in different situations. Another distinctive of Jesus is that his message to the crowds and his message to his disciples do not seem to have differed. Sometimes, to be sure, the Gospels present Jesus giving further explanations of his sayings and actions to his most intimate followers (see, for example, Matt. 13:1-53). Yet he was no esotericist, holding to a secret doctrine that was known only to a group of initiates.[3] Moreover the Jewish custom was for individuals to seek out a teacher for instruction, and then remain with him for a definite period of time or until the course of studies was completed. Jesus by contrast was a teacher who solicited his own students, thus reversing the usual procedure. He recruited them with a peremptory summons to follow him, and did not indicate that this appointment was temporary or would come to an end.[4]

Jesus' call for others to follow him must be understood in historical context. Most of those who accepted Jesus' preaching probably continued in their accustomed ways of life. At the same time, there was a group of disciples who made a break with their homes, families, villages, and a settled existence. In today's mobile society it is not at all shocking to hear of people who change their place of residence, exchange one job for another, or even leave behind family and friends in order to move to another region or country. Yet, as Pheme Perkins notes, "In Jesus' time such forms of 'uprooting' were evidence that disasters like war and famine had destroyed the traditional society of villages and towns. In that society children followed the occupations of their parents unless displaced by natural disaster, war, or enslavement. People lived in the same community for generations. . . . The traditional villager would have been quite shocked to have Jesus and his followers break with the ancestral ways of life."[5] It comes as no surprise that the Gospels portray Jesus' relatives as concerned about him (Mark 3:21) and his enemies as accusing him of insanity (John 10:20). In that time and culture, any person who broke with his or her family and home territory would have experienced a loss of identity. Almost everything about a person was determined by the place of birth and the patterns of social relationship into which he or she was born. Yet Jesus defended himself by insisting that his own preaching and healing were signs that God's reign was destroying the power of Satan. He also insisted that one's birth family and blood relationships were not ultimate. Eclipsing these in importance was one's relationship to God, and to other people through that relationship to God.[6] Jesus expressed this point rather stingingly when he announced: "'Who is my mother, and who are my brothers?' And pointing to his disciples, he said, 'Here are my mother and my brothers! For whoever does the will of my Father in heaven is my brother and sister and mother'" (Matt. 12:48-50).

Jesus' distinctiveness as a teacher can be grasped if we consider the conventional wisdom that prevailed within first-century Palestinian society.[7] At the heart of this ancient culture, as with almost any premodern culture, was a commitment to sacred traditions, or ways of thinking, acting, and feeling that were widely accepted within the society and seen as sanctioned by God. Living in accord with wisdom was a path of righteousness and blessing, while departing from it brought ruin and death. While some believed in rewards and punishments beyond the present life, there was no consensus on the matter. The great concerns of conventional wisdom in Jesus' day were family, wealth, honor, and religion, and this wisdom functioned by establishing social boundaries. Jews were distinguished from Gentiles, and also from Samaritans. More specific social distinctions existed between landowners and laborers, rich and poor, priests and laypersons, fathers and sons, elder and younger brothers, husbands and wives, and males and females generally. Those who followed the traditions were commended as righteous, and those who defied them were regarded as wicked. The underlying dynamic of this society is captured in Marcus Borg's phrase "the politics of holiness," wherein "to be holy meant to be separate from everything that would defile holiness."[8] The conventional wisdom of the culture was structured around polar oppositions between clean and unclean, purity and defilement, sacred and profane, Jew and Gentile, righteous persons and sinners.

This "politics of holiness" was an intensification of a cultural trend that had begun after the Jewish restoration from exile. In the period of the Babylonian exile and return, Israel's survival as a people depended on maintaining a sense of separate identity, and this in turn required the Jews to accentuate the practices and beliefs that made them distinct. The Jews had passed through a period of suffering and exile that the classical prophets attributed to God's anger, resulting especially from the people's adherence to foreign gods. Following the return from exile, many Jews were determined to be faithful to God and so to avoid another outpouring of divine judgment. As a small social group — and a conquered one at that, bereft of kingship and other national institutions — the Jews were in grave danger of assimilating to the surrounding cultures. Such has been the fate of most small social groups in history, and the culturally eclectic Hellenistic world made it quite easy for the Jews, if they had so wished, to blend in, intermarry with Gentiles, worship their gods and goddesses, and adopt Gentile customs. The Maccabean revolt of the second century B.C.E. arose in no small measure because of the effort of the ruler, Antiochus Epiphanes IV, to force the Jews to adopt Hellenistic culture and religion. The quest for holiness was thus especially attractive for the Jews because both God and worldly prudence seemed to require it. It was the path of social survival as well as religious fidelity. Thus "holiness" became the paradigm by which the Torah was understood. Interpreters of the Torah laid special emphasis on those portions of the law that spoke of the Jews' separateness from other peoples.

The Pharisees, as discussed above, were simply the most conspicuous instance of the drive toward holiness in this society. Their concern for strict tithing and observing the food laws led them to limit contact with Gentiles as well as with nonobservant Jews. Some of the Pharisees may have believed that the nonobservant Jews had lost their standing as Jews, and had in effect turned themselves into Gentiles. To be faithful to the law as they understood it, the Pharisees had no choice but to practice a kind of social ostracism. While the Gospels contain references to the Pharisees as "hypocrites" (for example, Matt. 23:13, 15, 23, 25, 27, 29), these statements should not be taken to mean that the Pharisees were not sincere in their beliefs and practices. What we know or surmise about the Pharisees from the various sources at our disposal would seem to indicate that they were passionately committed to fulfilling the letter of the ancient law. The burden of Jesus' criticisms of the Jewish teachers in Matthew 23 is not that they were completely wrong but that they failed to follow through on their own principles. "Do whatever they teach you and follow it; but do not do as they do, for they do not practice what they teach" (Matt. 23:3).[9] Jesus' disagreements with the Jewish leaders of his day — and disagreements there must have been, or else he would not have died as he did — were grounded in certain basic agreements. Jesus did not reject the Torah, but he interpreted it in a new way and so offered a differing conception of holiness.

Jesus was novel in his critique of the conventional wisdom of his day. Both subtly and overtly, he challenged the dominant ideas regarding family, wealth, honor, and religion. The family had tremendous importance in ancient Judaism, and indeed in almost all traditional societies. In a largely agricultural society, it was the primary economic unit. It was also the basis for an individual's identity, as each person was known as "the son or daughter of so-and-so." Yet many of Jesus' sayings challenged the idea of the family as an end in itself. At certain points in his teaching Jesus set the kingdom of God and its values in direct competition with those of the family.[10] Crossan even speaks of Jesus' "attack on the family."[11] One of his most radical sayings relates to the practice of burial, which was thought to be the most sacred of duties for a child to fulfill on behalf of parents. "To another he [Jesus] said, 'Follow me.' But he said, 'Lord, first let me go and bury my father.' But Jesus said to him, 'Let the dead bury their own dead; but as for you, go and proclaim the kingdom of God'" (Luke 9:59-60).[12] Sometimes Jesus seems to have disparaged his own family members (Luke 8:19-21; 11:27-28), and yet public criticism of one's family was not acceptable behavior within that society. Other radical sayings concerning the family appear in the Gospel of Matthew: "Whoever loves father or mother more than me is not worthy of me; and whoever loves son or daughter more than me is not worthy of me; and whoever does not take up the cross and follow me is not worthy of me. Those who find their life will lose it, and those who lose their life for my sake will find it" (Matt. 10:37-39). Such statements would have been even more surprising or shocking in the first century than they are today. They presuppose a conflict between Jesus' followers and others, and diminish the place of the family by insisting that loyalty to Jesus must come first.[13]

In Jesus' society, as in most, wealth and possessions were a major source of security and identity. Though the Jews of that era recognized that unrighteous people could have great wealth, the more fundamental idea was that great wealth was a sign of blessing from God. Yet Jesus regularly criticized wealth, and even is reported to have said that no one could be his disciple if he did not give up all his possessions (Luke 14:33). He told unfavorable stories about the pursuit of wealth, such as the so-called parable of the rich fool (Luke 12:16-21):

> The land of a rich man produced abundantly. And he thought to himself, "What should I do, for I have no place to store my crops?" Then he said, "I will do this: I will pull down my barns and build larger ones, and there I will store all my grain and my goods. And I will say to my soul, 'Soul, you have ample goods laid up for many years; relax, eat, drink, be merry.'" But God said to him: "You fool! This very night your life is being demanded of you. And the things you have prepared,

whose will they be?" So it is with those who store up treasures for themselves but are not rich toward God.

Jesus is said to have startled his closest followers with the words: "How hard it will be for those who have wealth to enter the kingdom of God! . . . It is easier for a camel to go through the eye of a needle than for someone who is rich to enter the kingdom of God" (Mark 10:23, 25). It is not clear that Jesus opposed wealth in principle, and among his followers there were some rich persons, such as wealthy women (Luke 8:1-3) and Joseph of Arimathea (Mark 15:43). Yet clearly Jesus saw the possession of wealth as a major hindrance to his message concerning God's reign, and viewed greed as one of the passions that blinded people to God and spiritual truths.[14]

Another pivotal value of Jesus' day was honor. To some extent it was the product of birth, family, and wealth, but it was also sustained by social recognition. Honor was not equivalent to social status, since it referred to the regard or esteem one received from others in light of one's status. Much time and energy went into the effort to acquire, preserve, and display one's honor. Yet Jesus disparaged and even ridiculed the pursuit of honor, speaking against those who sought the places of honor at a banquet (Luke 14:7-11), the best seats in the synagogue (Matt. 23:6), or respectful greetings in the marketplace (Matt. 23:7). Jesus also spoke against religious practices that were motivated by a desire for social recognition (Matt. 6:1-6, 16-18). "Whenever you give alms, do not sound a trumpet before you" (Matt. 6:2). He went so far as to claim that those who sought public recognition for their good deeds would have no recognition from God: "They love to stand and pray . . . so that they may be seen by others. Truly I tell you, they have received their reward. But whenever you pray, go into your room and shut the door and pray to your Father who is in secret; and your Father who sees in secret will reward you" (Matt. 6:5-6). Honor — the community's recognition of the individual — was a hindrance and a snare for Jesus' followers.[15]

Closely connected with honor was religion, and it might be regarded as the crowning aspect of conventional wisdom. The Jews regarded themselves as sons and daughters of Abraham and Sarah, and so their bloodline made them heirs of the covenant and its promises. To the Israelites, wrote the apostle Paul, "belong the adoption, the glory, the covenants, the giving of the law, the worship, and the promises; to them belong the patriarchs, and from them . . . comes the Messiah" (Rom. 9:4-5). By accepting their spiritual heritage and obeying the commandments of the Torah, the Jews stood within the covenant and shared in its assurances of blessing and an intimate relationship with God. Yet many of Jesus' harshest sayings are directed against religious people and pious practices. For Jesus, no one can count on his or her religious practice as a basis for security with God. Penitence, or a humble recognition of one's unworthiness before God, was more important to Jesus than outward conformity to the letter of the law. Consider the prayer that Jesus put on the lips of the Pharisee: "God, I thank you that I am not like other people: . . . I fast twice a week; I give a tenth of all my income" (Luke 18:11-12). This Pharisee does not seem to be a hypocrite in the usual sense, i.e., someone who said one thing and did another. Instead he is a model of what a faithful Jew should have been according to the strictest standards of the day. Yet Jesus' remarkable declaration was that the Pharisee did not go to his house "justified," but rather the tax collector who was too ashamed even to raise his eyes to heaven. The clear message is that no one can find security in religious practice, but only in the mercy of God.[16]

To understand Jesus' teaching, it is not enough to note where he differed from and critiqued his contemporaries. He was not a merry prankster who undermined other people's ideas but provided no alternative. On the contrary, the Gospels are filled with sayings and parables that delineate a way of life that Jesus laid out for his followers. One hallmark of this way, as Marcus Borg notes, is a call to *transformation*.[17] A purely outward or behavioral change was never enough for Jesus. His teaching again and again returns to the idea that people must change at their deepest level, or rather be changed, for them to live in a fashion that is pleasing to God. Jesus often spoke of "hearts" as soft or hard, good or bad, pure or impure. The term "heart" here, in accord with its Hebrew background, does not refer as in English to emotions only, but to all the deeper aspects of the self.[18] The "heart" represents the self in its innermost inclinations, where mind, affect, and will all coalesce into one. According to Jesus, the "heart" is where the problem resides: "This people honors me with their lips,/but their hearts are far from me" (Mark 7:6, quoting Isa. 29:13). Rather than actions making the person good or bad, Jesus taught the reverse, that the actions of a person flowed from the "heart" or essential character. "Either make the tree good, and its fruit good; or make the tree bad, and its fruit bad; for the tree is known by its fruit" (Matt. 12:33). "A good tree cannot bear bad fruit, nor can a bad tree bear good fruit" (Matt. 7:18).

It is striking how often Jesus' teaching makes reference to death, and these references are usually in the context of a general call for the transformation of the self. The disciples must "deny themselves and take up their cross" (Mark 8:34). "Those who find their life will lose it, and those who lose their life for my sake will find it" (Matt. 10:39). In Mark both "drinking the cup" and "baptism" are images for the death that Jesus and his followers must undergo (Mark 10:38-40; cf. Luke 12:50). "Unless a grain of wheat falls into the earth and dies, it remains just a single grain; but if it dies, it bears much fruit" (John 12:24). In its positive aspect, Jesus' teaching offered the prospect of a transformed self and a transformed way of thinking and acting. Yet in its negative aspect, it required that the disciples renounce falsehood and leave behind their former selves and former lives. "Dying" is a metaphor that stresses the once-for-all and decisive nature of the change intended in Jesus' teaching, as Borg explains: "A hardened heart must in a sense die in order that a new heart may be created; it cannot change itself. 'Dying' is something that happens to the self as opposed to it being something that the self accomplishes."[19]

With his death metaphor, Jesus taught renunciation. Yet his instruction was not based on a dualistic understanding of the material or natural world. Jesus' sayings contain no hint that he rejected the physical or material world and favored the spiritual world instead. Rather he seems to have delighted in the natural world as God's creation, and he appealed to his hearers to "look at the birds of the air" and "consider the lilies of the field" (Matt. 6:26, 28). The earthiness and everydayness of the parables and sayings confirm the point. They reflect a careful and caring observation of daily life, and they suggest apt analogies between ordinary experience and spiritual truths. The parables and sayings of Jesus are not what one would expect from a person who was hostile or indifferent to the present life or felt himself an alien to it.

Jesus was not an ascetic in the usual sense, since he was reputed to enjoy food and drink and his opponents contrasted him unfavorably with John the Baptist in this respect (Matt. 11:16-19).[20] Though apparently Jesus never married,[21] his teaching does not reflect any opposition to sexuality as such. Religious movements of a world-denying character usually involve some denigration of the body and of bodily appetites, and especially sexuality. What commonly goes with this is a denigration of women as spiritual hindrances to men or agents of carnal temptation. Despite a brief reference to "eunuchs" who forsake marriage for the sake of God's kingdom

(Matt. 19:12), Jesus' teaching is remarkable for its lack of antisexual animus. Jesus' followers were to renounce lust and a wandering eye (Matt. 5:27-30), just as they were to renounce covetousness and greed, but they were not in general called upon to abstain from sexual life. Dale Allison argues for Jesus as an "ascetic" in light of the fact that he asked some individuals to give away their money and goods, sent out itinerant preachers with less than the bare essentials for survival, and himself forsook work, family, and a stable home. While the definition of "ascetic" and its application to Jesus are both open to debate, there is no question that Jesus sounded a call to renunciation that was often rigorous indeed.[22] My point is that Jesus' teaching — however one labels it — did not reflect any opposition to the material world as such, or to the body and sexuality.

Jesus' teachings reflect a fresh observation of the social and natural worlds and the affairs of everyday life. "They have the ring of originality," writes C. H. Dodd. "They betray a mind whose processes were swift and direct, hitting the nail on the head without waste of words." In all of Jesus' teachings, there is a "sense for the concrete" and a "delight in imaginative picture-making."[23] The parables show an eye for human affairs that was sympathetic and yet unsentimental. They depict human virtues — the affection of a father for his wayward son (Luke 15:11-32), the devotion of a shepherd to his flock (Luke 15:3-7), and the compassion of a passerby for a man robbed and left to die (Luke 10:29-37). At the same time, the parables also show the odd mixture in human motives — a man arises at midnight to help a friend, but only because the friend was making a pest of himself (Luke 11:5-8), and a dishonest servant about to be dismissed cuts a business deal that defrauds his master and yet still evokes the master's praise because of his shrewdness (Luke 16:1-9). Jesus' parables are down-to-earth. To speak colloquially, they exhibit "horse sense" or "street smarts." They rest on the assumption that spiritual matters are not alien to worldly concerns, but can be understood on analogy with them. "The principles of human action," writes Dodd, "fall within a universal order . . . to be recognized at any level by those who have eyes to see and ears to hear. No circumstance of daily life is too trivial or too commonplace to serve as a window into the realm of ultimate values, and no truth too profound to find its analogue in common experience."[24]

An important yet neglected aspect of Jesus' teaching is its humor, paradox, wit, and irony.[25] Through most of Christian history, the exalted view of Jesus held within the church resulted in a rather solemn and even sanctimonious image of him. The impression was certainly not that of a witty or entertaining individual. Yet there is no need to think that humor is necessarily a sign of frivolity, or that humor always seeks laughter as an end in itself. Within the Jewish tradition, even the most serious subjects have often been treated in humorous stories.[26] As an oral teacher addressing himself mostly to rural and illiterate audiences, Jesus' wit may have played a strategic role, so that the "twinkle in Jesus' eye" became "that most effective device for puncturing the pomposity of those grave authority figures."[27] Humor is often a sign of intellectual freedom, of detachment from fixed categories, and of the ability to view human affairs from multiple perspectives and so perceive the incongruities of life. These qualities were necessary for Jesus' followers to grasp the significance of the elusive reality he referred to as the kingdom of God.

The sense of humor is a highly individual phenomenon, and also closely tied to language, time, and place. So the sayings and parables that may have seemed humorous to Jesus' contemporaries may not be so to us, and vice versa.[28] Yet it is still possible to identify statements that probably came across as comic, ironic, or hyperbolic. Some of Jesus' best-known statements are paradoxical word pictures, and occasionally the image evoked by the words borders on the absurd. A person blinded by an object in the eye is hardly able to perform a delicate operation on another person's eye! "Or how can you say to your neighbor, 'Let me take the speck out of your eye,' while the log is in your own eye?" (Matt. 7:4). While God can change someone's hair color, humans could not (at least in Jesus' day): "You cannot make one hair white or black" (Matt. 5:36). When blind people lead the blind, both fall into a pit (Matt. 15:14). Harsher in tone is the saying about the scrupulosity of the religious leaders: "You strain out a gnat but swallow a camel!" (Matt. 23:24).[29] Sometimes Jesus' paradoxes reveal some aspect of the kingdom of God: "Whoever wishes to be first among you must be slave of all" (Mark 10:44). The widow who had only two small coins to contribute to the Temple actually gave more than the wealthy with their large sums of money (Mark 12:41-44). Jonsson notes that these "paradoxes show that from the common point of view the life of the kingdom is in many ways contrary to the present aeon."[30]

Jesus was sometimes ironic, as in the saying at the time of his arrest: "Have you come out with swords and clubs to arrest me as though I were a bandit?" (Matt. 26:55). There is also an ironic saying associated with Jesus' visit to his hometown: "Doctor, cure yourself!" (Luke 4:23). At other times

Jesus' irony was like that of Socrates, who posed questions that forced others to reassess their own opinions or question themselves and their values. This feature of Jesus' teaching becomes especially evident in the conflict stories regarding his final week in Jerusalem. When asked regarding the source of his authority, he responded to the question with another question: "Did the baptism of John come from heaven, or was it of human origin?" (Matt. 21:25). The refusal of his interlocutors to answer him showed that their minds were already made up. Likewise, the interchange regarding the "Son of David" (Matt. 22:41-46) has a Socratic flavor to it, since Jesus elicits a response from others but then from the response draws out a further and unanticipated question.

Perhaps the best-known and most celebrated aspect of Jesus' teaching was his use of parables.[31] Prior to Jesus the Hebrew tradition made frequent use of the *mashal*, a term that referred to a similitude or comparison and had a wide range of meaning.[32] An example in the Hebrew Bible is found in the Song of the Vineyard, where Israel is compared to a vineyard and God to the keeper of the vineyard (Isa. 5:1-7). Although he took excellent care of the vine, it bore only worthless grapes. The story issues in God's call to "judge between me/and my vineyard" (v. 3). As this example shows, the genre of parable combines the qualities of narrative, metaphor, and brevity. The point of a parable is to tell, as concisely as possible, a story having a double meaning. One meaning is usually quite clear on the surface of the narration. Another, and presumably deeper meaning, lies hidden within the narrative. The underlying meaning or meanings are a challenge for the recipient to consider and interpret the words. "Parables," as Crossan says, "are lures for interpretation."[33]

One of the debated points regarding the Gospel parables concerns the presence of allegory within some of the parables. In allegory there is a whole set of correspondences between elements in the story and certain persons or objects in actual life. Thus, to use the familiar parable of the prodigal son (Luke 15:11-32), one can attempt to identify the father, the runaway son, and the elder brother with certain persons or certain types of person. Since the pioneering study of the parables by Adolf Jülicher at the close of the nineteenth century, there has been a tendency to interpret the Gospel parables as stories having a single, clearly defined point, and thus a single, clearly defined point of comparison.[34] Any apparent allegory in the Gospel texts, on this view, comes from the later expansion and editing of the original sayings of Jesus. Recently scholars have challenged this point of view, and today many accept that some of the parables as delivered by Jesus contained allegorical elements.[35]

The genre of parable or *mashal* in the Hebrew Bible tradition was broad enough to include many different kinds of comparison, ranging from short pithy sentences to lengthier narratives and allegories. The New Testament parables are comparably varied in their form, as indicated within a single chapter, such as Mark 4. The section opens with "he began to teach them many things in parables" (v. 2) and concludes by saying that "with many such parables he spoke the word to them" (v. 33). Yet within these two framing statements one finds both narrative parables (the sower, vv. 3-8; the harvest time, vv. 26-29; the mustard seed, vv. 30-32) and brief aphoristic parables (lamp and bushel, v. 21; measure for measure, v. 24). Both types of parable include the warning: "Let anyone with ears to hear listen!" (vv. 9, 23). The most famous of Jesus' parables are extended narratives, such as the prodigal son (Luke 15:11-32) and the good Samaritan (Luke 10:25-37). Since Jesus was an oral teacher, it is quite possible that the Gospel texts are in effect plot summaries of stories that took much longer for Jesus to tell his audiences.

Crossan, following Axel Olrik's work on oral storytelling, has identified some recurrent features in Jesus' parables. There is a "law of three" that appears in the path, the rocks, and the thistles of the parable of the sower (Mark 4:3-8), and also a "law of twins" whereby the first two servants in the parable of the talents (Luke 19:11-17) and the first two travelers in that of the good Samaritan (Luke 10:29-37) are in contrast to the third. The "law of contrasts," that is, of clearly polarized protagonists, appears in numerous parables: in the farmer and his enemy in the parable of the wheat and weeds (Matt. 13:24-30), in the rich man and Lazarus (Luke 16:19-31), in the Pharisee and the publican (Luke 18:10-13), in the former and latter guests of the parable of the marriage feast (Matt. 22:1-13), and in the wise and foolish bridesmaids (Matt. 25:1-13). An obvious feature of Jesus' parables is their normalcy — they speak of the realities of ordinary life in Galilee, of the weeds that spring up in a field along with the wheat, of a peasant woman who goes looking for a lost coin, of a rich farmer whose barns are filled with a bumper crop, and so forth.[36]

Together with their everyday quality, the parables of Jesus also point toward matters that are far from ordinary. Many parables relate to judgment. They are replete with dramatic images of crisis, reward, and retribution. The parables speak of the winnowing of wheat from chaff and the fire that burns up the chaff (Matt. 13:40-42), the owner of a vineyard who destroys his rebellious tenants (Matt. 21:33-44), and the household servant who is suddenly called to account for his stewardship (Matt. 24:45-51). There are maidens who awaken to find that their lamps have gone out (Matt. 25:1-13), people shut out of a banquet because they did not respond in time or came wearing inappropriate garb (Matt. 22:1-14), and a barren tree that is to be chopped down unless it bears fruit (Luke 13:6-9). Jesus' teaching is also filled with images of things that have lost their proper function. The foolish servant buries his money in the ground rather than investing it (Luke 19:11-27). Salt loses its taste and so must be thrown out (Matt. 5:13). A lamp shines and yet is hidden away under a basket so that its light cannot be seen (Matt. 5:14-16). Jesus' parables imply that Israel had become unfruitful and was not as God had intended for it to be. The leaders of the people were "blind guides of the blind" (Matt. 15:13-14). They followed a policy of business as usual, unaware of the crisis and the opportunity facing them.[37]

Jesus' parables not only called for interpretation but for personal or existential response. Their insistent and challenging tone is one of their most distinctive features, as John Meier explains:

> [Jesus'] parables *(meshalim)* served to tease the minds of his audience, throw them off balance, and challenge them to decide for or against his claim on their lives. The parables are not pretty Sunday-school stories. They are troubling riddles, meant to destroy any false sense of security and create a fierce feeling of urgency. Any moment may be too late: the hearer must stake all on Jesus' message *now,* no matter what the cost. For God is about to work his own kind of revolution: the poor will be exalted and the powerful dispossessed. This startling and disturbing program is at the heart of the parables. . . . It is a promise of radical reversal.[38]

The parables were linked with Jesus' proclamation of the kingdom of God: "The kingdom of heaven is like . . ." (Matt. 13:31, 33, 44, 45, 47). They called for a change of heart and a change of behavior in light of God's reign.

The parables and sayings show that judgment and grace were both important themes within the teaching of Jesus. God grants forgiveness to those who are penitent, and grants it apart from any spiritual or moral attainments on their part. Mercy is what God delights in. God is "long-suffering," or slow to condemn and reluctant to judge, and correspond-ingly quick to forgive and ready to receive sinners. When the prodigal son returns, the father comes running to meet him (Luke 15:20). In this respect Jesus' presentation of God is in accord with that of the Hebrew prophets. The book of Hosea presents God as profoundly ambivalent, both inclined to bring judgment on his erring people and reluctant to do so:

> How can I give you up, Ephraim?
> How can I hand you over, O Israel? . . .
> My heart recoils within me;
> my compassion grows warm and tender.
> I will not execute my fierce anger.
>
> (Hos. 11:8-9)[39]

Nonetheless, the God of Jesus' parables and sayings exercises judgment and does so decisively. A shibboleth of the Victorian era books on Jesus was the repudiation of the theme of judgment. Even a cursory study of the sayings and parables of Jesus shows how lopsided this interpretation was, and how much it represented a softening of Jesus' teaching to suit a later audience.

A striking feature of Jesus' teaching is its frequent reference to, and commentary upon, the texts of the Hebrew Bible. Bruce Chilton and Craig Evans note that "the sense of his teaching is often inaccessible unless its scriptural underpinnings are appreciated."[40] Some of the scriptural cita-tions in the Gospels are attributed to Jesus himself and others are not. In an environment in which scriptural language and imagery were the com-mon vehicles for religious reflection and discourse, references to the Bible would naturally appear in a presentation of Jesus' life and significance. The many scriptural citations in the Gospel of Matthew seek to demonstrate that Jesus fulfills the prophecies of the Hebrew Bible. Matthew has a for-mula for his scriptural citations: "This was to fulfill what had been spoken by the Lord through the prophet" (Matt. 2:15; cf. 1:22-23; 2:17-18, 23; 4:14-16; 8:17; 12:17-21; 13:35; 21:4-5; 27:9).[41] Nonetheless, the insertion of scriptural references by the Gospel authors does not suggest that Jesus himself never cited scripture in connection with his sayings and parables. There is wide agreement among New Testament scholars that the stringent sayings in the Gospels prohibiting divorce (Mark 10:11-12) are a departure from the gen-eral Jewish teaching on divorce and certainly go back to Jesus himself.[42]

These sayings attributed to Jesus are closely interwoven with scriptural citations that are also attributed to Jesus, and so there is good reason to think that Jesus on certain occasions cited scripture to make his points. He may not have been a typical "Torah sage," as Marcus Borg rightly notes, but this does not mean that reference to scripture was not a part of his public teaching.[43]

Even where Jesus is not quoting the Hebrew scripture, his manner of arguing often shows an affinity to that of the rabbinical tradition. The rabbis formulated some accepted principles of interpretation or midrash, and Jesus' sayings exemplify a number of them. One must be careful about drawing unwarranted conclusions, since the rabbinic principles seem to have been formalized only after 70 C.E., in the period of Jewish redefinition. At the same time, it is probable that some of these principles were already in common use in Jesus' day. The Jewish texts attribute a number of "measures" (Hebrew *middoth;* sg. *midda*) to the first-century sage Hillel. According to *qal wa-chomer* (light and heavy), what is true or applicable in a "light" or less important instance is surely true in a "heavy" or more important case. As God cares for the birds, so he will also care for Jesus' followers (Matt. 6:26; Luke 12:24). If God clothes the grass of the field, he will also provide clothing for human beings (Matt. 6:30; Luke 12:28; cf. Matt. 7:11; Luke 11:13). According to *gezera shawa* (equivalent regulation), one passage may be explained by another if similar words or phrases are present. In Mark 11:17 Jesus is said to have quoted phrases from Isaiah 56:7 and Jeremiah 7:11. What connects these two passages is the word "house" that occurs in the quoted verse from Isaiah and in an unquoted part of the verse from Jeremiah.

According to *binyan 'ab mikkatub 'echad* (constructing a father from one [passage]), a general principle may be established from one key verse or phrase. Since God is not the God of the dead but of the living, "I am the God of Abraham," as spoken at the burning bush (Exod. 3:14-15), implies that Abraham is to be resurrected. From this one text one may infer that there is a general resurrection. According to *kelal uperat uperat ukelal* (general and particular, and particular and general), general interpretations can be inferred from specific statements in scripture, or specific interpretations can be inferred from general statements. Thus the commandment of love (Mark 12:28-34) is a general commandment that sums up all of the particular commandments. According to *dabar halamed me'inyano* (a word of instruction from its context), the meaning of a given passage must be clarified by its context. This rule is exemplified in Jesus' teaching on divorce (Matt. 19:3-8; Mark 10:2-9).[44]

Despite these points of contact with the Judaic tradition, Jesus' references to and reflections on the Hebrew scriptures differ from the common rabbinical approaches. As Chilton and Evans observe, "Jesus was not a rabbi in the sense of the mishnaic authorities, but his approach to Scripture was governed by his sense of fulfillment."[45] This brings us back, once again, to the overriding significance for Jesus of the kingdom of God. Even the sacred scriptures, whose authority Jesus does not seem to have challenged in principle, had to be viewed in a new light because of the eschatological fulfillment that was a part of Jesus' proclamation of the kingdom of God. "Today this scripture has been fulfilled in your hearing" (Luke 4:21). The sense of fulfillment becomes most obvious in what John A. T. Robinson referred to as Jesus' "challenging use" of scripture, where he does not so much argue over the correct interpretation of a passage, or use a text to prove a point, as pronounce a text as a challenge.[46] Usually such challenges are posed as interrogatives: "Have you not read?" (Mark 2:25; 12:10, 26; Matt. 12:3, 5; 19:4; 21:16, 42; 22:31; Luke 6:3), "What do you think?" (Matt. 22:42), or a simple "How?" (Mark 9:12; 12:35; Matt. 22:43; Luke 20:41). Often the questions are posed to the disciples as well as to Jesus' opponents.[47] These sayings show that Jesus' sense of eschatological fulfillment was linked to the conflicts during his ministry — a subject we will now consider in greater detail.

The Public Figure

Career and Controversies

Having examined Jesus' works of wonder and the general character of his teachings, we turn now to what might be called Jesus' career. One thing known with certainty is that he died by crucifixion at the hands of the Roman authorities, and it seems just as certain that he died under the charge of being "the king of the Jews."[1] Given his acts of healing and exorcising, and the teachings that stressed God's love for the unworthy, the outcome of Jesus' life is rather surprising, and one of the chief aims in interpreting it is to show how and why he died as he did.[2]

The Gospels present Jesus as very popular and influential with the multitudes, and yet not winning favor with everyone. The "woes" he pronounced on the cities of Chorazin, Bethsaida, and Capernaum show that these cities did not respond to him in the way he had hoped or expected (Matt. 11:20-24). Also there are texts that speak of Jesus' rejection in his hometown of Nazareth (Mark 6:1-6). As mentioned earlier, Jesus does not seem to have gone out of his way to enter the larger urban areas, and the reason for this is unclear. His frequent travels from place to place and his willingness to face opposition indicate a strong sense of mission,[3] and this could well have led him directly to the cities where there was the greatest concentration of wealth, power, and influence. Yet it seems that Jesus did not reckon the effectiveness of his ministry as modern people might, in terms of winning over the greatest number of persons or the most influential individuals. Instead Jesus spent his time with the same people he had known throughout his life — village dwellers, craftsmen, tradesmen, farmers, and fishermen. His mode of life, according to the Gospels, was itinerant. Or, in one of Jesus' more memorable utterances: "Foxes have holes, and birds of the air have nests; but the Son of Man has nowhere to lay his head" (Luke 9:58).[4]

During Jesus' lifetime the core of the movement was centered on a person. Wherever Jesus was, there the movement was.[5] Of the people attracted to Jesus, not everyone followed him literally in the sense that they left their homes and families and moved with him from place to place. Most probably remained in their original communities as local sympathizers. No exact figure can be given for the number of such sympathizers Jesus may have won over before his death, but there probably were hundreds if not thousands. Among the sympathizers were Simon the Pharisee (Luke 7:36-50), Zacchaeus the tax collector (Luke 19:1-10), and Joseph of Arimathea, a member of the Sanhedrin (Mark 15:42-47). Yet there were others who followed Jesus on the road, and, as noted already, it was a remarkable thing for anyone in the rural Palestine of that day to leave behind home and family and take up a rootless way of life.[6] The Gospels indicate that Jesus and his first followers were supported with food, temporary lodging, and financial donations from others (Matt. 10:9-13; Luke 8:1-3; cf. 1 Cor. 9:14). They depict Jesus or his disciples dining as guests in various houses (Mark 2:15-17; Luke 7:36-50; 11:37-44; 19:1-10). According to John 21:1-3, Jesus' disciples returned again to fishing right after his death, though this may have been merely transitional. In Acts the apostles were active in Jerusalem immediately after Jesus' death, and there they had no visible means of support. Some early followers were men and women of means who sold property for the benefit of the entire congregation (Acts 4:32-37).[7]

One of the most interesting questions relates to the role of women in the early movement surrounding Jesus. Did Jesus have female followers who were as closely connected with him as were the male followers? There are two sides to this issue, both of which need to be considered. On the one hand there were no women among the core group of the Twelve. If women had made a regular practice of physically following Jesus on the road, as the men did, this would have been scandalous in the eyes of their contemporaries. In that day there were firm boundaries between men's and women's spheres. A man was not even to mention aloud the name of a respectable woman in a public place. If Jesus' women followers had been his usual traveling companions, and had spent the night in proximity with him, one would expect some echo of this directed as a criticism against him in the Gospels. It is more likely, then, that the female disciples accompanied Jesus only on special occasions, such as pilgrimages, and that generally they played a more traditional role by providing food and lodging.[8]

On the other hand the Gospels contain indications that the female disciples of Jesus did not always conform to their traditional roles, and that Jesus encouraged them to depart from these roles.[9] In the story of Mary and Martha (Luke 10:38-42), Martha has taken on the occupation of hostess, and she finds herself shorthanded because her sister Mary is listening to Jesus' teaching rather than helping with the household tasks. Mary has violated her "job description" by sitting with the men. In his response to Martha, however, Jesus affirms Mary's right to sit and learn at his feet, and he even commends Mary by saying that she has "chosen the better part, which will not be taken away from her" (Luke 10:42). This is all the more remarkable when one considers that later rabbinic teaching, as indicated by the Mishnah, often condemns those who taught Torah to women.[10] Kathleen Corley has argued that some of Jesus' early female followers may have been slandered as "prostitutes" because they were seen publicly with men and shared meals with them. These were probably not peasant women, but upper-class women who had highly circumscribed social roles that did not allow for this kind of open association with men.[11] So the general conclusion would seem to be that Jesus' female followers were not treated just as the men were, and yet they were also freed from some of the social constraints that applied to women within first-century Jewish society.[12]

All four canonical Gospels and the Acts of the Apostles agree that there were twelve special disciples (collectively called "the Twelve"), but they differ in their listing of names (see Matt. 10:1-4; Mark 3:13-19; Luke 6:12-16; and Acts 1:13). This could be because the number was a symbolic one, representing the restoration of the twelve tribes of Israel (Matt. 19:28), and the actual number of close disciples varied from time to time and from place to place during the ministry of Jesus. A more likely explanation is that the disciples had more than one name. "Matthew," for instance, is sometimes called by the name of "Levi," and so it may have been with others. John Meier draws some interesting conclusions regarding the Twelve. First, he notes that the inclusion of Judas within the Twelve argues strongly for the historical authenticity of this group during Jesus' lifetime. If the whole idea of the Twelve were a later Christian invention, a projection back in time from twelve leaders in the early church, it is not plausible to think that Judas would have been included among their number. Second, the choice of the Twelve argues against an interpretation of Jesus' movement as sectarian. The number twelve signified the totality of Israel, not a separated sect, and his twelve "patriarchs" were "to be the exemplars and center of a renewed people of God in the endtime." Third, the fact that Jesus was not himself included in the Twelve argues that he stood over and against them, and that he was to play a distinctive role in the renewal of Israel.[13]

Three disciples represent an inner circle: Peter, and the two sons of Zebedee, James and John. They alone are with Jesus at such important moments as the transfiguration (Mark 9:2-8) and the prayer in Gethsemane (Mark 14:33). It is clear that Jesus had followers with differing degrees of responsibility and intimacy. Peter seems to have been the acknowledged leader of the disciples. There was the small circle of three, then the Twelve, and larger than this a much more numerous group of "disciples," and still larger a collection of sympathizers and well-wishers. Luke records that Jesus commissioned not only the Twelve for a preaching and healing mission (Luke 9:1-11), but also a group of seventy that went out and later reported success in casting out demons (Luke 10:1-20). Visually, these groupings could be represented as a series of concentric circles. While Jesus proclaimed the gospel or "good news" of God's kingdom to multitudes, it was only a smaller group that he called to follow after him in the stricter sense of the word.[14]

The role played by the twelve close disciples varies in the Gospel accounts. In the Gospel of Mark their role is largely negative, and they again and again fail to grasp the significance of Jesus' words and actions and person. Remarkably, the miracle of the feeding of the five thousand does not bring insight to the spiritually dim-witted disciples: "They did not understand about the loaves, but their hearts were hardened" (Mark 6:52). Just as surprisingly, outsiders and even Gentiles like the Syro-Phoenician woman prove to be better models of faith than the closest disciples. It is also noteworthy that Jesus' own family members do not seem to have been followers. With the exception of certain sayings about Mary, most of the material in the Gospels casts them in a negative light. At one point his family members tried to seize him and take him away, fearing that he "has gone out of his mind" (Mark 3:21). Jesus, for his part, depreciates the importance of blood relation to himself when he says: "Who are my mother and my brothers? . . . Whoever does the will of God is my brother and sister and mother" (Mark 3:33, 35). Yet, after the resurrection, Jesus' mother Mary and his brothers joined the disciples in prayer (Acts 1:14), and one of Jesus' brothers, James, served as a leader of the early church in Jerusalem.[15]

What was it that made Jesus controversial? And why was he put to death? These two simple questions have evoked answers of enormous range, subtlety, and complexity among biblical scholars, historians, and theologians. Any response to them involves an interlocking set of judgments on Jesus' character, his possible alignment with or aloofness from the political and religious parties of his day, the defection of Jesus' own followers, the varying responses of the crowds, the policies of the Roman government, the relationship between Pontius Pilate and the high priestly clique, the legal procedures used by the Romans in governing their provinces, the customs of the Sanhedrin in judicial affairs, and the exercise of capital punishment in that time and place. The scholars' reconstructions of the issues are balanced as delicately as an artist's mobile: touch one piece and all the rest tremble in their places. Unfortunately there is just not enough information to provide an adequate social, religious, and political backdrop for understanding the Gospels' accounts of the controversies, trial, and death of Jesus. Even on so basic a matter as Roman legal procedure, far more is known of what happened in the city of Rome than in a provincial capital such as Jerusalem. With regard to the Sanhedrin, the later rabbinical statements regarding judicial procedure may or may not be an accurate reflection of the situation prior to 70 C.E. We cannot be certain.

In the last thirty to forty years, a few points of broad consensus have emerged regarding Jesus' controversies and death. First, almost all recent authors have recognized the inappropriateness of reading the Gospels as though Jesus were opposed in principle to something called "Judaism" and was put to death for this reason. This viewpoint, though common among Gentile Christians in the past and present, signally fails to recognize Jesus' Jewishness, his adherence to Jewish practices, and the wide disagreements on fundamental issues that existed among the subgroups within first-century Judaism. If Jesus engaged in disputes with other Jews on matters of Torah observance, this hardly proves that he opposed "Judaism." On the contrary, it proves just the reverse, namely, that he was within the circle of those who took legal or halakic observance seriously, and so seriously debated it. Second, although the bulk of the Gospel narratives make frequent references to the Pharisees as Jesus' opponents, the Pharisees are conspicuous by their absence in the account of the arrest, trial, and death of Jesus. The Pharisees as a group played little or no role in Jesus' death. Third, it is agreed that the final legal responsibility for Jesus' death lay with the Roman governor, Pontius Pilate. Thus Jesus was executed as a perceived political threat and according to a Roman mode of punishment. He died under a placard bearing the words "the king of the Jews." Fourth, it is agreed that if any Jews were likely to have played an instrumental role in Jesus' arrest, trial under Pilate, and execution, it would have been the high priest and his associates. The exact degree of involvement by the high priests and elders in the events leading up to Jesus' death continues to be debated. They have been variously regarded as the instigators of the proceedings against Jesus, as active collaborators with the Romans, as unwilling agents, or as passive spectators.[16] The issue of Jesus' trial and death will be treated in the next chapter, following a discussion of the earlier controversies during his ministry.

The Gospels portray Jesus as being in conflict with some of the religious leaders of the Jews, and it may be helpful to make note of some of the specific conflicts that are mentioned. In the second and third chapters of the Gospel of Mark, there is a whole sequence of conflicts.[17] Jesus cured a paralytic with the words "your sins are forgiven," and this led the scribes to murmur that Jesus presumed to have the authority to forgive sins. They called it blasphemy. Jesus sensed their opposition but proceeded with the cure anyway (2:1-12). Jesus called a tax collector to follow as one of his disciples, and subsequently he dined with many other tax collectors. The scribes of the Pharisees complained about this to Jesus' disciples, and Jesus responded by defending his right to call sinners (2:13-17). People asked Jesus why his disciples did not fast in the way that the disciples of John the Baptist and the Pharisees were fasting. Jesus defended his disciples by saying that while the bridegroom was with them, the wedding guests should not fast (2:18-22). On a Sabbath day Jesus and his disciples were traveling through a grain field and, since the disciples were hungry, they began to pluck the heads of grain and eat them. When the Pharisees saw this and criticized them, Jesus cited the example of David, who when he and his men were hungry ate the consecrated bread that was for the priests alone. Jesus also made two statements in defense of what had happened, that "the sabbath was made for humankind, and not humankind for the sabbath," and "the Son of Man is lord even of the sabbath" (2:23-28). On another Sabbath day Jesus entered a synagogue where there was a man with a withered hand, and he asked those present whether it was legitimate to heal on the Sabbath day. They remained silent, and Jesus went ahead and healed the man, which led the Pharisees to go out and confer with the Herodians as to how to kill Jesus (3:1-6).

As E. P. Sanders has noted, these stories show a kind of progression, in which the conflict escalates in severity. At first Jesus' opponents merely murmur their opposition to themselves, addressing neither Jesus, nor the disciples, nor the people at large. Next they complain to the disciples about

Jesus. In the third and fourth stories they object to Jesus himself about his disciples. In the final story they move beyond complaint and objection and intend to kill Jesus. There is also an escalation in the number of Jesus' opponents. At first they are simply the "scribes" or legal experts, but soon they are "scribes of the Pharisees," that is, those who belonged to the Pharisaic party. Then they are unidentified, but perhaps Pharisees or the disciples of John. At the end they are Pharisees again, though they have consulted with the Herodians.[18]

To understand what is at stake in these stories of conflict, it is important to understand what is and is not being disputed regarding the Torah. Laws may be disputed in differing ways, as Sanders indicates.[19] (1) One could argue that a certain law is wrong in itself and should be revoked or repealed. This is a very radical step, and although overt dissent and disobedience are common enough in modern history, it would have been much rarer in ancient times. Because of the Jewish view that the Torah was given by God, any assertion that the law was wrong would be tantamount to saying that God had made a mistake. (2) As an alternative, one could argue that a law is wrong and should be repealed, but should still be obeyed. (3) As a less radical step, a person may allege that there are certain mitigating circumstances that justify transgression on some occasions. (4) Yet another approach would be to interpret the law in such a way as in effect to change it. (A possible example might be the U.S. Supreme Court decision that "equal" schooling was not compatible with racially "separate" schooling.) (5) In some cases it may be possible to avoid or evade some laws without actually repealing them. (6) One may propose that the law be extended and criticize it for not going far enough. This is compatible with a continued adherence to the law in its present form. (7) Finally one may create a lot of supplementary rules and practices that govern precisely how laws are to be fulfilled. People who follow such supplemental rules may believe that those who do not are transgressing the law, and vice versa.

As we have seen already, first-century Judaism was rife with controversies regarding the observance of the Torah, and yet these almost always fell into categories 3-7 above and not categories 1-2. Much of early Pharisaic Judaism and later rabbinic Judaism was devoted to the explication of supplemental rules (referred to as "the tradition of the elders" in Matt. 15:2), and the strictest groups, such as those in the Dead Sea community, regarded those who did not follow their particular interpretations of Sabbath, food, and other laws as flagrant transgressors. Yet, once one distinguishes the rejection of the law in principle from disagreements over the proper application of the law, Jesus basically appears as an observant Jew. Nowhere does he ride roughshod over the prescriptions of the Torah, or simply assert that they are not to be observed.[20] If Jesus had done this, there would have been no basis for an argument with the Pharisees. Jesus would have been self-condemned.[21] Even when he healed a leper, Jesus is said to have told the leper to show himself to the priest, as prescribed in the Law of Moses (Matt. 8:4) — a detail not likely to have been inserted into the narrative by the early church. Jesus is said to have paid the required Temple tax, albeit reluctantly (Matt. 17:24-27). Moreover, the practice of the earliest Jewish Christians in the "Jerusalem church" under the leadership of James (the brother or kinsman of Jesus),[22] Peter, and John corroborates that Jesus did not advocate any fundamental break with Jewish law. These first followers of Jesus were pious adherents of Judaism who observed circumcision, the Sabbath (on Saturday), the dietary laws, festivals and fasts, and other traditions. If Jesus had decisively broken with these Jewish practices, then it is quite unlikely that his earliest followers would have continued in them.[23] Peter's vision, as reported in Acts, confirms the point, for it takes a special revelation from God to convince Peter to begin associating with Gentiles. And when the heavenly voice tells him to "kill and eat," he objects by saying, "I have never eaten anything that is profane or unclean" (Acts 10:14; cf. 11:8). In other words, the leading disciple of Jesus kept kosher during the period following Jesus' death. The bald statement in the Gospel of Mark that Jesus "declared all foods clean" (Mark 7:19) must be taken, then, not as a report of Jesus' teaching per se, but as an interpretation of that teaching.[24]

E. P. Sanders has stated that the whole picture of Jesus' conflict with the Pharisees in the Gospels is a retrojection or reading back into Jesus' lifetime of the later controversies between the church and synagogue toward the end of the first century. He asserts that there was no substantial conflict between Jesus and the Pharisees with regard to Sabbath, food, and purity laws, and he finds the general picture of conflict in the Gospel accounts to be unrealistic and unhistorical.[25] Yet Jacob Neusner, in his detailed study on the Pharisees, has shown that "the central traits of Pharisaism concerned observance of dietary laws" and that "Pharisees furthermore ate only with other Pharisees, to be sure that the laws were appropriately observed." Thus the Pharisees were akin to the group known as *haberim* (associates), mentioned in rabbinical literature as a table-fellowship group. Aside from the invective in the Gospels, Neusner says, the basic picture of the Pharisees in the Gospels as concerned with ritual purity fits in with the rabbinical traditions about the Pharisees.[26] In light of their intense concern for ritual purity, it is ipso facto probable that Jesus would have come into conflict with them over matters of purity, and indeed it would be remarkable had there been no conflicts along these lines. According to the rabbinic traditions, the Pharisees had several disputes with the Sadducees over issues of purity, and so it would not be unexpected for them to have had similar disputes with Jesus.[27]

One of the most frequent and obvious points of controversy in the Gospels concerned Jesus' sharing of meals with "sinners." Who were these "sinners"? Some authors have tended to overemphasize the gap between the Pharisees and everyone else, and to portray the Pharisees as superbigots and supersnoopers, ready to take offense at Jesus for associating with the common people. According to this account, the bulk of the populace or "people of the land" (Heb. ʿam ha-aretz) were cut off from God in the eyes of the Pharisees and other stricter Jews.[28] Sanders has offered a corrective to this viewpoint, pointing out that the Pharisees had in effect applied the stricter rules of ritual purity for the Temple priests to themselves in everyday life. They regarded the whole world as, in effect, a Temple. The question then was not moral worth but ritual purity. Not to observe these stricter rules of ritual purity was not the same thing as spurning God's law. Yet there were some whom the Pharisees and other stricter Jews regarded as "wicked" or "sinful." They were Jews who had no intention of observing God's law. They failed not through inadvertence or occasional lapses into ritual impurity, but through habitual inattention to the prescriptions of the Torah. Jesus incurred the wrath of the Pharisees, scribes, and other strict Jews by sharing meals with these people.

If we read the Gospels from a social-scientific perspective, it is not at all surprising that the controversies concerning Jesus should involve the issue of shared meals. Anthropologists, through cross-cultural study, have concluded that "in all societies both simple and complex, eating is the primary way of initiating and maintaining human relationships." For this reason "to know what, where, how, when, and with whom people eat is to know the character of their society."[29] In short, the rules for shared eating are a mirror image of the general rules for associating and socializing in a given society. Sharing food brings an individual into a certain economy or exchange that typically involves obligations to give, receive, and then repay

after receiving. One often finds fine nuances of meaning attached to particular practices of eating. As Crossan points out, if beggars appear at one's
front door, there is a difference between giving them some food to go, in-
viting them into one's kitchen for a meal, bringing them into the dining
room for a meal with the family, or having them return on the weekend for
a supper with a group of one's friends. These examples show a steady progression in the level of social intimacy.

From the Gospels, it seems that Jesus had the most intimate kinds of
shared eating experiences with some of the most disreputable characters of
his society. Is it any wonder that he raised both objections and eyebrows
with his behavior? Yet, like his healings and his parables, this too commu-
nicated something regarding God's reign. Crossan explains that "the Kingdom of God as a process of open commensality, of a nondiscriminating
table depicting in miniature a nondiscriminating society, clashes fundamentally with honor and shame, those basic values of ancient Mediterranean culture and society."[30] When some Jews called other Jews "sinners"
and refused to share meals with them, this created a partition within Israel
that Jesus' table practice directly challenged. The breaking of this bound-
ary between observant Jew and nonobservant Jew in Jesus' lifetime foreshadowed the overcoming of the still greater rift between Jews and
Gentiles in the early church.[31]

Yet it was not only the act of associating with habitually nonobservant Jews that aroused opposition to Jesus. And it was not only the
act of sharing meals with such nonobservant Jews, though everything we
know or surmise about the Pharisees and other stricter Jews makes it likely
that such shared meals would have provoked them to criticize Jesus. Above
all else, it was Jesus' confident declarations of *divine forgiveness* for such
nonobservant Jews that must have touched off a firestorm of controversy.
"The promise of salvation to sinners," writes Sanders, "is the undeniably
distinctive characteristic of Jesus' message."[32] The forgiveness that Jesus
announced did not require the offering of the Temple sacrifices that were
the prescribed means of atoning for sin.[33] Jesus proclaimed God's love to
"sinners" *before* they repented. Sanders explains: "The novelty and offense
of Jesus' message was that the wicked who heeded him would be included
in the kingdom even though they did not repent as it was universally understood — that is, even though they did not make restitution, sacrifice,
and turn to obedience to the law." Perhaps most shocking of all is that Jesus
seemed to regard the association of "sinners" with himself as the func-

tional equivalent of repentance. He even went so far as to suggest that such association with himself and participation in his group of followers was equivalent to admission into the kingdom of God. That, for clear-cut reasons, was "offensive to normal piety — not just to trivial, externalistic super-piety."[34]

So the scandal or offensiveness of Jesus has to be understood on a number of different levels. By openly associating with notoriously nonobservant Jews, Jesus cast a shadow across his own reputation. By sharing meals with these "sinners," he announced to the world that he did not abide by the stricter principles of Pharisees or *haberim*. By proclaiming divine forgiveness to these same Jews while they remained nonobservant, Jesus seemed to be setting aside the prescribed means of atonement or ritual purification set down in the Torah. By intimating that association with himself was equivalent to repentance, Jesus appeared to be setting himself altogether above the Torah and Temple alike. These were very serious matters indeed for Jews of the first century, and the issues came to a head when Jesus made his final and fateful journey to Jerusalem.

Approaching the End

The Final Week

Why did Jesus make his final journey to Jerusalem? Did he do so in full recognition of his impending death? Did he not only foresee his own death, but actually intend it in some way? While Jesus remained in Galilee there was probably little or no danger to his life, but this was not the case once he arrived in Jerusalem at the time of the Passover festival. There may have been some 300,000 to 400,000 pilgrims in or around the city at this time,[1] in addition to the year-round population of about 40,000 to 60,000, and the chief concern of the Roman governor together with the Jewish high priest was to maintain public order. Religious festivals were potentially volatile situations and would have been the most likely time for an attempted political strike of some kind. Albert Schweitzer surmised that Jesus went to Jerusalem believing that his mission was to bear the woes of the end time. He was to die "on behalf of the many," that is, in their stead. In Schweitzer's account, Jesus deliberately provoked the leaders to kill him.[2] His death was not merely the outcome but the purpose of the journey. N. T. Wright has recently expressed agreement with Schweitzer that Jesus went to Jerusalem intending to die.[3] Alternatively Marcus Borg suggests that Jesus' death was the outcome and not the purpose of his going to Jerusalem.[4] In Luke Jesus identified himself with the succession of prophets sent to Jerusalem, and in bitter irony spoke the words: "It is impossible for a prophet to be killed outside of Jerusalem" (Luke 13:33). The Gospels contain repeated predictions of the sufferings that Jesus was to endure in Jerusalem, in language concerning the suffering "Son of Man" (Matt. 17:9, 22-23; 20:17-19; Mark 9:31; 10:32-34; Luke 9:22, 44; 18:31-33). Although the authenticity of these and other "Son of Man" sayings is disputed, there is no reason to think that Jesus would not have been able to foresee some of the events that would transpire in Jerusalem. Especially if Jesus had already intended to take decisive action at the Temple mount at the time of the Passover festival, then certain consequences were bound to follow.

Jerusalem was the most Jewish of cities in first-century Palestine, and was occupied by a garrison of Roman troops that received additional reinforcements at the time of the major festivals. At the season of the Passover, Roman troops arrived in the city from the west in a procession led by the Roman governor and with all the trappings of Roman power. Jesus and his followers arrived from the east, perhaps on the same day.[5] During his last week, there are five major scenes in the drama of Jesus' life. First, Jesus entered Jerusalem on a donkey, with people shouting acclamations. According to Matthew and Luke, they explicitly called him "Son of David" or "king" (Matt. 21:9; Luke 19:38). Second, Jesus went into the Temple, where he overturned the tables of the money changers and the seats of those who sold pigeons (Mark 11:15-19). The Gospel of Mark attributes to Jesus the words (partly based on Isa. 56:7 and Jer. 7:11): "'My house shall be called a house of prayer for all the nations[.]'/But you have made it a den of robbers" (Mark 11:17). Third, Jesus shared a final meal with his disciples, saying that he would not drink wine again until the day that he would "drink it new" with them in God's kingdom (Mark 14:22-25). Fourth, the guards belonging to the high priest arrested Jesus and took him before the high priest and his council. Although some witnesses accused him of threatening to destroy the Temple, their testimony was not consistent and so could not be used to condemn him. According to the Gospel of Mark, Jesus, in direct questioning by the high priest, acknowledged that he was both the "Messiah" and the "Son of God," and this led to a charge of blasphemy against him (Mark 14:43-64). Fifth, Jesus' captors sent him to Pilate, who interrogated him and then ordered him to be crucified under the charge of claiming to be "king of the Jews" (Mark 15).[6]

Both the entry into the city and the action at the Temple are probably to be understood as prophetic actions. The Hebrew prophets of earlier centuries not only delivered oracles from God, but also performed actions that carried symbolic significance. Thus we read in the Hebrew Bible that God commanded Jeremiah to break a pot and proclaim that Jerusalem would be destroyed (Jer. 19:1-13) and, on another occasion, to wear a yoke to indicate that Judah should submit to Babylon (Jer. 27–28). Isaiah and Ezekiel also performed symbolic actions (Isa. 20:3; Ezek. 4–5; 12:1-16; 24:15-24). Jesus' entrance into the city, riding on a donkey's colt, fulfilled the passage in Zechariah which spoke of a king of peace riding "on a colt, the foal of a donkey" (Zech. 9:9-10). Marcus Borg suggests that Jesus chose this particular symbolism to stress that his kingdom was a kingdom of peace and not of war.[7] An interesting feature of the final week is that certain actions are *not* recorded during this period: there are no reported healings or exorcisms. Instead the Gospel narratives highlight the prophetic and challenging teaching of Jesus to the multitudes.

Jesus' second prophetic action, which was even more provocative than the first, was done in the Temple area, a large flat platform of about thirty-five acres. This area included various courts and buildings, and the Temple itself. This was understood by the Jews to be the dwelling place of God on earth. Public worship occurred in the courts surrounding the sanctuary. There were graded levels of holiness in this place: beginning with the Holy of Holies — where the high priest entered once each year on the Day of Atonement, the priests' court, the court reserved for male Israelites alone (where Gentiles were forbidden to enter on pain of death), and the court of the women. The Temple grounds also included a place where sacrificial animals could be purchased and pilgrims could exchange their image-bearing coins (needed to pay the Temple tax) for coins without images. In what the Jewish scholar Joseph Klausner called Jesus' "greatest public deed,"[8] he expelled the money changers and the sellers of sacrificial animals. This was a highly provocative action that must have caused a stir. Yet the onlookers must not have regarded it as an attempt to take over the Temple area, for otherwise the Romans, whose garrison overlooked the Temple courts, would immediately have intervened. It was a symbolic act that made a powerful statement but did not change the way business was done in the Temple.[9] The force exerted was Jesus' personal authority in confronting the crowd.[10]

The action at the Temple can be interpreted in more than one way, and there may be some truth in each viewpoint. E. P. Sanders argues that Jesus' action should not be regarded as a "cleansing" of the Temple, or as a protest against the Temple priests and their alleged greed, abuse of power, or negligence of duty. Instead it was a symbolic destruction of the Temple that prefigured a future eschatological intervention in which God would replace the existing Temple with a new one.[11] Sanders notes that this understanding of the action at the Temple explains why the Temple came up as an issue during the Jewish trial of Jesus. The action at the Temple was the basis on which Jesus was taken into custody, though it was not ultimately the ground for Jesus' condemnation. So in a real sense, the action at the Temple triggered the series of events that led to Jesus' death.[12] While Sanders is right to emphasize the importance of the Temple action, the opposition to Jesus was based on a number of considerations that mutually reinforced one another, as noted already in the discussion of the controversies during the ministry in Galilee. It was not merely the action at the Temple that made Jesus a potential threat to public order. Furthermore, Craig Evans has argued that Jesus' action, in historical context, can appropriately be seen as a "cleansing" or a critique of the existing priestly leaders and their policies. The Judaic literature of the period is filled with attacks on the high priests for their greed, corruption, and oppressive policies toward the common people and even their fellow priests. The household of the high priest Annas was reputed to be especially corrupt. If Jesus' dramatic words and action were in fact an expression of indignation at the way business was done in the Temple precincts, then Jesus would not have been alone in his protest.[13] N. T. Wright views Jesus' action from a different angle, stressing that the Temple was actually — not symbolically — destroyed in the generation after Jesus: "The Temple, as the central symbol of the whole national life, was under divine threat, and, unless Israel repented, it would fall to the pagans." Thus Jesus "enacted judgment" against the Temple, and consequently the action at the Temple is "the most obvious act of messianic praxis within the Gospel narratives."[14]

If Jesus ever gave his followers some explanation of how he viewed his approaching death, the most likely occasion for doing so would be the last opportunity that he had, namely, the Last Supper. The tradition regarding this final meal is especially well attested, since it is independently supported in Mark and the Gospel of John, in special traditions in Luke, and in an early formula that is preserved in Paul's first letter to the Corinthians. The variation in wording among these different accounts indicates that they are based on an actual event and not an effort by early Christians to concoct a last supper after the fact. One might expect there to be some harmonization of the divergent accounts if they were constructed after Jesus' death and without reliable traditions to support them.[15] The date of the meal has been debated, since the Gospel of John speaks of Jesus' death on the day of "preparation" and this would seem to place the crucifixion one day earlier (14 Nisan) than the synoptic Gospels (15 Nisan). At least two theories have been proposed to reconcile the Gospel of John with the synoptic Gospels, one proposing that the Jews followed different calendars for celebrating the Passover, and another claiming that "preparation" was a term for the day preceding the Sabbath, i.e., Friday, and thus that John agrees with the chronology of the other Gospels.[16] During his final meal, Jesus used bread and wine to represent tangibly his impending death, which he accepted as a part of God's will for bringing in the kingdom of God. Though some scholars feel that the original form of Jesus' words may be hidden behind the variations in form (reflecting the influence of the later liturgical traditions of the church), the core sayings seem to be that "this is my body [or flesh]" and "this is the covenant [sealed] in my blood." This final meal, as Meier explains, "was a pledge that, despite the apparent failure of Jesus' mission to Israel, God would vindicate him even beyond death and bring him and his followers to the final banquet in the Kingdom."[17] By drinking from *one* cup, *his* cup, they were pledging themselves to hold their fellowship with Jesus even in death, and to await the renewal of that fellowship in the coming kingdom.[18]

To what extent, or in what fashion, were the leaders of the Jewish people involved in Jesus' death? The issue is highly volatile, if not incendiary, since it ties directly into the tragic history of anti-Semitism whereby Gentile Christians regarded the Jewish people as collectively responsible for Jesus' death.[19] The notion of hereditary guilt became the pretext for unspeakable crimes against the Jewish people throughout the history of the Christian church. It is only within recent generations that a sizable number of Christians have become aware of the pervasive and virulent anti-Semitism that has existed within, and been fostered by, the church.[20] As early as the second century Gentile Christians came to see the actions of a ruling clique in Jerusalem as somehow representative of all Jews past and present.[21] Even earlier, while many New Testament texts were being written, from about 60 to 90 C.E., a struggle ensued between the Jesus movement and the larger Jewish community that disputed the claims of the earliest Christians. The question is: To what extent does this first-century conflict color the Gospels' presentation of Jesus' relation with the Jewish leaders, and especially the presentation of the events that led directly to Jesus' death?

Regarding an anti-Jewish bias in the earliest church, the evidence is mixed. On the one hand are numerous verses in the Gospel of John where those who oppose Jesus are simply designated as "the Jews," and such texts may convey the unfortunate impression that Jesus and his first followers were not Jews themselves![22] Another text in Matthew has the people of Jerusalem call out for the release of Barabbas rather than Jesus, and then say regarding Jesus: "His blood be on us and on our children!" (Matt. 27:25). A text in the book of Revelation refers to some in the city of Smyrna, probably persecutors of the Christians there, as "a synagogue of Satan" (Rev. 2:9). On the other hand, one finds texts where Nicodemus and Joseph of Arimathea — said to be members of the Sanhedrin — are both singled out as respectable persons (Matt. 27:57-60; Mark 15:43; Luke 23:50-53; John 3:1; 19:38-42). Even Gamaliel, an outstanding Jewish sage of the era, comes across as neutral and not hostile toward the early followers of Jesus (Acts 5:33-40). At the culmination of Jesus' ministry in the Gospel of Mark, there is a scribe who is said to be "not far from the kingdom of God" (Mark 12:34). The Gospel of John speaks of certain Pharisees who were favorably disposed toward Jesus (John 9:16). Acts refers to a multitude of priests who turned to the faith (Acts 6:7). Even the high priest Caiaphas is described as a man with prophetic gifts (John 11:51), which is ironic since one might expect the Gospels to blacken his portrait as much as possible.[23] In light of these passages, it is not possible to make blanket assertions about a consistent anti-Judaic tendency in the New Testament. Some texts may reflect the struggle of church and synagogue, and some may not. The reality behind the texts is too complex to fit into a single pattern.

The question about the Jewish leaders and Jesus, despite its disturbing resonances with the later tortuous history of Jews and Christians, has to be answered in terms of historical sources and historical methods. By far the most thorough and wide-ranging examination of the arrest, trial, and execution of Jesus is the magisterial study of Raymond Brown in *The Death of the Messiah*.[24] Brown concludes that, despite the very early theologizing of the events connected with Jesus' death, the Gospel narratives are based on actual events. "It is inconceivable that they [i.e., the Twelve] showed no concern about what happened to Jesus after the arrest," writes Brown. While there is "no Christian claim that they were present during the legal proceedings against him, Jewish or Roman," he adds that "it is absurd to think that some information was not available to them about why Jesus was hanged on a cross."[25] The whole point of crucifixion, after all, was to *publicize* that certain crimes would be severely punished. Crossan disputes this, claiming that "Jesus' first followers knew almost nothing whatsoever about the details of his crucifixion, death, or burial." Into this void, according to Crossan, the early Christians brought new interpretations of Hebrew Bible texts to create a meaningful narrative of what happened to Jesus their leader. Thus the passion accounts are not "history remembered but prophecy historicized."[26]

As Brown has demonstrated in his massive work, the passion narratives in the Gospels are an interweaving of historical remembrance and theological reflection, an almost seamless garment of event and interpretation. Yet the texts are grounded in actual events. Given the working relationship that existed between the Roman governor and the high priest and his cohorts, it is unlikely that Jesus would have been executed apart from some collaboration of the Jewish leaders with the Romans. Josephus summarized the trial and death of Jesus by noting that "Pilate . . . hearing him [i.e., Jesus] accused by men of the highest standing among us . . . condemned him to be crucified."[27] Even Crossan, despite his general skepticism regarding the passion narratives, says that Josephus is not likely to have invented a tradition of Jewish responsibility for Jesus' death, and therefore he takes it "as historical that Jesus was executed by some conjunction of Jewish and Roman authority."[28] If the trial of Jesus had been a *purely* Roman affair, apart from any Jewish involvement, then this would imply that Jesus' conduct in religious affairs was offensive but that the trial bypassed all this. It would also lead to the implausible conclusion that Jesus was not involved in any indictable political activities but was nonetheless tried for such. On the other hand the known teachings and activities of Jesus do provide a coherent and logical prelude for a hearing before the Sanhedrin.[29]

There are a number of different reconstructions of the series of events constituting Jesus' arrest, trial, and condemnation.[30] One scenario is that a night trial was held before the Sanhedrin, presided over by Caiaphas the high priest (who held that office from 18 to 36 C.E.), and that this session lasted until dawn or else was followed by a brief session at dawn. This seems to be the general picture presented in Matthew and Mark. Another version of the events holds that the Sanhedrin held only an early morning session, as appears to be the case in the Gospel of Luke. A third account holds that an informal session with Jesus was held by some Jewish official, perhaps Annas, the father-in-law of Caiaphas, who had been high priest previously (6-15 C.E.), but that no formal trial took place before the Sanhedrin. This scenario is based on the Gospel of John. Paul Winter has argued in favor of the last option on the basis of the Mishnaic teaching on the trial procedures of the Sanhedrin. If either of the two other scenarios were true, then the Sanhedrin in trying Jesus would have been violating several of its stated rules (e.g., holding a trial at night, etc.).[31] Yet the problem is that the later rabbinical rules, written down about 200 C.E., may or may not have been in effect in the period prior to 70 C.E. Whether or not the meeting with Jewish leaders was a full-scale trial or simply an informal hearing, some accusation against Jesus must have come under consideration.[32]

One feature of the passion narrative that is reliably reported in the Gospels is Peter's cowardly denial of Jesus. This detail, though embarrassing, is noteworthy since it places one of the early disciples as an eyewitness during the first stages of Jesus' trial. Historians have debated whether or not the Jewish authorities needed to have recourse to Pilate for a death sentence to be executed. The various pieces of evidence are ambiguous, but it is more plausible than not that during this period the Sanhedrin no longer had the authority to enact a death sentence.[33] Pontius Pilate, who was prefect of Judea from 26 to 36 C.E., is described by some ancient sources as a ruthless ruler.[34] He would have been entirely uninterested in legal or theological disputes that divided Jews from one another. His only concern would have been with accusations that involved a threat to Roman rule. Hence Jesus was brought before Pilate on the charge that he had claimed to be "king of the Jews," which indicates that the Jewish interrogation and discussion had probably already touched on the issue of messiahship. Thus it was on the charge of kingship, understood no doubt in the sense of being a revolutionary, that Pilate tried and condemned Jesus. It is notable that Jesus alone was arrested and executed, and not his followers. This indicates that the Romans did not regard the Jesus movement as a potential military threat.[35]

Roman crucifixion was commonly preceded by scourging,[36] which apparently weakened Jesus to the point that he was no longer able to carry the crossbeam for the cross on which he died. (The upright stake probably remained in place at the site of the execution.) To aid Jesus the soldiers pressed into service a certain Simon from Cyrene (a province in North Africa), and this African man carried Jesus' cross to the place of execution. His sons, Alexander and Rufus, were well known as members of the early church (Mark 15:21). Just as with Peter's denial, this is a detail in the Gospel narrative that places an early member of the church as an eyewitness of the events of Jesus' last day. The crucifixion took place outside the walls of the Holy City, at a spot called "Golgotha" (Aramaic for "skull place"), possibly an abandoned quarry by the side of the road. Despite the traditional references to "Mount Calvary," the Gospels in fact say nothing about a hill. The best archaeological candidate for the site of Jesus' death is the Church of the Holy Sepulchre in Jerusalem. Despite some debates over the contours of the city walls in earlier times, it seems that the site of this church was outside the walls early in the first century. The passion narrative does not say whether Jesus was tied to the cross or nailed to it, though nail marks are mentioned in the accounts of Jesus' resurrection, and a recent archaeological find of the remains of a crucified man indicates that he had been nailed to his cross.[37]

The horror and brutality associated with crucifixion may be difficult for us to visualize today. It was inflicted by the Romans on the lower classes, including slaves, violent criminals, and the unruly elements in the provinces, not least in Judea. Jesus' death by the method of crucifixion was not an indication of the heinousness of his crime but rather a sign of his complete lack of social standing. This was how the Romans disposed of a slave, or nobody, in their society. A chief reason for its use was its supreme efficacy as a deterrent. It was a form of state terrorism, intended to astonish and terrify the onlookers. Martin Hengel writes: "By the public display of a naked victim at a prominent place — at a crossroads, in the theatre, on high ground, at the place of his crime — crucifixion also represented his uttermost humiliation."[38] The cruelty of those who performed crucifixions is indicated in Josephus's description of the entertainment offered to the Roman soldiers at the end of the Jewish War in 70 c.e.: they competed with one another to find new and interesting positions in which to nail their victims to the wood.[39]

Jesus died relatively quickly, and Jewish law (Deut. 21:22-23) specified that the body not be left hanging overnight, all the more so when the Passover day that year (15 Nisan) came before a Sabbath day. An influential Jew, Joseph of Arimathea, interceded with Pilate to provide a burial, perhaps only temporarily, in a tomb that he owned nearby. The Galilean women who were said to be at the cross witnessed the preparation of the body for burial. The name of Mary Magdalene occurs in all the Gospel traditions about Jesus' burial. With Friday coming to an end and the Sabbath day beginning at sunset (according to the Jewish reckoning of the week), the burial of Jesus took place in haste, and those who deposited the body in the tomb hurried to reach their homes before the sunset.[40]

The story of Jesus was at an end — or rather, was just beginning.

A New Beginning

The Resurrection

The earliest Christians insisted that Jesus' death on the cross was not the end of his life, and that he reappeared to many of them, alive again.[1] Their claim was not that he was resuscitated from death and simply returned again to the same kind of existence he had had prior to his crucifixion. Instead the resurrection narratives suggest that Jesus had passed into a new mode of existence. On the one hand he had a physical body, and in the Gospel of Luke he invited them to verify this for themselves with the words: "Touch me and see; for a ghost does not have flesh and bones as you see that I have" (Luke 24:39). Luke also states that Jesus ate a piece of fish in their presence (Luke 24:42-43; cf. John 21:13). On the other hand Jesus presents himself in the Gospels as victorious over death and therefore no longer existing in a mortal or perishable body. In the Gospel of John Jesus suddenly appears with the disciples in a room where the doors were shut and locked (John 20:19-20). In John, as in the Gospel of Luke, he shows them his hands and sides (John 20:20), presumably so that they could see the marks of his suffering and know that the one they saw was also the one who had died on the cross.

The narratives of Jesus' after-death appearances differ in their details. Matthew and Mark present the disciples as traveling to Galilee to see Jesus there (Matt. 28:7, 16; Mark 16:7), while in Luke they remain in the vicinity of Jerusalem (Luke 24:33-36, 50-53). There are also differences in the accounts of Jesus' ascension into heaven in Luke 24:50-53 and Acts 1:6-11, even though these were authored by the same person. In Matthew Jesus appears twice, once to Mary Magdalene and another woman named Mary (Matt. 28:9) and once to the surviving eleven disciples (Matt. 28:16-20; Judas had killed himself). Luke includes nothing about Jesus' appearance to the women (Luke 24:1-12), but rather tells of "two men in dazzling clothes" who announced to them that Jesus had risen from the dead. Luke then tells of Jesus showing himself to Cleopas and an unnamed disciple (Luke 24:13-35), and then to all the disciples, before whom he ate (Luke 24:36-49). According to Acts, Jesus was with the disciples, appearing on and off, over a period of forty days (Acts 1:3). Even earlier than the Gospels and Acts is Paul's discussion of the resurrection in 1 Corinthians, which may have been written in the early 50s. Here Paul claims that he is passing on what was "handed down" to him, a list of the appearances of the risen Lord: an appearance first to Cephas (i.e., Peter), then to the Twelve, then to more than five hundred persons at one time, then to James (Jesus' brother or kinsman), then to "all the apostles" (apparently not only the Twelve), and finally to Paul himself (1 Cor. 15:3-8).[2]

In 1 Corinthians Paul devotes considerable space to discussing the nature of Jesus' resurrection (1 Cor. 15), and seems to be steering a middle path between some who were denying the resurrection of the dead altogether and others who failed to understand that the resurrected body was something other than just a resuscitated corpse. It was a "spiritual body" (1 Cor. 15:44).[3] In Paul's letters the resurrection is a sign for the present age, perhaps the ultimate sign, of Jesus' vindication by God. In this event he triumphed over his enemies and "was declared to be Son of God with power . . . by resurrection from the dead" (Rom. 1:4). Paul also taught that the resurrection of Jesus was a sign that God would raise from the dead those who believe in Jesus. His resurrection was the "firstfruits" (1 Cor. 15:20, 23), which, as it were, pointed forward to a coming harvest.

Among the earliest Christians, no one claimed to have seen Jesus at the time that he rose again and left the grave. What they claimed instead was that they had seen Jesus alive again after his death. They also did not describe these afterdeath appearances of Jesus as public events, seen by disciples and nondisciples alike. They were only for the eyes of the disciples, and so the basis for asserting that Jesus was alive a second time is the testimony of those who claimed to be eyewitnesses to these occurrences. Believing in the resurrection of Jesus means believing in the apostles' and disciples' testimony.

Throughout the history of Christianity, those who have affirmed Jesus' bodily resurrection have shown differences of emphasis in the way in which they understand it. Some have seen Jesus' resurrection as a matter of simple faith, unrelated to historical evidence or logical argumentation.

Others have been convinced that an impartial consideration of the historical evidence proves Jesus' bodily resurrection to be an actual occurrence. William Lane Craig, in his numerous books and articles, claims that Jesus' empty tomb can be established as an historical fact — a point indirectly acknowledged even by the opponents of the early Christians. Craig argues further that the disappearance of Jesus' body requires an explanation, and that the bodily resurrection is the theory that best fits the historical data.[4]

In the modern period there has been a tendency among some scholars to interpret the resurrection language of the New Testament as referring to the experiences of the disciples rather than to the person and body of Jesus. Such writers will say that the meaning of the resurrection is continuing hope in God, or a sense of divine presence, or joy in the face of tragedy, or some other experience that is religiously significant but not necessarily connected with the body of Jesus. In this vein, Marcus Borg claims that "the truth of the resurrection is not dependent upon an empty tomb or a vanished corpse. Rather, the truth of the resurrection is grounded in the experience of Christ as a living reality before his death." Similarly, John Dominic Crossan explains that "the resurrection of Jesus means for me that the human empowerment that some people experienced in Lower Galilee . . . is now available to any person in any place at any time."[5] While Borg and Crossan have stated what the resurrection means for them personally, this is not what the resurrection of Jesus meant for the earliest Christians. Paul, for example, writes to the Corinthians that if the physical body of Jesus had not been raised, then "your faith is futile and you are still in your sins" (1 Cor. 15:17). Paul's apostolic ministry depended on his conviction that Jesus rose again. If Jesus were still dead and buried, then so was the gospel. Nor was Paul alone in assigning overriding importance to the resurrection of Jesus. The various New Testament writers viewed the resurrection as both central to their message and as an event involving Jesus' body, as Pheme Perkins notes: "The resurrection kerygma [i.e, proclamation] found in the canonical texts would not have assumed its present shape without the belief that Jesus' body was no longer in the grave."[6]

The historical question posed by the biblical texts is what the first Christians meant when they wrote narratives of postdeath appearances or used the term "resurrection" in reference to Jesus. Their entire way of speaking and acting indicates that they believed that Jesus, having died, was now actually alive again. The Acts of the Apostles contains an amusing reference to Porcius Festus (appointed procurator of Judea in 60 c.e.), who heard Paul defend himself before his accusers and did not really grasp the "points of disagreement" except for "a certain dead man, Jesus, whom Paul asserted to be alive" (Acts 25:19 NASB).

Apart from the event of Jesus' resurrection, it might be impossible to explain the vital faith, fervent evangelism, charismatic ministry, willingness to suffer, and rapid expansion of the earliest Christians. The resurrection underlay their conviction that Jesus, having conquered death, was now reigning with the Father, and would soon return to judge the world, overthrow all forces of evil, and make his kingdom manifest and glorious. Thus the resurrection ties directly into the issue of Jesus' identity — the topic of the next chapter.

Wisdom, Apocalypse, and the Identity of Jesus

Some Historical Reflections

The latest scholarship on Jesus presents two distinct paradigms: an eschatological or apocalyptic Jesus and a sapiential or wisdom-based Jesus. Much of this literature also assumes that Jesus was *either* a sage who gave instruction on how to live wisely and well in the present world *or* a prophet who announced the speedy end of the world.[1] Marcus Borg expresses the contrast when he writes that "the difference between an apocalyptic eschatology and a sapiential eschatology is enormous; the latter involves no objective change in the world whatsoever."[2] Apparently Borg presupposes that Jesus could not have been sapiential as well as apocalyptic or eschatological, and that the two images of Jesus exclude one another as fire excludes water or darkness excludes light.

Yet the Gospels allow both interpretations of Jesus. Numerous sayings present him as a teacher of wisdom and many others refer to a coming kingdom and cosmic transformation of some sort. The kingdom that Jesus envisaged is not like any age that has existed in the past, or any that is conceivable apart from divine intervention. The Beatitudes (Matt. 5:3-11) point toward an eon in which the meek will inherit the earth, those who hunger and thirst for righteousness will be satisfied, and the pure in heart will see God. In that day "the righteous will shine like the sun in the kingdom of their Father" (Matt. 13:43). Then "the last will be first, and the first will be last" (Matt. 20:16). In other words, the coming kingdom will not be the kind of world we now live in. On the other hand Jesus instructed his disciples on the proper use of possessions, marriage and divorce, relationships with others, living without anxiety, and so forth. He offered not only the hope of a coming kingdom but a wisdom to be practiced in everyday life. The parables and sayings embrace both the mundane and the extramundane. At one time the teaching is down-to-earth and worldly-wise, and at another it verges on full-blown apocalypticism.

So then why should there be an argument as to whether Jesus was sapiential or eschatological? Why not affirm both? The objections to finding a harmony of the two have not been textual or exegetical so much as philosophical. Schweitzer, as noted above, interpreted the eschatological language of the New Testament as an indication that Jesus expected the immediate end of the world. Beginning with Schweitzer, one of the major foci of discussion was whether an expectation of the immediate ending of the world was consistent with Jesus' ethical exhortations. In other words, if the world were ending in three months, would that spur you on to become a better person or a worse one? Would a firm expectation that life as we know it would soon be over encourage ethical exertion or moral laxity? This is an interesting psychological question that can be answered in contradictory ways. Martin Luther once declared that if the world were to end tomorrow, he would still plant a tree today. A fine sentiment, to be sure, but one wonders how many would act similarly. Schweitzer developed the notion that Jesus' teaching was an "interim ethic" intended for only a short period. Jesus could be quite rigorous and even perfectionistic in his moral instruction because his imperatives had to be obeyed for only a brief period. The commands were stamped with an expiration date.

This theory makes too much of a few isolated Gospel sayings that might hint at an immediate ending of the world and it ignores many more that suggest that the world in its present order is going to be around for some time. Schweitzer took his starting point in a text where Jesus says to his disciples: "When they persecute you in one town, flee to the next; for truly I tell you, you will not have gone through all the towns of Israel before the Son of Man comes" (Matt. 10:23). This is one of a very few passages that might be taken to mean that Jesus expected the world to end within a few years or decades. Yet even this statement is ambiguous, and could simply be a way of saying: the task is great, and actually so great that you will always have more work to do; and so, if you are persecuted in one place, continue your work in another. Many parables and sayings present the kingdom of God as undergoing a process of growth and development through time. "The kingdom of heaven is like a mustard seed that someone took and sowed in his field; it is the smallest of all the seeds, but when it has grown it is the greatest of shrubs and becomes a tree, so that the birds of the air come and make nests in its branches" (Matt. 13:31-32). Here there is no Technicolor description of cosmic cataclysm but rather a description of gradual emergence. Jesus' simile is organic, suggesting that each new stage in the growth of the kingdom of God builds on that which preceded it. Another analogy appears in the same context in Matthew: "The kingdom of heaven is like yeast that a woman took and mixed in with three measures of flour until all of it was leavened" (Matt. 13:33). A further organic image is in Mark: "The kingdom of God is as if someone would scatter seed on the ground, and would sleep and rise night and day, and the seed would sprout and grow, he does not know how. The earth produces of itself, first the stalk, then the head, then the full grain in the head. But when the grain is ripe, at once he goes in with his sickle, because the harvest has come" (Mark 4:26-29). This parable in Mark adds something not in the parables of the mustard seed and yeast. There is not only gradual growth, but also a conclusion to the process, a time of harvest (cf. Matt. 13:23, 30). These parables weigh against the idea that Jesus expected the world to end immediately.

Jesus instructed his followers on how to live in the present world in the light of the world to come. His parables and sayings imply both the kingdom's gradual growth and the deferral of its final arrival. Jesus' "unconventional wisdom," to use Borg's phrase, was for people living in the present world — marrying and sometimes divorcing, setting up households, raising children, trying to make a living, suffering wrong and committing it, tempted by greed and lust, prone to distraction as well as devotion, and sometimes harassed and misunderstood for Jesus' sake. These teachings do not show the marks of what Schweitzer called an "interim ethic," if this means a teaching that was clearly limited to a brief span of time (e.g., don't leave your home — there's an air raid under way). Crossan emphasizes the countercultural and inclusive community called into being by Jesus' ministry. Yet if Jesus was concerned with the formation of a new kind of human community, and planned and prepared for it with the call and instruction of his first followers, then this too is an argument against thinking that he believed that God was just about to intervene in history, abolish the present world, and start separating the sheep from the goats.

On strictly textual and exegetical grounds, Jesus was both a sapiential and eschatological figure. He might be termed an eschatological sage or sapiential prophet.[3] He called his followers to a new way of living and intended for them to embody a transformed social order among themselves. His teachings pointed forward to an ultimate transformation of the cosmos that might occur in the remote rather than the near future. In the end, the individual, society, and cosmos were all to be changed. To be sure, difficulties appear in attempting to fit together the various pieces of Jesus' teaching. A critic might point out, for instance, that the *gradual growth* of the kingdom of God, suggested in the parables enumerated above, is not the same thing as the *deferred arrival* of an otherworldly or apocalyptic sort of kingdom. This is true. In the former case the kingdom is always advancing and emerging from what preceded, while in the latter it bears little relation to what preceded it and falls like a stone from the sky. Yet this objection does not undermine the position proposed here. My point is simply that the sapiential and eschatological aspects of Jesus' teaching need to be coordinated and not set against each other. How one does this remains an open question, susceptible to a number of answers.

A second matter to address briefly is the origin of Christology or the early Christian images of Jesus. Sometimes this question is posed in terms of Jesus' view of himself and his role, or what is sometimes called his self-understanding. My readers may have noticed that this book has used little or no "psychologizing" language regarding Jesus: "Jesus thought," "he intended," "feeling anger as he turned over the tables," "his compassion for the multitudes," and so on. As Henry Cadbury showed in his book *The Peril of Modernizing Jesus*, the nineteenth- and twentieth-century biographers of Jesus often erred in this respect. They slipped into wholesale psychologizing, and typically did so without first reconstructing any kind of social and historical background within which to understand Jesus. It is hardly surprising, then, that when they attempted to understand Jesus' inner life, they simply attributed to him the kinds of thoughts and feelings that they themselves might have had under similar circumstances. Undoubtedly the issue of Jesus' "self-understanding" is a legitimate question, and one that falls within the bounds of historical Jesus research. To understand any human being involves an assessment of his or her thoughts, feelings, and self-awareness. A number of recent authors have done careful work on the issue of Jesus' self-understanding.[4] What is more, certain acknowledged features of Jesus' life, such as his address to God as *Abba* (my dear Father), could be a basis for claiming that Jesus had a distinctive sense of intimacy with God or "filial consciousness."[5] Yet, having said this, there are plenty of pitfalls for anyone seeking to reconstruct the inner life of Jesus. How might one *disprove* a given assertion about what Jesus thought or felt? And if one cannot disprove such statements, then does this not show that claims about Jesus' subjective state are themselves very subjective? One hopes for a surer route to firm conclusions regarding Christology.

Another common way of approaching the origin of Christology is through a study of the various titles attributed to Jesus in the New Testament and early Christian literature: "Son of God," "Son of Man," "Messiah," and so forth.[6] Generally the authors who write on this subject have sought to determine the first-century meanings of these various titles, and then to show whether there is a basis for affirming that Jesus applied these titles to himself. If Jesus referred to himself as "Messiah" or "Lord" or with some other title, then the origin of Christology would lie within Jesus' own teaching. The problem with this approach, as E. P. Sanders points out, is that in first-century Judaism these titles may not have had fixed and unambiguous definitions that were understood alike by everyone. Knowing the term that Jesus applied to himself, or that others applied to Jesus, does not tell us exactly what was meant by the term.[7] The phrase "Son of God," for instance, had a very wide range of meaning in Jesus' day. In one sense all the people of Israel were "sons or daughters of God," while in another sense the phrase could denote a special individual. To recount the most famous case of ambiguity, the phrase "Son of Man" has generated widely differing interpretations. Some scholars hold that the term refers to an exalted heavenly figure who will appear at the end of the world.[8] Barnabas Lindars argues that Jesus used the phrase not as a title but as a modest circumlocution, "a man like myself," and that it was the early church that turned the phrase into a title.[9] John Meier maintains that Jesus used "Son of Man" as "an enigmatic designation of himself" as the lowly and yet powerful servant of God's kingdom, and "may also have used the title to affirm his assurance of final triumph and vindication by God."[10] Other scholars are not convinced that Jesus ever used the phrase at all.[11] As with the issue of Jesus' self-understanding, there are many perplexities in approaching the issue of Christology by means of the early titles applied to Jesus.

My modest suggestion regarding the origin of Christology is simply this: The root of the early Christian images of Jesus lies not in any isolated statements or actions attributed to Jesus, such as titles he might have used for himself or references he made to God as his Father. Rather the origin of Christology lies in Jesus' entire mode of self-presentation, his whole way of acting and speaking. John Meier writes: "The crux of the problem lies in the paradox that, although Jesus rarely spoke directly about his own status,

he implicitly made himself *the* pivotal figure in the final drama he was announcing and inaugurating. The Kingdom was somehow already present
in his person and ministry, and on the last day he would be the criterion by
which people would be judged."[12] Similarly E. P. Sanders observes:
"Through him, Jesus held, God was acting directly and immediately, bypassing the agreed, biblically sanctioned ordinances, reaching out to the
lost sheep of the house of Israel with no more mediation than the words
and deeds of one man — himself."[13] Jesus startled his contemporaries not
because he somehow opposed the law in principle but because he implied
that his own mission was what really counted. To cite Sanders again, the
"most important point that can be made about Jesus' view of himself" is
that "he regarded himself as having full authority to speak and act on behalf of God," and thus he might have thought of himself as God's "vice-
roy."[14] Jesus presented himself neither as an Israelite prophet who speaks
in God's name — "thus says the Lord" — nor as a Jewish sage who speaks
in the name of another teacher — "Rabbi Abba in the name of Samuel
said." He had a very different way of presenting himself.[15] This modest
suggestion — that the root of Christology lies in Jesus' entire self-
presentation — is not without significance. For it implies that the divergent reactions to Jesus, ranging from shock and offense to skepticism,
faith, and devotion, flow not from his incidental characteristics but from
the central features of his life, teaching, and actions.

Thinking Outside the Boxes

A Critique of Contemporary Images of Jesus

Everyone seems to agree that Jesus' life was significant, and yet the meanings assigned to that life diverge, based on the assumptions made and questions posed by the interpreters. In surveying the history of Jesus research, Albert Schweitzer observed that "there is no historical task which so reveals a man's true self as the writing of a Life of Jesus."[1] All renderings of Jesus — whether by erudite scholars or breezy popularizers — run the risk of projecting onto him what later generations have wanted to find.[2] Adolf von Harnack's learned volume *What is Christianity?* (1900), evoked a telling response from a Roman Catholic critic: "The Christ that Harnack sees . . . is only the reflection of the Liberal Protestant face, seen at the bottom of a deep well."[3] Some readers may judge that I have done as Harnack did, and discovered my own face mirrored back to me. It would be presumptuous to deny this possibility. Yet if we become aware of our own tendencies to refashion Jesus according to our preconceptions, then we will be in a better position to grasp what is most unexpected and challenging in him. Robert Funk states that the ground rule of the Jesus Seminar is, "Beware of finding a Jesus entirely congenial to you."[4] N. T. Wright, despite his differing approach to the Gospels, says much the same thing: "We have often muted Jesus' stark challenge, remaking him in our own image and then wondering why our personal spiritualities have become less than exciting and life-changing."[5] Both Funk and Wright insist that the proper approach is to let the evidence speak for itself, and not to sift or skew it to support any cherished image of Jesus.

The figure of Jesus revealed by historical investigation shatters not one but many stereotypes, and by considering and critiquing them together it may be possible to counteract our biases — whichever direction they may run. As a step along this line, I will start with four admittedly provocative statements to open up some new ways of viewing Jesus, or thinking outside the boxes:

- Jesus was a homewrecker.
- Jesus sided with the poor.
- Jesus preached fire-and-brimstone.
- Jesus was a totalitarian.

Each of the above is a response to one of four currently popular images of Jesus, which I will term the "family values Jesus," "end-of-the-world Jesus," "socially inclusive Jesus," and "global spirituality Jesus." Since I am writing in a North American context, these images may have greater relevance in that geographical and cultural region. Yet I suspect that the same underlying issues appear in the current interpretations of Jesus in other parts of the globe. To explain the four statements above, I will discuss what is worthwhile and what is problematic in each of the images of Jesus in turn.

The hallmark of the "family values Jesus" is the call to ethical integrity. Jesus' followers must keep their promises, care for spouses and children, work hard to support themselves and provide for others, and practice honesty in the workplace. Celibacy outside of marriage, sexual fidelity within marriage, and the continuity of marriage (i.e., the rejection of divorce) play a large role within this portrayal of Jesus. The "family values" outlook stresses the intergenerational links within the Christian community. Parents carry a heavy responsibility for teaching and exemplifying ethical conduct to their children. In effect, this viewpoint interprets the New Testament as a "Book of Virtues" — to borrow the title of a recent bestseller — that gives specific direction and instruction on living a worthwhile and worthy life.

Without a doubt, this understanding of Jesus builds on important themes in the Gospels. Most scholars regard Jesus' prohibition of divorce — or near prohibition (Matt. 5:32) — as a distinguishing feature of his message and a point of departure from rabbinical teaching. Jesus' concern for children is well-known, as in the episode in which his disciples "spoke sternly" to those who brought children to him and he replied: "Let the little children come to me, and do not stop them" (Matt. 19:14). In a society that was far less sentimental toward children than our own, Jesus surprised his hearers by using children as models of faith and of the spiritual life:

"Truly I tell you, whoever does not receive the kingdom of God as a little child will never enter it" (Mark 10:15). In his teaching on those who "have made themselves eunuchs for the sake of the kingdom of heaven" (Matt. 19:12), Jesus suggested that some of his followers would renounce sexual fulfillment in the pursuit of a higher calling in the service of God. This text played a role in the emergence of an ethic of sexual self-restraint among the early Christians. Concerning a work ethic, the parables of sowing and reaping (Matt. 13:1-9) and of invested money (Luke 19:11-27) carry an implicit message. To reap one must first sow, and to gain interest one must put money in the bank. Consequently, the various elements of the "family values Jesus" all have a basis in the Gospels: care for children and their instruction, hard work and investment in the future, celibacy outside of marriage, and lifelong fidelity within marriage.

At this point we may be basking in a kind of warm domestic glow, like a Norman Rockwell portrait of a family gathered around the hearth at Christmastime. One is tempted to draw a circle around the family and proclaim it a sacred and inviolable sphere. What is wrong here? It is simply this: *Jesus was a homewrecker.* Anyone who views the family as the end-all or be-all of human life will be disappointed and disturbed by much of what Jesus says. John Dominic Crossan may exaggerate when he speaks of Jesus' "attack on the family,"[6] but there is no question that the claims of Jesus' kingdom override those of the family. Jesus saw that his call to discipleship would turn families against themselves, and he described the sad outcome with breathtaking clarity:

> Do not think that I have come to bring peace to the earth; I have not come to bring peace, but a sword. For I have come to set a man against his father, and a daughter against her mother, and a daughter-in-law against her mother-in-law; and one's foes will be members of one's own household. Whoever loves father or mother more than me is not worthy of me; and whoever loves son or daughter more than me is not worthy of me; and whoever does not take up the cross and follow me is not worthy of me. Those who find their life will lose it, and those who lose their life for my sake will find it. (Matt. 10:34-38)

It is no accident that Jesus speaks of death in the same breath as the breakup of the home. To lose one's family in ancient times was a kind of social death. A young man was called after his father's name, and to have one's father as an enemy was to be disowned, exiled, and utterly lost. Jesus' words thus have a terrible poignancy. What compensates for the loss of one's family and identity is the gaining of a new identity as Jesus' follower and a new family in the community of disciples: "Peter began to say to him, 'Look, we have left everything and followed you.' Jesus said, 'Truly I tell you, there is no one who has left house or brothers or sisters or mother or father or children or fields, for my sake and for the sake of the good news, who will not receive a hundredfold now in this age — houses, brothers and sisters, mothers and children, and fields, with persecutions — and in the age to come eternal life" (Mark 10:28-30).

The Gospels do not encourage sentimentality toward the family. As E. P. Sanders notes, one of the texts most jarring to first-century Jewish sensibilities is the passage where Jesus tells a would-be follower not to bother with his father's burial: "Let the dead bury their own dead" (Luke 9:60). Jesus thus sets aside a son's most sacred obligation toward his father. Furthermore, the Gospels do not allow us to romanticize Jesus' family any more than our own, for we read that "not even his brothers believed in him" (John 7:5). When Jesus was informed that his mother and brothers were waiting outside to see him, he brushed aside their claim: "My mother and my brothers are those who hear the word of God and do it" (Luke 8:19). In response to a woman who says to Jesus, "blessed is the womb that bore you," he replies: "On the contrary, blessed are those who hear the word of God, and observe it" (Luke 11:28).

An exclusive emphasis on the family brings a disastrous narrowing of outlook. A major issue in contemporary society, discussed by sociologists and theologians alike, is the privatization of religion. The "family values" outlook easily falls into the trap of privatism. Religion becomes a spare-time activity or recreation that is divorced from public policy and the workaday world. Secularists for the most part do not object to faith so long as it remains in the privacy of someone else's living room. Strangely, "family values" Christians and secularists may have something in common to the extent that they think of spiritual life as something that finds its proper place within a private, domestic sphere. What is more, the call to rally round the family hearth is cold comfort to those who have never felt the warmth and love that ought to be experienced there. Throughout the world there are broken homes, lonely people, orphaned children, displaced persons, and victims of oppression, and it is not the "nuclear family" as such but rather the whole community of Jesus' disciples — single, married, separated, divorced, and widowed — that must respond to those in need. Lastly, Jesus' teaching on celibacy suggests that the family, while important, is not ultimate. The Gospels portray Jesus as celibate and unmarried, and record Jesus' saying that the saints in heaven "neither marry nor are given in marriage, but are like angels in heaven" (Matt. 22:30). Thus Jesus' life provides an example of singleness, and his teaching portrays eternal life with God as a state transcending marriage and family. This, too, limits the role of the family in Jesus' teaching.

Another popular construal of Jesus might be called the "end-of-the-world Jesus," to borrow a phrase from Marcus Borg. This viewpoint rests squarely on the apocalyptic and eschatological texts of the New Testament. Whereas the "family values Jesus" stresses ethical integrity, the "end-of-the-world Jesus" emphasizes eschatological hope. According to this viewpoint, Jesus offers the hope of a future that is unlike anything yet seen in this world. In accordance with the promises of Scripture, God will transform the entire cosmos into a "new heaven and new earth" (Rev. 21:1). Unquestionably there are innumerable texts in the Gospels — not to mention the Old Testament and other New Testament books — that foster the hope for a changed world. In Mark 13 we read: "But in those days, after that suffering, the sun will be darkened, and the moon will not give its light, and the stars will be falling from heaven, and the powers in the heavens will be shaken. Then they will see the Son of Man coming in clouds with great power and glory. Then he will send out the angels, and gather his elect from the four winds, from the ends of the earth to the ends of heaven" (Mark 13:24-27). This passage is hardly exceptional. Eschatological and apocalyptic themes are woven so tightly through the sayings and parables of Jesus that one could not remove them from the Gospels without unraveling Jesus' whole teaching.

In many ways the earliest Christians shared the apocalyptic outlook of contemporary believers in the "end-of-the-world Jesus." A text from the late first century or early second century, known as *The Didache* or *The Teaching of the Twelve Apostles,* records the prayer of the primitive church: "Let Grace come and let this world pass away!"[7] I wonder how many today could sincerely pray these words. If the reader is a Christian, then he or she can pose the questions: Could I rejoice at the cessation of this present world? Would I be happy to let go of the possessions I have acquired during my life? Or would these words of the earliest Christians stick in my throat if they were a part of the Sunday service? Evidently those who are most comfortable and well connected, and thus have the greatest stake in the present world, are also the least likely to long for a "new heaven and new earth." Conversely when the times are darkest for Jesus' disciples, the light of eschatological hope burns brightest. Today this hope may be best exemplified in China, the Sudan, Indonesia, and other nations where Christians are suffering persecution and harassment.

So what is wrong with the "end-of-the-world Jesus"? The problem is with the way Jesus' eschatological teaching has been construed and applied. Affluent Christians in North America have misunderstood the drift and aim of the texts. The point of the Gospel teaching is to create alert and attentive disciples who are detached from material things and from materialistic greed. Yet contemporary apocalyptic doctrine often encourages complacency and a do-nothing philosophy — the very opposite of what is intended in Jesus' instruction. Apocalypticism has been allied with social conservatism and the maintenance of the status quo, with the affluent indulging in luxurious and wasteful consumption while hundreds of millions all around the globe lack food, clothing, medical care, and basic housing.

To return to the second statement above: *Jesus sided with the poor.* A genuine understanding of Jesus' eschatological teaching ought to begin with Matthew 25:31-46, which is one of the Gospels' most explicit and elaborate portrayals of the coming of the Son of Man and his manner of judging the world:

> When the Son of Man comes in his glory, and all the angels with him, then he will sit on the throne of his glory. All the nations will be gathered before him, and he will separate people one from another as a shepherd separates the sheep from the goats, and he will put the sheep at his right hand and the goats at the left. Then the king will say to those at his right hand, "Come, you that are blessed by my Father, inherit the kingdom prepared for you from the foundation of the world; for I was hungry and you gave me food, I was thirsty and you gave me something to drink, I was a stranger and you welcomed me, I was naked and you gave me clothing, I was sick and you took care of me, I was in prison and you visited me." Then the righteous will answer him, "Lord, when was it that we saw you hungry and gave you food, or thirsty and gave you something to drink? And when was it that we saw you a stranger and welcomed you, or naked and gave you clothing?

And when was it that we saw you sick or in prison and visited you?" And the king will answer them, "Truly I tell you, just as you did it to one of the least of these who are members of my family, you did it to me." Then he will say to those at his left hand, "You that are accursed, depart from me into the eternal fire prepared for the devil and his angels; for I was hungry and you gave me no food, I was thirsty and you gave me nothing to drink, I was a stranger and you did not welcome me, naked and you did not give me clothing, sick and in prison and you did not visit me." Then they will answer, "Lord when was it that we saw you hungry or thirsty or naked or sick or in prison, and did not take care of you." Then he will answer them, "Truly I tell you, just as you did not do it to one of the least of these, you did not do it to me." And these will go away into eternal punishment, but the righteous into eternal life.

Many biblical interpreters have tried unsuccessfully to soften this passage by reading into it a doctrine of salvation by grace or by limiting the scope of the good works that the text enjoins. Yet, as R. T. France points out, Jesus here locates "the criterion of judgment in sheer undiscriminating good deeds to the needy."[8]

A prosperous Christian who takes the Bible seriously should be disturbed by Matthew 25. The point may come across more forcefully if we translate it into the contemporary context. The rich in America live in gated communities that block out the world, and hire private security guards to remove unwanted persons who stray into their neighborhood. If you live in this sort of exclusive development, then Matthew 25 is your worst nightmare become reality. The fence around the community is broken down, the security guards are absent, the police phone line is off the hook, the neighbors are on vacation, and every hobo and drifter from the entire region shows up to hold a meeting in your living room. You look out your carpet-to-ceiling picture windows and these strangers are all converging toward your lot from every direction. Collectively they are going to decide whether or not you get to stay in your home, and the outcome will be based on your past treatment of the poor! One after another speaks up: "I remember asking her for money to buy food, and she just pretended I wasn't there." You begin to ransack your memory and search the faces of those gathered to see if there is *anyone* whom you have helped. In Matthew 25, Jesus says that this is the way God's judgment will be.

Unfortunately, the apocalyptic *Left Behind* novels — which have now sold an astonishing fifty million copies — have little to say concerning the poor and needy and the ways in which they enter into the New Testament teachings on the coming kingdom. Consistently the Gospel texts regarding eschatology depict social and economic *reversal:* "So the last will be first, and the first will be last" (Matt. 20:16). Mary's words in the so-called *Magnificat* are as startling as any attributed to Jesus: "He has brought down the powerful from their thrones, and lifted up the lowly; he has filled the hungry with good things, and sent the rich away empty" (Luke 1:52-53). In light of passages like these, Peter Maurin, the co-founder with Dorothy Day of the Catholic Worker movement, used to say that the Gospels are dynamite but the church keeps the dynamite wet so that it will not explode.[9] To sum up, the Jesus of the Gospels ought to be a deeply disturbing figure for affluent and comfortable people who would seek to use biblical eschatology to insulate themselves from the cry of the poor and the call to practical works of mercy.

The "socially inclusive Jesus," in distinction to the first and second viewpoints, stresses the inclusive community that Jesus initiated and prescribed among his followers. As with the earlier images of Jesus, there is much in the Gospels to commend this perspective. In a society in which shared meals were an indication of intimate relationships, Jesus scandalized his contemporaries by dining regularly with some of the most disreputable people of his day. This led to accusations against Jesus, captured in the words he put on the lips of his opponents: "Look, a glutton and a drunkard, a friend of tax collectors and sinners!" (Matt. 11:19). The varied cast of characters who receive commendation from Jesus in the Gospel narratives include a Roman centurion (Matt. 8:5-13), a woman of dubious reputation (Luke 7:36-50), a Syro-Phoenician woman with a demon-possessed child (Matt. 15:21-28), and a leading tax collector in Jericho (Luke 19:1-10). In Jesus' teaching, a Samaritan rather than a Jewish priest serves as an example of good deeds (Luke 10:25-37), and a humble tax collector rather than an arrogant Pharisee becomes a model of repentance (Luke 18:9-14). Women held an inferior place in first-century Palestine, and yet Jesus publicly honored women by addressing them directly, giving them a place among his followers, and assuring them of God's love and concern. He spoke of a woman he had healed with the honorific designation "daughter of Abraham" (Luke 13:16). He allowed women to hear his teaching alongside of males. In the famous episode of the sisters Mary and

Martha, Jesus refused to send Mary into the kitchen to help her sister Martha in preparing food, and states that her place is to be listening to his teaching (Luke 10:38-42).

There was nothing narrow or parochial about Jesus, and the "social justice" perspective underscores the breadth and range of Jesus' ministry. It takes seriously the call to imitate Jesus, and regards discipleship as a process in which the pupil is to become like the teacher (Matt. 10:25). In contrast with the "family values Jesus," for whom charity begins at home, this viewpoint engages issues of public life and social policy. So what then is missing? The difficulty is a subtle one. It is that Jesus' inclusiveness is often turned against Jesus' call for faith in God and repentance from sin, as though these two things were somehow in opposition to one another. When confronted with the woman caught in adultery, Jesus not only said to the accusing bystanders, "Let anyone among you who is without sin be the first to throw a stone at her," but also, to the woman in question, "From now on do not sin again" (John 8:7, 11).[10] He commanded her to change her ways. The Gospels show that Jesus often spoke of the wrongfulness of sin and called on his hearers to amend their lives. An interpretation that omits Jesus' call for behavioral change is seriously mistaken. The "inclusiveness" of Jesus — however one interprets it — is not a basis for avoiding the so-called "hard teachings" on forgiveness, money, sex, self-denial, and servanthood. In certain ways the Jesus of the Gospels is anything but inclusive. He clearly did not endorse a plurality of viewpoints on God, but instead required his hearers to buy into his own specific vision, challenge, and claim. This leads me to the third statement: *Jesus preached fire-and-brimstone.*

The Gospels indicate that Jesus spoke frequently of hell and damnation. Almost a third of what Jesus says in the Gospel of Mark revolves around the themes of judgment, heaven, and hell. Strewn through the Gospels are images of hell as "the outer darkness" (Matt. 8:12) in which "their worm never dies, and the fire is never quenched" (Mark 9:48), and contrasting pictures of heaven as a place of banqueting, joy, light, abundance, and reward from God (Matt. 8:11-12; 13:40-43; 22:13; 25:34, 41; Mark 9:43-48; Luke 19:17; etc.). While some may regard heaven, hell, and salvation as irrelevant or even antithetical to the concerns of earthly justice and community, I would argue the opposite. The social and communal emphasis in Jesus' teaching does not make sense apart from Jesus' teaching on God and divine judgment. Considered in terms of natural endowments, human beings are plainly *disparate and unequal* — rich and poor, bright and dull, pretty and plain, honored and outcaste. Yet these distinctions fade in God's presence, so that everyone is equally in need of divine grace and equally able to receive it. Jesus' followers are an inclusive group precisely because they are *a community of the forgiven.* The point is strikingly conveyed in the Eucharist. Because of Jesus' broken body and shed blood, each participant receives assurance of God's forgiveness. Along with forgiveness of sins and communion with God, each is united with all the others who share in the meal. The inclusiveness of the sacrament has everything to do with Jesus' sacrifice and God's offer of forgiveness. On the other hand, if sin, sacrifice, and grace are left out of the picture, then the basis for inclusive community ceases to exist and one is left with a vague humanitarianism. A salient criticism of John Dominic Crossan is that he says much about the kingdom but little about the King — the one who establishes and reigns over what he calls the "kingdom of nuisances and nobodies." The burden of the apostles' preaching was not an ideal of human equality but rather a crucified King, who had died, risen from the dead, and was to come again in glory. Social inclusiveness was not a taught doctrine but an embodied reality in the early Christian communities, where Jews and Gentiles, rich and poor, highborn women and slave girls all gathered together to worship Jesus.

A fourth viewpoint to be considered is the "global spirituality Jesus." While the first three viewpoints were concerned with the transformation of the home (family values), the cosmos (apocalypticism), and society (justice and inclusiveness), this last perspective has to do with the transformation of the self. On this account, Jesus appears as a master teacher and practitioner of the inner life, rather like the great Asian teachers Buddha, Confucius (K'ung-fu-tzu), and Lau Tse. Along with his public ministry in the Gospels, Jesus was devoted to spiritual practice, and withdrew from even his closest followers to pray privately: "In the morning, while it was still very dark, he got up and went out to a deserted place, and there he prayed. And Simon and his companions hunted for him. When they found him, they said to him: 'Everyone is searching for you'" (Mark 1:35-37). Jesus seems to have regarded solitude with God as a part of his vocation.

In Jesus' spiritual teaching, as noted earlier, an outward or behavioral change was never enough. Repeatedly he returns to the idea that people must change at their deepest level, or rather be changed, to be able to live in a manner pleasing to God. Jesus often spoke of "hearts" as either soft or hard, good or bad, pure or impure. For the "heart" is where the problem resides: "This people honors me with their lips,/but their hearts are far from me" (Mark 7:6, quoting Isa. 29:13). Rather than actions making the person good or bad, Jesus taught the reverse, that the actions of a person flowed from the "heart" or essential character. "Either make the tree good, and its fruit good; or make the tree bad, and its fruit bad; for the tree is known by its fruit" (Matt. 12:33). "A good tree cannot bear bad fruit, nor can a bad tree bear good fruit" (Matt. 7:18). Jesus' teaching makes frequent reference to death, and these references appear in the context of a general call for the transformation of the self. The disciples must "deny themselves and take up their cross" (Mark 8:34). "Those who find their life will lose it, and those who lose their life for my sake will find it" (Matt. 10:39). "Unless a grain of wheat falls into the earth and dies, it remains just a single grain; but if it dies, it bears much fruit" (John 12:24). Jesus required that the disciples renounce falsehood and leave behind their former selves and former lives. The death metaphor stresses the once-for-all transformation that Jesus' disciples needed to undergo.

The "global spirituality" perspective shows an appreciation for the deeper dimensions of human life. It is not enough to engage in a new social praxis, or to practice personal ethical integrity, or to await the coming of God's kingdom. Instead Jesus' followers must be changed from the inside out and become a different sort of person. Liberation theologians, who in the 1960s and 1970s interpreted the Christian gospel as a call to economic and social change, have begun to put greater emphasis on the spirituality needed to sustain the struggle for a just and liveable society. Gustavo Gutiérrez's We Drink from Our Own Wells (1984) is an effort along these lines. The Franciscans for almost eight centuries have practiced a way of life in which spirituality and the concern for social justice are inextricably intertwined, and the same more recently has been true of the Jesuits and some other Catholic orders and Christian communities. Thus a call for personal transformation would seem to be an essential part of any public ministry or practice of discipleship, and the merit of the "global spirituality Jesus" is to emphasize this point.

Yet a difficulty with the "global spirituality Jesus" lies in the temptation to eclecticism. People today often pride themselves on being independent of any one religious tradition or community, and seek instead to draw selectively on many sources of insight — whether Christian spirituality, Jewish qabbalah, Islamic Sufism, Native American ritual, Buddhist meditation, Hindu mythology, or Jungian analysis. To be tied to one tradition, on this viewpoint, is to be shackled. Martin Marty has referred to this as an "unmoored spirituality," in contrast to the "moored spirituality" that seeks personal growth by adherence to a particular set of disciplines and beliefs.[11] In Robert Bellah's study of contemporary American life, *Habits of the Heart* (1985), a nurse named Sheila listed her religious affiliation as "Sheilaism," and described her faith as a matter of following after "my own little voice."[12] Wade Clark Roof in *A Generation of Seekers* (1993) and *Spiritual Marketplace* (1999) has documented a growing trend among younger Americans away from formal religious membership and toward a spirituality that is tailor-made for each individual.[13] Today in some American homes one can find an altar or shrine containing such disparate objects as a picture of Jesus or a crucifix, a seated Buddha, a yin-yang symbol, a menorah, a dancing Shiva, and a Hopi Indian Kachina. In this kind of spiritual practice, Jesus is not a permanent focus but rather one among many gurus. Critics view it as a "cafeteria" religiosity, where individual choice trumps the need for constancy and discipline in following a religious path.[14]

In response to this eclectic approach to Jesus, I will turn to my fourth statement: *Jesus was a totalitarian*. Throughout the Gospels, he made stark claims to the allegiance of his followers. Their commitment was to be unlimited and unqualified, and in that sense Jesus led his followers in a totalitarian fashion. The conclusion to the Sermon on the Mount illustrates the point. Jesus states that the one who hears his words and acts on them will be like a "wise builder" whose house will withstand the coming storm of divine judgment. Alternatively, anyone who spurns his teaching is a "foolish builder" whose house will collapse (Matt. 7:24-27). Jesus' audacity seems boundless: every person will ultimately stand or fall based on whether they have responded appropriately to him![15] E. P. Sanders grasps this point clearly: "Through him, Jesus held, God was acting directly and immediately, bypassing the agreed, biblically sanctioned ordinances, reaching out to the lost sheep of the house of Israel with no more mediation than the words and deeds of one man — himself."[16] A number of Jewish scholars have drawn similar conclusions. Jacob Neusner says that he accepts Moses and the Jewish sages but rejects Jesus. The former speak in the name of Yahweh or the Torah, but Jesus does what is unacceptable by speaking in his own name and by his own authority.[17] Ahad Ha'am stated: "Israel cannot accept with religious enthusiasm, as the Word of God, the utterances of a man who speaks in his own name — not 'thus saith the Lord' but 'I say unto you.' This 'I' is in itself sufficient to drive Judaism away from the Gospels for ever."[18] The same point regarding Jesus appears in the writings of C. S. Lewis, though he writes as a Christian believer. According to Lewis, Jesus' claims in the Gospels are so intimidating and overweening that one cannot engage in "patronizing nonsense about His being a great human teacher. He has not left that open to us."[19]

The Jesus of the Gospels makes startling claims to authority over his followers and requires unconditional faith and obedience. The Buddha, Siddhartha Gautama — so far as we are able to reconstruct him historically — appears to have been quite different. The Pali Canon records the saying that "the Buddha has not the closed fist of a teacher," and often Siddhartha seems to have disclaimed any and all personal authority.[20] One was to follow the Buddha's teaching not because the Buddha taught it, but because the teaching proved itself in practice. By contrast, Jesus was to be believed and obeyed because of who he claimed to be. What is perhaps the most far-reaching statement appears in the Gospel of John: "I am the way, and the truth, and the life. No one comes to the Father except through me" (John 14:6). The Jesus of the Gospels thus insists on being in the center and being in charge, and today's eclectic spirituality is often at odds with the ethos of the New Testament.

Having surveyed these four images of Jesus, it should be clear that neither conservatives nor liberals, neither traditionalists nor radicals, have a monopoly on misinterpretation. All social groups and ideological parties tend to accommodate Jesus to their own point of view.[21]

In the first chapter, I noted that Jesus did not fit comfortably into any of the existing cultural or religious categories in first-century Palestine. Though his life displayed analogies with those of the prophet, wisdom teacher, philosopher-sage, apocalypticist, and wonder-worker, Jesus could not be reduced to a single pattern. "No one title or label adequately explains a figure as complex as Jesus," writes Ben Witherington, and so "multiple complementary models are needed to deal with the man who fits no one formula."[22] To find an analogy for this, one naturally thinks of the so-called Renaissance man. A typical Italian of the fifteenth-century might be described rather simply. Leonardo da Vinci, in contrast, was a painter, inventor, writer, architect, philosopher, engineer, and mathematician. There is no simple way to depict a complex person. Why not construe Jesus as a man of manifold aspects, dimensions, capabilities, perspectives, and activities? Would this not be the interpretation that arises most naturally out of a reading of the Gospels?

In *Deconstructing Jesus* (2000), Robert Price argues that the biblical representations of Jesus all cancel one another out, since Jesus could not have been an eschatological figure *and* a wisdom teacher *and* a teller of parables *and* a wonder-worker *and* a founder of a new religious community.[23] My conclusion is different. The various aspects of Jesus' image are not fictional. If we have difficulty in applying them to the same person, it is because Jesus is too large to be pigeonholed. The interpreter's most common and most characteristic error regarding Jesus is to narrow down the figure in the Gospels until he fits into some box chosen by the interpreter. My point about the first-century context thus applies to the twenty-first century as well. Jesus does not conform to any contemporary category, whether that of social activist, spiritual guru, alternative healer, ethical teacher, textual scholar, gadfly, hippie, corporate executive, political revolutionary, doomsday prophet, inspirational speaker, or commune founder. Jesus was and is uncategorizable, and this is one reason why he remains a perpetual challenge to believers and nonbelievers alike, a figure instantly recognizable and yet ever elusive.

Notes

Note to the Preface

1. Luke Timothy Johnson, "The Humanity of Jesus," in John Dominic Crossan et al., *The Jesus Controversy: Perspectives in Conflict* (Harrisburg, Pa.: Trinity Press International, 1999), p. 74.

Notes to "Jesus"

1. See E. P. Sanders, *The Historical Figure of Jesus* (London: Allen Lane/Penguin Press, 1993), pp. 10-11, and the fuller discussion in Craig A. Evans, "Authenticating the Activities of Jesus," in Bruce Chilton and Craig A. Evans, eds., *Authenticating the Activities of Jesus* (Leiden: Brill, 1999), pp. 3-29, esp. pp. 3-5. James H. Charlesworth provides a listing of the "possible aspects" and "relatively certain aspects" of Jesus' life in "The Historical Jesus: Sources and a Sketch," in James H. Charlesworth and Walter P. Weaver, eds., *Jesus Two Thousand Years Later* (Harrisburg, Pa.: Trinity Press International, 2000), pp. 106-13. See also N. T. Wright, *Christian Origins and the Question of God*, vol. 2, *Jesus and the Victory of God* (Minneapolis: Fortress Press, 1992-), pp. 147-49; Robert W. Funk, ed., *The Acts of Jesus: What Did Jesus Really Do? The Search for the Authentic Deeds of Jesus* (San Francisco: HarperCollins, 1998); and Paula Fredriksen, *Jesus of Nazareth, King of the Jews: A Jewish Life and the Emergence of Christianity* (New York: Alfred Knopf, 1999), pp. 8-9. Gerd Lüdemann provides "A Short Life of Jesus," in *Jesus After Two Thousand Years: What He Really Said and Did* (London: SCM, 2000), pp. 686-93.

2. The following is largely based on Sanders, *Historical Figure*, pp. 11-14, and Helmut Koester, *Introduction to the New Testament*, 2 vols. (Philadelphia: Fortress Press/Berlin and New York: Walter de Gruyter, 1982), 2:73-86.

3. Opinions differ regarding the tradition of Jesus' birth in Bethlehem and his birth from a virginal mother. Some scholars affirm both points, while others view these ideas as later theological embellishments. Crossan sees the infancy narratives in the Gospels as "overtures, condensed intertwinings of the dominant themes in the respective gospels to

which they serve as introduction and summary" (*Jesus: A Revolutionary Biography* [San Francisco: HarperCollins, 1994], p. 5). He compares the twin births of Jesus and John the Baptist in Luke, showing the structural similarities (pp. 6-10): (1) the angelic announcements to Zechariah and Mary (1:5-25, 26-38); (2) the publicized birth of each child (1:57-58; 2:7-14); (3) the circumcision and naming (1:59-63; 2:21); (4) the public presentation and prophecy of destiny for each child (1:65-79; 2:25-38); and (5) the description of the child's growth (1:80; 2:40-52). Crossan also points out the parallels between the infancy story of Moses in Exodus and that of Jesus (p. 15). Concerning the virginal conception of Jesus, Crossan calls this "a confessional statement about Jesus' status and not a biological statement about Mary's body" (p. 23). Elsewhere Crossan states that either one must accept *all* claims to literally miraculous births in history (e.g., the "divine" births of Alexander the Great, Augustus Caesar, Jesus, Buddha, etc.), or else *none* of these claims ("Why is Historical Jesus Research Necessary?", in Charlesworth and Weaver, *Jesus Two Thousand Years Later,* p. 16). His claim that it is "not morally acceptable" to assert one miraculous birth but not others seems to be a philosophical assumption rather than a conclusion from his historical research. Bruce Chilton treats the paternity of Jesus in *Rabbi Jesus: An Intimate Biography* (New York: Doubleday, 2000), pp. 5-17, and asserts that "Joseph and Mary . . . broke with custom and slept together soon after meeting and well before their marriage was publicly recognized," and that this fact was known during Jesus' upbringing and rendered him a *mamzer,* or "Israelite of suspect paternity" (pp. 5-17, citing pp. 6-7, 12). Yet evidence is lacking for Chilton's claims. Raymond Brown argues that the authors of both the Gospel of Matthew and the Gospel of Luke regard Jesus' virginal conception as an historical event, and concludes that the later Jewish charge of Jesus' illegitimacy may be dependent on the Gospel narratives or alternatively could have preexisted prior to the circulation of the Gospels (*The Birth of the Messiah: A Commentary on the Infancy Narratives in Matthew and Luke* [Garden City, N.Y.: Doubleday, 1977], esp. pp. 25-38, 517-42). For further discussion, see John P. Meier, *A Marginal Jew: Rethinking the Historical Jesus,* 3 vols. to date (New York: Doubleday, 1991-), 1:208-30; George J. Brooke, ed., *The Birth of Jesus: Biblical and Theological Reflections* (Edinburgh: T&T Clark, 2000); and the extensive bibliography edited by Watson E. Mills, *Bibliographies on the Life and Teachings of Jesus,* vol. 1, *The Birth Narratives* (Lewiston, N.Y.: Edwin Mellen Press, 1999).

4. The major traditions in Christianity present differing explanations of the "brothers and sisters" mentioned in the Gospel narratives. (1) Traditional Roman Catholicism has insisted on the perpetual virginity of Mary both before and after the conception and birth of Jesus. Thus Jesus was miraculously conceived by Mary as a virgin, Jesus was Mary's only child, and Jesus' siblings could not have been Mary's biological children. Instead they were "kinfolk," and the term translated as "brothers" (Gk., *adelphoi*) carries its extended meaning of "kinsmen." (2) Some Orthodox Christians hold that Joseph was a widower at the time he married Mary, and that Joseph had children from this earlier marriage who were related to Jesus as stepbrothers and stepsisters, and yet are simply denoted "brothers and sisters" in the Gospels. (3) Traditional Protestants have held to the doctrine of the virginal conception and birth of Jesus, but maintain that Joseph and Mary had ordinary marital relations after Jesus' birth (perhaps implied by the word "until" in Matt. 1:25), and so the resulting children of Joseph and Mary are called the "brothers and sisters" of Jesus. Technically they would not be

Jesus' full siblings, since biologically Joseph would have played no role in Jesus' conception. (4) Nontraditional Christians have rejected the doctrine of the Virgin Birth, and this opens the door to viewing Jesus as the child of both Joseph and Mary, and Jesus' "brothers and sisters" as full siblings.

5. Koester expresses the point more strongly: "He was certainly able to read and write" (*Introduction*, p. 74). Yet it is not clear how one can draw this conclusion, in the absence of any clear traditions regarding Jesus' education. Meier argues that Jesus probably possessed very good reading skills (*A Marginal Jew*, 1:268-78).

6. Sanders, *Historical Figure*, pp. 52-55, 282-90.

7. Luke 2:2 is usually translated along these lines: "This was the first census that took place while Quirinius was governor of Syria" (New International Version). Luke's statement seems to conflict with what is stated by other ancient authors. Quirinius was "imperial legate" of Syria in 6-7 C.E., and conducted a well-known and unpopular census in Palestine in or around 6 C.E. Yet no record exists of a previous census in Palestine. The Gospel of Matthew asserts that Jesus was born during the reign of Herod the Great, which ended in 4 B.C.E. So the census already known to have occurred under Quirinius took place about ten years after the death of Herod. Even if a previous census were established during the reign of Herod, this would no longer lie within the period when Quirinius was imperial legate of Syria. To resolve this difficulty, three proposals have been presented. (1) The Greek word *prote* in Luke 2:2 might be adverbial rather than adjectival, so that the verse would be translated as "this census was taken before Quirinius was governor," or, "this census was before that while Quirinius was governor." Some scholars, though, dispute whether this is a possible translation. (2) The usual translation of Luke 2:2 might be correct, and yet the term for "governor" (Greek, *hegemoneuontos*) is a general term that describes officials functioning in a number of different capacities. Quirinius was conducting military expeditions in the eastern provinces of the Roman Empire during the period that Quintillus Varus was imperial legate in Syria (6-4 B.C.E.). It is possible that Quirinius was the procurator of this province while Varus — or his predecessor, Sentius Saturninus, 9-6 B.C.E. — was imperial legate, and Quirinius could have been responsible for a census during this period. It is also worth noting that the early Christian writer Tertullian claimed that Jesus was born while Saturninus was legate, and that the imperial record (no longer extant) showed that censuses were conducted under Saturninus. (3) Quirinius may have served as the imperial legate of Syria prior to his appointment as such in 6-7 C.E. A Latin inscription discovered in 1764 near Tivoli (outside of Rome) refers to an individual who had twice served as "imperial legate" or governor of Syria. While the individual in question is not named in the surviving portion of the inscription, it is possible that Quirinius is the person intended, and that he was legate of Syria a first time during the reign of Herod the Great and a second time in 6-7 C.E. For further discussion and analysis of the issues, see: Jack Finegan, *Handbook of Biblical Chronology* (Princeton, N.J.: Princeton University Press, 1964), pp. 234-38; George Off, "Quirinius Question To-day," *Expository Times* 79 (1968): 231-36; Harold W. Hoehner, *Chronological Aspects of the Life of Christ* (Grand Rapids, Mich.: Zondervan, 1977), pp. 12-23; Wayne A. Brindle, "The Census and Quirinius: Luke 2:2," *Journal of the Evangelical Theological Society* 27 (1984): 43-52; Kenneth F. Doig, *New Testament Chronology* (San Francisco: EMText, 1991); John M.

Lawrence, "Publius Sulpicius Quirinius and the Syrian Census," *Restoration Quarterly* 34 (1992): 193-205; and Ronald L. Conte, Jr., at www.biblicalchronology.com/census.htm.

8. Koester, *Introduction*, 2:78.

Notes to "Piles of Books"

1. Rudolf Bultmann, *Jesus and the Word* (New York: Scribner, 1934), p. 14.

2. E. P. Sanders, *Jesus and Judaism* (Philadelphia: Fortress, 1985), p. 2.

3. Paul Winter, *The Search for the Real Jesus* (London, 1982); cited in James H. Charlesworth, "Jesus Research Expands with Chaotic Creativity," in Charlesworth and Walter P. Weaver, *Images of Jesus Today* (Philadelphia: Trinity Press International, 1994), p. 11. Edgar V. McKnight states that "a revolution has taken place!" as researchers have set aside their "scholarly timidity" in investigating Jesus (*Jesus Christ in History and Scripture: A Poetic and Sectarian Perspective* [Macon, Ga.: Mercer University Press, 1999], p. vii).

4. Sanders, *Historical Figure*, pp. xiii-xiv, 1-6, 56. Marcus Borg writes: "We can be relatively sure of the *kinds* of things he said, and of the main themes and thrust of his teaching. We can also be relatively sure of the kinds of things that he did: healings, association with outcasts, the deliberate calling of twelve disciples, a mission directed to Israel, a final purposeful journey to Jerusalem. Moreover, as we shall see, we can be relatively certain of the kind of person he was: a charismatic who was a healer, sage, prophet, and revitalization movement founder. By incorporating all of this, and not preoccupying ourselves with the question of whether Jesus said *exactly* the particular words attributed to him, we can sketch a fairly full and historically defensible portrait of Jesus" (*Jesus: A New Vision; Spirit, Culture, and the Life of Discipleship* [San Francisco: HarperSanFrancisco, 1987], p. 15).

5. A discussion of recent archaeological findings and their significance for the interpretation of the New Testament is given in James Charlesworth, *Jesus within Judaism: New Light from Exciting Archaeological Discoveries*, Anchor Bible Reference Library (New York: Doubleday, 1988).

6. Among the pioneering works in applying a social-scientific approach to the Bible were Norman K. Gottwald, *The Tribes of Yahweh: A Sociology of the Religion of Liberated Israel, 1250-1050 B.C.E.* (Maryknoll, N.Y.: Orbis, 1979); Abraham J. Malherbe, *Social Aspects of Early Christianity* (Baton Rouge: Louisiana State University Press, 1977); Gerd Theissen, *The Sociology of Early Palestinian Christianity* (Philadelphia: Fortress, 1978); and the summary volume by Theissen (with Annette Merz) *The Historical Jesus: A Comprehensive Guide* (Minneapolis: Fortress, 1998). Theissen's work has been critiqued in Richard A. Horsley, *Sociology and the Jesus Movement* (New York: Crossroad, 1989). The writings of Bruce J. Malina also deserve mention, especially *The New Testament World: Insights from Cultural Anthropology* (Atlanta: John Knox, 1981); *The Social World of Jesus and the Gospels* (London and New York: Routledge, 1996); and *The Social Gospel of Jesus: The Kingdom of God in Mediterranean Perspective* (Minneapolis: Fortress Press, 2001).

7. Among the recent comparative studies of millennialism are the following: the essays contained in Sylvia L. Thrupp, ed., *Millennial Dreams in Action: Studies in Revolutionary Religious Movements* (New York: Schocken Books, 1970); Bryan R. Wilson, *Magic and the*

Millennium: A Sociological Study of Religious Movements of Protest among Tribal and Third-World Peoples (New York: Harper & Row, 1973); Michael Barkun, *Disaster and the Millennium* (New Haven: Yale University Press, 1974); Hillel Schwartz, "Millenarianism: An Overview," in *The Encyclopedia of Religion*, ed. Mircea Eliade (New York: Macmillan, 1987), 9:521-32; and the articles in *The Encyclopedia of Apocalypticism*, ed. John J. Collins, Bernard McGinn, and Stephen J. Stein, 3 vols. (New York: Continuum, 1998).

8. See Sanders, *Jesus and Judaism*, and Hyam Maccoby, *Judaism in the First Century* (London: Sheldon Press, 1989).

9. Pinchas Lapide, *Israelis, Jews, and Jesus* (Garden City, N.Y.: Doubleday, 1979), pp. 31-32, cited in Donald A. Hagner, *The Jewish Reclamation of Jesus: An Analysis and Critique of Modern Jewish Study of Jesus* (Grand Rapids: Zondervan, Academie Books, 1984), p. 25.

10. See especially: Geza Vermès, *Jesus the Jew: An Historian's Reading of the Gospels* (New York: Macmillan, 1973); Schalom Ben-Chorin, "The Image of Jesus in Modern Judaism," *Journal of Ecumenical Studies* 11 (1974): 401-30; Pinchas Lapide and Ulrich Luz, *Jesus in Two Perspectives: A Jewish-Christian Dialogue* (Minneapolis: Augsburg, 1985); Harvey Falk, *Jesus the Pharisee: A New Look at the Jewishness of Jesus* (New York and Mahwah, N.J.: Paulist, 1985); David Flusser, in collaboration with R. Steven Notley, *Jesus* (Jerusalem: The Magnes Press, 1997); Susannah Heschel, *Abraham Geiger and the Jewish Jesus* (Chicago and London: University of Chicago Press, 1998); Schalom Ben-Chorin, *Brother Jesus: The Nazarene Through Jewish Eyes*, trans. and ed. by Jared S. Klein and Max Reinhart (Athens, Ga., and London: The University of Georgia Press, 2001); and Beatrice Breteau, ed., *Jesus Through Jewish Eyes: Rabbis and Scholars Engage an Ancient Brother in a New Conversation* (Maryknoll, N.Y.: Orbis Books, 2001). Flusser may be the leading contemporary Jewish interpreter of Jesus, and he seeks to situate Jesus within first-century Judaism and yet do justice to Jesus' "high self-awareness" (R. Steven Notley, "Foreword," in Flusser, *Jesus*, p. 10). Ben-Chorin provides a commentary on the major segments and themes of the Gospels in light of Jewish tradition, while Breteau's anthology exhibits the variety of personal responses to Jesus among contemporary Jews.

11. On the study of Jesus throughout the history of Christianity, see Harvey K. McArthur, *The Quest through the Centuries: The Search for the Historical Jesus* (Philadelphia: Fortress, 1966); Warren S. Kissinger, "Historical Overview," in Kissinger, *The Lives of Jesus: A History and Bibliography* (New York and London: Garland, 1985), pp. 3-111; Walter P. Weaver, *The Historical Jesus in the Twentieth Century, 1900-1950* (Harrisburg, Pa.: Trinity Press International, 1999); and the edited volume, with selections from major authors since 1600, Gregory W. Dawes, ed., *The Historical Jesus Quest: Landmarks in the Search for the Jesus of History* (Louisville: Westminster/John Knox Press; Leiderdorp, The Netherlands: Deo Publishing, 2000). A valuable survey of Jewish, Islamic, Hindu, and Buddhist responses to Jesus is provided in Clinton Bennett, *In Search of Jesus: Insider and Outsider Images* (London and New York: Continuum, 2001), while a new anthology of three hundred and forty texts, David F. Ford and Mike Higton, eds., *Jesus*, Oxford Readers (Oxford: Oxford University Press, 2002), exhibits almost every conceivable point of view on Jesus.

12. Henry J. Cadbury, *The Peril of Modernizing Jesus* (New York: Macmillan, 1937), p. 17.

13. Throughout this chapter I am indebted to N. T. Wright's insightful article, "Jesus,

Quest for the Historical," in *Anchor Bible Dictionary*, ed. David Noel Freedman et al., 6 vols. (New York: Doubleday, 1992), 3:796-802. Another broad overview, focusing on current issues, may be found in William R. Telford, "Major Trends and Interpretive Issues in the Study of Jesus," in *Studying the Historical Jesus: Evaluations of the State of Current Research*, ed. Bruce Chilton and Craig A. Evans (Leiden: Brill, 1994), pp. 33-74. Donald Capps has used psychological theory to assess the reconstructions of Jesus by E. P. Sanders, John P. Meier, John Dominic Crossan, and Marcus J. Borg, in *Jesus: A Psychological Biography* (St. Louis: Chalice Press, 2000), pp. 3-45. Raymond Martin uses philosophical analysis to probe the reconstructions of Jesus by Marcus Borg, John Dominic Crossan, Elisabeth Schüssler Fiorenza, John Meier, E. P. Sanders, and N. T. Wright, in *The Elusive Messiah: A Philosophical Overview of the Quest for the Historical Jesus* (Boulder, Colo.: Westview Press, 1999).

14. The story of Reimarus's impact on the learned world is as complex as it is interesting. Following Reimarus's death in 1768, the German man of letters Gotthold Ephraim Lessing published as the "Wolfenbüttel Fragments" in 1774-78 several anonymous extracts from a vast manuscript left behind by Reimarus under the title *Apologie oder Schutzschrift für die vernünftigen Verehrer Gottes*. A part of the *Apologie* has been translated into English with a helpful introduction in Charles H. Talbert, ed., *Reimarus: Fragments*, trans. Ralph S. Fraser (Philadelphia: Fortress, 1970).

15. John Dominic Crossan, *The Historical Jesus: The Life of a Mediterranean Jewish Peasant* (San Francisco: HarperSanFrancisco, 1991), p. xxviii.

16. For an interpretation of Jesus in light of first-century Jewish Zealotism, see S. G. F. Brandon, *Jesus and the Zealots: A Study of the Political Factor in Primitive Christianity* (New York: Scribner, 1967), esp. pp. 350-58. Brandon's view is discussed and critiqued in Oscar Cullmann, *Jesus and the Revolutionaries*, trans. Gareth Putnam (New York: Harper & Row, 1970); and J. P. M. Sweet, "The Zealots and Jesus," and Ernst Bammel, "The Revolution Theory from Reimarus to Brandon," in *Jesus and the Politics of His Day*, ed. Ernst Bammel and C. F. D. Moule (Cambridge: Cambridge University Press, 1984), pp. 1-9, 11-68 respectively. John Dominic Crossan seems to associate both John the Baptist and Jesus with movements of popular revolt when he describes "the Baptism movement of John and the Kingdom movement of Jesus" as representing "two popular resistance movements" (John Dominic Crossan and Jonathan L. Reed, *Excavating Jesus: Beneath the Stones, Behind the Texts* [San Francisco: HarperSanFrancisco, 2001], p. 274). Yet Crossan breaks from the model of Jesus as revolutionary when he says that Jesus promoted not violent revolution but "a programmatically nonviolent resistance."

17. On Strauss see James C. Livingston, *Modern Christian Thought: From the Enlightenment to Vatican II* (New York: Macmillan; London: Collier Macmillan, 1971), pp. 173-80, and Albert Schweitzer, *The Quest of the Historical Jesus: A Critical Study of Its Progress from Reimarus to Wrede*, trans. W. Montgomery (New York: Macmillan, 1968), pp. 68-120.

18. See Daniel L. Pals, *The Victorian "Lives" of Jesus* (San Antonio: Trinity University Press, 1982).

19. Ernest Renan, *Life of Jesus*, pp. 392-93, cited in Jaroslav Pelikan, *Jesus through the Centuries: His Place in the History of Culture* (New York: Harper & Row, 1985), p. 199. On the sentimentalizing of Jesus in nineteenth-century America, see the illuminating work by Stephen Prothero, *American Jesus: How the Son of God Became a National Icon* (New York:

Farrar, Straus & Giroux, 2003), especially pp. 43-86. My thanks are due to Professor Prothero of Boston University for showing me this work in manuscript form.

20. Heinrich Julius Holtzmann was not the first to propose a two-source theory of Mark and Q, and yet he was a leading figure in what David L. Dungan has called a "period of consolidation" in the mid-nineteenth century. See Dungan, *A History of the Synoptic Problem: The Canon, the Text, the Composition, and the Interpretations of the Gospels*, Anchor Bible Reference Library, ed. David Noel Freedman (New York: Doubleday, 1999), esp. pp. 326-29.

21. Johannes Weiss, *Die Predigt Jesu vom Reiche Gottes* (Göttingen: Vandenhoeck & Ruprecht, 1892), and later editions, translated as *Jesus' Proclamation of the Kingdom of God* (Chico, Calif.: Scholars Press, 1985).

22. Albert Schweitzer, *The Quest of the Historical Jesus: A Critical Study of Its Progress from Reimarus to Wrede*, trans. W. Montgomery (New York: Macmillan, 1968 [1910]).

23. Schweitzer, *Quest*, pp. 398-99, 402.

24. Wright, "Jesus," p. 798.

25. Rudolf Bultmann, "The New Testament and Mythology," in Bultmann et al., *Kerygma and Myth: A Theological Debate* (New York: Harper & Row, 1961), pp. 1-44, citing 5.

26. Bultmann made it his principle never to visit any of the sites of the Holy Land — "a bad old German tradition with dangerous results," in the words of Martin Hengel (in Richard Ostling, "Who Was Jesus?" *Time*, August 15, 1988, pp. 37-42, quoting p. 38).

27. A roster of the "fellows" of the Jesus Seminar is given in Robert W. Funk, Roy W. Hoover, and the Jesus Seminar, *The Five Gospels: The Search for the Authentic Words of Jesus* (New York: Macmillan, 1993), pp. 533-37.

28. Funk et al., *The Five Gospels*, pp. 36-37. This volume contains the results of the seminar's deliberations on all the sayings attributed to Jesus in the synoptic Gospels and the noncanonical *Gospel of Thomas*. *The Gospel of Jesus According to the Jesus Seminar*, Robert W. Funk et al. (Santa Rosa, Calif.: Polebridge Press, 1999) gathers into one volume all the material in the Gospels judged by the Jesus Seminar to be probably authentic.

29. Funk et al., *The Five Gospels*, p. 5.

30. Funk et al., *The Five Gospels*, p. 4.

31. Robert Funk, in *Foundations and Facets Forum* 1, no. 1 (1985): 11-12, cited in Luke Timothy Johnson, *The Real Jesus: Misguided Quest for the Historical Jesus and the Truth of the Traditional Gospels* (San Francisco: HarperSanFrancisco, 1996), p. 8. Johnson's book is a rebuttal of the methods and conclusions of the Jesus Seminar. Yet Johnson in some statements seems to reject not only the Jesus Seminar but all attempts at reconstructing the historical Jesus, and to favor an attitude of faith in the biblical Christ: "The main accomplishment of the quest, both early and late, has been the discrediting of the gospel portraits of Jesus, at an enormous cost. The alternatives offered by historical reconstruction reveal themselves as fantasies and abstractions, held together by scholarly cleverness, incapable of sustaining even close examination, much less of galvanizing human lives. The Jesus they present is a dead person of the past. For those, in contrast, whose lives are being transformed by the Spirit of the Living One, the Jesus depicted in the literary compositions of the New Testament is recognized as true, both to his life and theirs" (Luke Timothy Johnson, "The Hu-

manity of Jesus," in John Dominic Crossan et al., *The Jesus Controversy: Perspectives in Conflict* [Harrisburg, Pa.: Trinity Press International, 1999], p. 74).

32. Philip Jenkins interprets the Jesus Seminar in terms of "a kind of inverted fundamentalism, a loving consecration of the noncanonical" (*Hidden Gospels: How the Search for Jesus Lost Its Way* [New York: Oxford University Press, 2001], p. 20). He views the writings of the Jesus Seminar as academically unsound but rhetorically effective: "The marketing of alternative Christianity represents a model case study in effective rhetoric, in which a potential audience is first identified, and a message is then tailored to its particular needs and interests. . . . Generally, the hidden gospels offer wonderful news for liberals, feminists, and radicals within the churches, who challenge what they view as outdated institutions and prejudices" (p. 16). N. T. Wright, in "Five Gospels but No Gospel: Jesus and the Seminar," in Chilton and Evans, *Authenticating the Activities of Jesus*, pp. 83-120, describes the Jesus Seminar as "fundamentally antifundamentalist" (p. 89).

33. Robert Funk, in *Atlanta Journal-Constitution*, September 30, 1989, cited in Johnson, *The Real Jesus*, pp. 12-13.

34. Johnson, *The Real Jesus*, pp. 15-16.

35. Bruce Chilton offers his criticism that "'the Jesus Seminar' . . . has explored intriguing possibilities and sparked much useful controversy and debate, yet it fails to grapple with the complex issue of Jesus' own religious orientation as a Jew" (*Rabbi Jesus*, p. xix).

36. See Crossan, *The Historical Jesus*, and, more concisely, *Jesus: A Revolutionary Biography*; F. G. Downing, *Jesus and the Threat of Freedom* (London: SCM, 1987) and *Cynics and Christian Origins* (Edinburgh: T&T Clark, 1992).

37. Crossan, *The Historical Jesus*, pp. 115, 117-18, 120.

38. Recounted in Cicero, *Tusculan Disputations*, Loeb Classical Library (London: William Heinemann; New York: Putnam, 1927), 5.92.

39. Marcus Borg writes: "There is a friendly joke circulating among Jesus scholars: Burton Mack's Jesus was killed in a car accident on a freeway in Los Angeles. The point: for Mack, there is no significant connection between what Jesus was like and the fact that he was executed. His death was, in an important sense, accidental" (*Jesus in Contemporary Scholarship* [Valley Forge, Pa.: Trinity Press International, 1994], p. 38 n. 28).

40. Burton L. Mack, *A Myth of Innocence: Mark and Christian Origins* (Philadelphia: Fortress, 1988) and *Who Wrote the New Testament? The Making of the Christian Myth* (San Francisco: HarperSanFrancisco, 1995).

41. Crossan, *The Historical Jesus*, pp. 117-18; cf. Horsley, *Sociology*, p. 117.

42. Charlesworth, "Jesus Research Expands," p. 16. Compare the statement of Sean Freyne that the early Jesus movement did not "espouse the kind of social and personal withdrawal that was associated with various kinds of Cynicism. . . . Rather it proposed an alternative way of life that adopted and adapted the kinship and familial values which were being eroded in the larger culture" ("The Geography, Politics, and Economics of Galilee and the Quest for the Historical Jesus," in *Studying the Historical Jesus*, pp. 75-121, quoting p. 120).

43. See Matt. 10:5-15, 24-33; 19:27-30.

44. Evans, "Authenticating the Activities of Jesus," in Chilton and Evans, *Authenticating the Activities of Jesus*, pp. 27-28.

45. Wright, "Jesus," p. 800. On the "third quest," see Craig A. Evans, "The Third Quest

of the Historical Jesus: A Bibliographic Essay," *Christian Scholars' Review* 28 (1999): 532-43, and John P. Meier, "The Present State of the 'Third Quest' for the Historical Jesus: Loss and Gain," in *Biblica* 80 (1999): 459-87. Stanley E. Porter questions whether N. T. Wright's unifying label of "third quest" is helpful at all. In fact, he challenges the entire periodization proposed by Wright, arguing that the so-called "no quest" period described only certain (and especially German) scholars, that the "second quest" and "third quest" are not really distinct, and that "there is a great deal of evidence that there has always been just one multi-faceted quest for the historical Jesus." The research shows "an unbroken line of scholarly investigation" (*The Criteria for Authenticity in Historical-Jesus Research: Previous Discussions and New Proposals*, Journal for the Study of New Testament Supplement Series, 191 [Sheffield, England: Sheffield Academic Press, 2000], pp. 47, 51-52, 238-39). Despite Porter's caveats, Wright's interpretive framework is still widely accepted as a way of understanding the history of Jesus research.

46. Ben F. Meyer, *The Aims of Jesus* (London: SCM, 1979). For a condensation of Meyer's position, see his article "Jesus," in *Anchor Bible Dictionary*, 3:773-96.

47. A. E. Harvey, *Jesus and the Constraints of History* (Philadelphia: Westminster, 1982), p. 65.

48. Among his works on Jesus are the following: *Conflict, Holiness, and Politics in the Teachings of Jesus* (New York: Mellen, 1984); *Jesus* (see n. 4 above); *Jesus in Contemporary Scholarship;* (with N. T. Wright) *The Meaning of Jesus: Two Visions* (San Francisco: Harper SanFrancisco, 1998); and the essay "An Orthodoxy Reconsidered: The 'End-of-the-World' Jesus," in *The Glory of Christ in the New Testament*, ed. N. T. Wright and L. D. Hurst (Oxford: Clarendon, 1987), pp. 207-17.

49. Borg, *Jesus*, p. 114.

50. Sanders's most important books include the following: *The Historical Figure of Jesus; Jesus and Judaism; Jewish Law from Jesus to the Mishnah* (London: SCM, 1990); and *Judaism: Practice and Belief, 63 B.C.E.–66 C.E.* (London: SCM; Philadelphia: Trinity Press International, 1992).

51. Sanders, *Historical Figure*, p. 56.

52. "Let the dead bury their own dead" (Luke 9:60), discussed in Sanders, *Jesus and Judaism*, pp. 252-55.

53. Meier, *A Marginal Jew*, 1:1.

54. Meier, *A Marginal Jew*, 1:7-9.

55. Meier, *A Marginal Jew*, 1:123-41.

56. Meier, *A Marginal Jew*, 2:237-506.

57. Meier, *A Marginal Jew*, 2:509-1038. The quoted phrase is from Josephus, *Antiquities* 18.3.3.

58. On the Jesus Seminar, see Wright's extensive critique in *Jesus and the Victory of God*, pp. 28-74. See also the discussion of the forgiveness of sins as a return from exile (p. 268), the possible meanings of eschatological language (pp. 208-9), and Jesus' identity and his coming to Jerusalem as the return of Yahweh himself (pp. 477, 608-9, 631-32, 653). Ben Witherington III, in *Jesus the Seer: The Progress of Prophecy* (Peabody, Mass.: Hendrickson, 1999), pp. 269-77, criticizes Wright's construal of eschatological language, arguing that Wright is not consistent with himself in *Jesus and the Victory of God*.

59. Bart D. Ehrman, *Jesus: Apocalyptic Prophet of the New Millennium* (New York: Oxford University Press, 1999), pp. x, 3, 17-18, 244, citing p. x.

60. Dale C. Allison, *Jesus of Nazareth: Millenarian Prophet* (Minneapolis: Fortress, 1998).

61. Fredriksen, *Jesus of Nazareth*, esp. pp. 11, 107, 197-207, 257, citing p. 266.

62. Chilton, *Rabbi Jesus*, esp. pp. 50, 53, 93, 108-9, 272-74, 283. One of Chilton's basic themes is that "Jesus' purifications had celebrated the innate purity of Israelites" (pp. 92, 140). Jesus' "trick was to activate the purity which came from inside a person" (p. 136), since he believed that each human being "possessed the angelic likeness" (pp. 242-43). Thus Chilton's Jesus teaches that salvation comes from within each person, and Chilton exhibits a corresponding lack of interest in such Gospel themes as sin and grace, divine forgiveness, and Jesus' death as a sacrifice. The "fundamental mistake" of Christianity is the identification of Jesus as "the one and only 'son of God'" (p. 172). Jesus never claimed uniqueness, says Chilton, but rather claimed to have the power to transform his followers into children of God (pp. 191-92, 292). Chilton writes that "John was like a guru" (p. 53), and the same is true of Jesus in this book. On Jesus as short, fat, and balding, see p. 138.

63. According to the Gospels (e.g., Luke 5:1-11), Jesus *did* go on fishing trips, and yet they were laborious rather than recreational!

64. John H. Hayes, *Son of God to Superstar: Twentieth-Century Interpretations of Jesus* (Nashville: Abingdon, 1976), pp. 82, 187-88, 184, 170. Concerning popular renderings of Jesus, see also Walter P. Weaver, *The Historical Jesus in the Twentieth Century, 1900-1950* (Harrisburg, Pa.: Trinity Press International, 1999), pp. 313-59. See also two works on Jesus and American culture: Stephen Prothero, *American Jesus*, and Richard W. Fox, *Jesus in America: Personal Savior, Cultural Hero, National Obsession* (San Francisco: HarperCollins, 2004). See also Fox's essay, "Jefferson, Emerson, and Jesus," *Raritan* 22 (2002): 62-75.

65. Adele Reinhartz, "Jesus of Hollywood: A Jewish Perspective," in *The Historical Jesus Through Catholic and Jewish Eyes*, edited by Leonard J. Greenspoon, Dennis Hamm, and Bryan LeBeau (Harrisburg, Pa.: Trinity Press International, 2000), pp. 131-46. On the place of Jesus in film, see also: Roy Kinnard and Tim Davis, *Divine Images: A History of Jesus on the Screen* (New York: Citadel Press, 1992); Gerald E. Forshey, "The Jesus Cycle," in *American Religious and Biblical Spectaculars* (Westport, Conn.: Praeger, 1992), pp. 83-121; Lloyd Baugh, *Imaging the Divine: Jesus and Christ-Figures in Film* (Kansas City: Sheed and Ward, 1997); W. Barnes Tatum, *Jesus at the Movies* (Santa Rosa, Calif.: Polebridge Press, 1997); and Peter T. Chattaway, "Jesus in the Movies," *Bible Review* (February 1998): 28-35, 45-46.

66. The best recent discussion of the nonexistence theory is found in Robert E. Van Voorst, *Jesus Outside the New Testament: An Introduction to the Ancient Evidence* (Grand Rapids, Mich., and Cambridge, U.K.: Eerdmans, 2000), pp. 6-16. Earlier treatments include: Shirley J. Case, *The Historicity of Jesus* (Chicago: University of Chicago, 1912); Arthur Drews, *Die Leugnung der Geschichtlichkeit Jesu in Vergangenheit und Gegenwart* (Karlsruhe: Braun, 1926); Maurice Goguel, *Jesus the Nazarene: Myth or History?* (London: Fisher & Unwin, 1926), esp. pp. 19-29; and Herbert G. Wood, *Did Christ Really Live?* (London: SCM, 1938), esp. pp. 18-27.

67. See C.-F. Volney, *The Ruins, or a Survey of the Revolutions of Empires* (New York: Davis, 1796; French, 1791), and C. F. Dupuis, *The Origin of All Religious Worship* (New York:

Garland, 1984; French, 1794, 1822). Quotation from F. M. Voltaire, "De Jesus," in *Dieu et les hommes*, in *Oeuvres completes de Voltaire* (Paris: Societe Litteraire-Typographique, 1785), 33:273, cf. 279; cited in Van Voorst, *Jesus Outside the New Testament*, p. 8.

68. George A. Wells's six books on the issue of Jesus' historicity include, most recently, *The Jesus Myth* (Chicago and LaSalle, Ill.: Open Court, 1999), which, despite its title, "represents a departure from my earlier position that the Jesus of the gospels resulted purely from attempts to make the vaguely conceived . . . Pauline Jesus into something more definitely historical" (p. 273 n. 40). Now Wells seems to have drawn closer to the position of Burton Mack, according to which Jesus existed but not at all in the way described in the canonical Gospels. Robert M. Price, in *Deconstructing Jesus* (Amherst, N.Y.: Prometheus Books, 2000), appeals to Burton Mack as well as Bruno Bauer, and calls his position "agnosticism" rather than "atheism" on the question of Jesus' existence (pp. 9, 16-17). He is not convinced of a real crucifixion under Pontius Pilate (pp. 248-49), sees the Gospel of Mark as fiction (p. 253), criticizes "liberal Christians" for retaining a historical Jesus while rejecting the reliability of the Gospels (p. 16), and concludes that "the various scholarly reconstructions of Jesus cancel each other out" (p. 16). Jack Nelson-Pallmeyer, in *Jesus Against Christianity: Reclaiming the Missing Jesus* (Harrisburg, Pa.: Trinity Press International, 2001), is almost as skeptical as Price as he "attempts to solve the mystery of Jesus' disappearance from Christianity" (p. vii), and explain how the nonviolent message of Jesus was replaced by the vengeful images of God and Jesus contained in the New Testament Gospels (pp. X-xv).

69. Barbara Thiering, *Jesus the Man* (New York: Doubleday, 1975), pp. 88, 103-4, 115-16, 133, 146-48, 221-22, 229, 237, 254, 262-63, discussed by Telford, "Major Trends," p. 46.

70. A. Faber-Kaiser, *Jesus Died in Kashmir: Jesus, Moses, and the Ten Lost Tribes of Israel* (London: Gordon Cremonesi, 1977). Recently, Joshua M. Benjamin in *The Mystery of Israel's Ten Lost Tribes and the Legend of Jesus in India* (New Delhi: Mosaic Books, 2001) has woven together various forms of pseudo-scholarship by asserting that Jesus was brought up by the Essenes (i.e., the Dead Sea Scroll sect), that he survived the cross, went to India, and was linked to the lost tribes of Israel and early Buddhism. Philip Jenkins writes that "the whole idea of hidden gospels and a lost Christianity has a deeper resonance, in that it appeals at the level of myth, using that word in its anthropological sense." "The real Jesus," according to this perspective, "was hidden behind the deceptive facade of Christianity, until hidden documents were found which exposed the truth and overthrew a conspiracy that had lasted for centuries" (*Hidden Gospels*, pp. 20-21). This is the stuff not of sound scholarship, but overwrought imagination or tabloid journalism. Thus Joshua Benjamin asserts that "the mystery of the survival of Jesus on the Cross and his travel to India can be solved if the 'Dark Treasury' at the Hemis Monastery . . . is opened for the public, as also the 63 manuscripts brought to Rome by missionaries from India, China, Egypt, and Arabia, which are said to be stored in the Vatican Library in Rome" (p. ix). Neil Douglas-Klotz, *The Hidden Gospel: Decoding the Spiritual Message of the Aramaic Jesus* (Wheaton, Ill.: Quest Books/ Theosophical Publishing House, 1999), appeals to the purported Aramaic texts that underlie the existing New Testament Gospels and thereby presents Jesus as a kind of guru: "Until now, the 'hidden Gospel' has lain buried deep within the Western psyche, perhaps awaiting just this moment to be discovered" (p. 24).

Notes to "Sources and Methods"

1. Koester, *Introduction*, 2:13.

2. Here I am indebted to the fine summary of recent scholarship in Chilton and Evans, *Studying the Historical Jesus*, and in particular the following chapters: Craig A. Evans, "Jesus in Non-Christian Sources," pp. 443-78; Evans, "Appendix: The Recently Published Dead Sea Scrolls and the Historical Jesus," pp. 547-65; and James H. Charlesworth and Craig A. Evans, "Jesus in the Agrapha and Apocryphal Gospels," pp. 479-533. A discussion of the issues treated in this chapter, for a popular readership, is given in E. P. Sanders, "How Do We Know What We Know About Jesus?," in Charlesworth and Weaver, *Jesus Two Thousand Years Later*, pp. 38-61.

3. *b. Sanh.* 106a. This and the other Talmudic and Judaic references in this chapter are taken from the following texts: *The Babylonian Talmud*, ed. I. Epstein, trans. Maurice Simon et al., 39 vols. (n.p.: Rebecca Benet Publications, 1959); *The Talmud of the Land of Israel: A Preliminary Translation and Explanation*, trans. Tzvee Zahary et al., 35 vols. (Chicago and London: University of Chicago Press, 1982-93); *The Mishnah*, trans. with notes by Herbert Danby (London: Oxford University Press, 1933); *The Tosefta*, ed. Jacob Neusner et al., 6 vols. (Hoboken, N.J.: Ktav Publishing House, 1977-86); Jacob Neusner, *The Fathers According to Rabbi Nathan: An Analytical Translation and Explanation* (Atlanta: Scholars Press, 1986). Following the usual scholarly conventions, the initial letter "b" stands for *The Babylonian Talmud*, "y" stands for *The Jerusalem Talmud* or *The Talmud of the Lord of Israel*, "m" stands for *The Mishnah*, "t" stands for *The Tosephta*, and "Abot de-Rabbi Nathan" stands for *The Fathers According to Rabbi Nathan*.

4. *b. Sanh.* 107b; *b. Sota* 47a.

5. *b. Sanh.* 43b.

6. *b. Sanh.* 107b; *b. Sota* 47a; *t. Shabb.* 11:15.

7. *b. Ber.* 17b; *b. Sanh.* 107b.

8. *b. Sanh.* 43a.

9. The same can be said regarding the picture of Jesus presented in the Qur'an and other Islamic sources. Non-Muslim scholars are generally in agreement that the Islamic teachings on Jesus are literarily dependent on the New Testament and/or other early Christian writings. Hence they cannot serve as independent sources of information regarding Jesus.

10. Suetonius, *Divus Claudius* 25.4; cited in Evans, "Jesus in Non-Christian Sources," p. 457.

11. Pliny the Younger, *Epistles*, bk. 10, letter 96, in Henry Bettenson, ed., *Documents of the Christian Church*, 2nd ed. (London: Oxford University Press, 1963), pp. 3-4.

12. Rowan Williams argues that the available evidence suggests that Jesus was worshipped by his earliest followers: "There is little or no trace in the first Christian decades of a Christianity unmarked by devotion to Jesus as a living agent. Even allowing for the most sceptical reading of the Gospels and Acts, we can say that within about twenty-five years from the likeliest date of Jesus' crucifixion, he was being invoked by Christians as a source of divine favour and almost certainly addressed in public prayer at Christian assemblies" ("A History of Faith in Jesus," in Markus Bockmuehl, ed., *The Cambridge Companion to Jesus* [Cambridge: Cambridge University Press, 2001], p. 220). This observation has significance

for interpreting the rise of Christianity, since it suggests that there is no basis for thinking that Jesus' earliest followers regarded him as purely human or non-divine.

13. See Origen, *Contra Celsum* 1.6, 38, 46, 68, 71; 2.9, 14, 16; 3.1; 5.51; 6.42; cited in Evans, "Jesus in Non-Christian Sources," p. 460.

14. Justin Martyr, *Dialogue with Trypho* 69, in Alexander Roberts and James Donaldson, eds., *The Ante-Nicene Fathers*, 10 vols. (Grand Rapids, Mich.: Eerdmans, 1985 [1885]), 1:233.

15. There are other notable references to Jesus in classical authors, as for instance in Lucian of Samosata (ca. 115–ca. 200), who writes of those who "revered him [Jesus] as a god, used him as a lawgiver, and set him down as a protector" (*Passing of Peregrinus* 11.13). Lucian refers disdainfully to early Christian egalitarianism ("their first lawgiver persuaded them that they are all brothers of one another") and to martyrdom ("the poor wretches despise death and most even willingly give themselves up"). Another sneering comment comes from Cornelius Tacitus (ca. 56–ca. 118), who in *Annals* 15.44 speaks of the Christians as "those hated for their vice" and followers of a "pernicious superstition" (citations from Evans, "Jesus in Non-Christian Sources," pp. 461-65). Tacitus confirms that Jesus died under the authority of Pontius Pilate, and that he was the founder of a religious movement called after his name. On this whole subject of outsiders' perceptions of Jesus and the early Christians, see the fascinating book by Robert Louis Wilken, *The Christians as the Romans Saw Them* (New Haven: Yale University Press, 1984).

16. Josephus, *Antiquities* 18.63; cited from *Josephus*, English translation by H. St. J. Thackeray, Ralph Marcus, Allen Wikgren, and L. H. Feldman, Loeb Classical Library, 9 vols. (Cambridge: Harvard University Press, 1926-83).

17. Meier discusses the *Testimonium*, with customary thoroughness, in *A Marginal Jew*, 1:56-88.

18. Josephus, *Antiquities* 20.200; Evans, "Jesus in Non-Christian Sources," pp. 468-73.

19. Mack, *A Myth of Innocence*, p. 282.

20. David Seeley, "Was Jesus like a Philosopher? The Evidence of Martyrological and Wisdom Motifs in Q, Pre-Pauline Traditions, and Mark," in *Society of Biblical Literature 1989 Seminar Papers*, ed. David J. Lull (Atlanta: Scholars Press, 1989), pp. 540-49, citing p. 548. Both cited in Evans, "Jesus in Non-Christian Sources," pp. 471-72.

21. Before leaving the topic of non-Christian sources, I should mention some recent discussions concerning the Dead Sea Scrolls (summarized in Evans, "Dead Sea Scrolls," pp. 547-65, esp. 553-54, 563-65). A stir was caused by the recent publication of the remaining scrolls from Cave 4 at Qumran. The original texts are given in Robert H. Eisenman and J. M. Robinson, *A Facsimile Edition of the Dead Sea Scrolls*, 2 vols. (Washington: Biblical Archaeology Society, 1991), and a selection of them with translations is found in Robert H. Eisenman and M. O. Wise, *The Dead Sea Scrolls Uncovered: The First Complete Translation and Interpretation of Fifty Key Documents Withheld for Over Thirty-five Years* (Shaftesbury: Element, 1992). The text catalogued as 4Q285 quickly became controversial when Eisenman claimed that it speaks of a slain Messiah (Eisenman and Robinson, pp. 224, 321, 409, 739, 1352; and Eisenman and Wise, pp. 27-29). He translated the key passage as "they will put to death the Leader of the Community, the Branch of David." Yet the context suggests that it is not the Messiah who is overcome, but rather the enemies who are overcome by the Messiah. Thus

the translation should read: "The Prince of the Community, the Branch of David, will put him to death." Another text worth mentioning is 4Q491, discussed by Morton Smith in "Two Ascended into Heaven — Jesus and the Author of 4Q491," in *Jesus and the Dead Sea Scrolls,* ed. James H. Charlesworth (New York: Doubleday, 1992), pp. 290-301. The text seems to describe a human being who ascends into heaven and there takes a seat among celestial beings. This text could have some relevance for the Gospel verse "'you will see the Son of Man seated at the right hand of the Power,' and 'coming with the clouds of heaven'" (Mark 14:62), since it provides evidence that notions of heavenly exaltation were entertained in certain branches of Judaism in Jesus' day.

22. Joachim Jeremias, *The Unknown Sayings of Jesus* (London: SPCK, 1957). See also the older classic in German, A. Resch, *Agrapha: Aussercanonische Schriftfragmente,* Texte und Untersuchungen 15 (Leipzig: Hinrichs, 1906).

23. O. Hofius, "Unknown Sayings of Jesus," in *The Gospel and the Gospels,* ed. Peter Stuhlmacher (Grand Rapids, Mich.: Eerdmans, 1991), pp. 336-60; Van Voorst, *Jesus Outside the New Testament,* pp. 179-85. See also William D. Stroker, *Extracanonical Sayings of Jesus,* Society of Biblical Literature Resources for Biblical Study, 18 (Atlanta: Scholars Press, 1989).

24. Cited from Charlesworth and Evans, pp. 484-86.

25. Charlesworth and Evans, p. 487 n. 22.

26. Meier, *A Marginal Jew,* 1:114.

27. Hofius, "Unknown Sayings of Jesus," p. 357, citing Joachim Jeremias, "Die Zuverlässigkeit der Evangelien-Überlieferung," *Junge Kirche* 6 (1938): 580, quoted in Charlesworth and Evans, "Jesus in the Agrapha," p. 490; Van Voorst, *Jesus Outside the New Testament,* p. 215. Christopher Tuckett agrees regarding the agrapha that "the overall value of such sayings is uncertain" ("Sources and Methods," in Bockmuehl, *The Cambridge Companion to Jesus,* p. 128).

28. Rudolf Bultmann, *History of the Synoptic Tradition,* trans. John Marsh (New York: Harper & Row, 1963), p. 374.

29. Meier, *A Marginal Jew,* 1:123-24, referring to the *Gospel of Philip* 63:25-30, and 73:8-15.

30. John Dominic Crossan has proposed a complex theory according to which the second-century *Gospel of Peter* is a revision of a much earlier "Cross Gospel," which was in fact so early that it served as the sole basis for the passion narrative in the Gospel of Mark. Meier (*A Marginal Jew,* 1:116-18) and Charlesworth and Evans ("Jesus in the Agrapha," pp. 503-14) demonstrate the weaknesses in Crossan's theory.

31. For a collection of these texts in English translation, see James M. Robinson, ed., *The Nag Hammadi Library in English,* 3rd ed. (San Francisco: Harper & Row, 1988).

32. A defense of these claims may be found in Stephen J. Patterson, *The Gospel of Thomas and Jesus* (Sonoma, Calif.: Polebridge Press, 1993), and Richard Valantasis, *The Gospel of Thomas,* New Testament Readings (London and New York: Routledge, 1997). Some of the recent authors overstate their case, however, in claiming that a "consensus is emerging in American scholarship that the *Gospel of Thomas* is a text independent of the Synoptics and that it was compiled in the mid to late first century" (Stevan L. Davies, "The Christology and Protology of *The Gospel of Thomas*," *Journal of Biblical Literature* 111 [1992]: 663, quoted in

Charlesworth and Evans, "Jesus in the Agrapha," p. 497 n. 41). Marcus Borg makes a similar claim regarding a "consensus" in *Jesus in Contemporary Scholarship*, p. 165.

33. John Meier argues that Matthew, Mark, Luke, and John fall into a distinct literary genre of "gospel" that necessarily includes reference to Jesus' deeds, death, and resurrection, as well as his teaching. On this basis Thomas does not qualify as a "gospel" (*A Marginal Jew,* 1:143-45 n. 15). Helmut Koester by contrast seems to define a "gospel" as including all writings that pertain to Jesus of Nazareth (*Ancient Christian Gospels: Their History and Development* [London: SCM; Philadelphia: Trinity Press, 1990], pp. 44-47).

34. E. P. Sanders says: "I share the general scholarly view that very, very little in the apocryphal gospels could conceivably go back to the time of Jesus. They are legendary and mythological. Of all the apocryphal material, only some of the sayings in the Gospel of Thomas are worth consideration" (*Historical Figure,* p. 64). Van Voorst, in his book-length analysis of the extracanonical evidence for Jesus, concludes that the *Gospel of Thomas* "belongs in the second century among gnosticizing Christians" and comments: "Despite noisy proposals that reconstruct Jesus and early Christianity on the basis of second- and third-century documents, actual and hypothetical, recent scholarship in general rightly sees the value of these writings as primarily witnesses to their own time" (*Jesus Outside the New Testament,* p. 217). Christopher Tuckett writes that the problems posed by the *Gospel of Thomas* are "probably ultimately insoluble" though "at least in the form of the text we have, some influence of the canonical gospels has taken place" ("Sources and Methods," in Bockmuehl, *The Cambridge Companion to Jesus,* p. 130). Tuckett's arguments are more fully presented in *Nag Hammadi and the Gospel Tradition: Synoptic Tradition in the Nag Hammadi Library* (Edinburgh: T&T Clark, 1986), and "Thomas and the Synoptics," *Novum Testamentum* 30 (1988): 132-57.

35. Meier, *A Marginal Jew,* 1:140.

36. An excellent analysis of the issues is found in Van A. Harvey, *The Historian and the Believer: The Morality of Historical Knowledge and Christian Belief* (New York: Macmillan, 1966).

37. Crossan, *Jesus,* p. x.

38. On historical tradition in John, see the following: C. H. Dodd, *The Fourth Gospel* (Cambridge: Cambridge University Press, 1960), pp. 444-53; A. J. B. Higgins, *The Historicity of the Fourth Gospel* (London: Lutterworth, 1960); C. H. Dodd, *Historical Tradition in the Fourth Gospel* (Cambridge: Cambridge University Press, 1963); Raymond Brown, *The Gospel according to John,* 2 vols., Anchor Bible, ed. David Noel Freedman (Garden City, N.Y.: Doubleday, 1966-70), esp. 1:xli-li; and Craig L. Blomberg, *The Historical Reliability of John's Gospel: Issues and Commentary* (Downers Grove, Ill.: InterVarsity Press, 2001).

39. For an interpretation of John in light of Gnostic, Hermetic, Mandaean, or Manichaean materials, see the classic studies by Wilhelm Bousset, *Kyrios Christos,* trans. John E. Steely (New York and Nashville: Abingdon, 1970 [German 1913]), pp. 211-44; and Rudolf Bultmann, *The Gospel of John* (Oxford: Basil Blackwell, 1971 [German 1941]).

40. Craig L. Blomberg notes that in 1993 the Jesus Seminar accepted only three of Jesus' attributed sayings in the Gospel of John as likely to be authentic (*Historical Reliability,* p. 17). He argues for the literary independence of John from the synoptic Gospels based on verbal analysis showing common ideas and episodes described in differing vocabulary.

Blomberg concludes: "If John is largely or exclusively independent, in a literary sense, from the Synoptics, then the numerous points at which criteria like multiple attestation and coherence apply help us to authenticate large portions of this Gospel" (p. 291).

41. Concerning the sayings of Jesus included in the Gospels, we should note that the earliest Christians believed that Jesus had ascended into heaven and they could communicate with him in prayer. They spoke to him, and sometimes he spoke back through visions or voices. Some of their prayers evoked verbal answers that could then be attributed to "the Lord." Thus in 2 Corinthians 12:7-9, Paul prays that God will remove an unnamed ailment, a "thorn in the flesh," and Paul recounts that the Lord responded: "My grace is sufficient for you, for power is made perfect in weakness." This is in effect a direct quotation of the heavenly Lord (Sanders, *Historical Figure*, p. 62). While there is considerable debate over the amount and quality of historical information in the Gospel of John, some regard the discourses of Jesus there as consisting in sayings of the "heavenly Lord," transmitted through recognized prophets. If that is the case, then the Fourth Gospel would be based on the assumption of a continuity between the sayings of the earthly Jesus and the Spirit-inspired utterances that came from the heavenly, exalted Jesus through the early Christian prophets. Supporting the theory that the sayings of the early Christian prophets were attributed to Jesus is M. Eugene Boring, in "How May We Identify Oracles of Christian Prophets in the Synoptic Tradition? Mark 3:28-29 as a Test Case," *Journal of Biblical Literature* 91 (1972): 501-21, and *Sayings of the Risen Jesus: Christian Prophecy in the Synoptic Tradition* (Cambridge: Cambridge University Press, 1982). A rebuttal may be found in D. Hill, "On the Evidence for the Creative Role of Christian Prophets," *New Testament Studies* 20 (1974): 262-74, and David E. Aune, in *Prophecy in Early Christianity and the Ancient Mediterranean World* (Grand Rapids, Mich.: Eerdmans, 1983), pp. 233-45. James D. G. Dunn supports Boring's hypothesis and yet suggests that prophetic utterances among the earliest Christians were always tested by their degree of coherence with the existing traditions regarding Jesus, and that this "implies the existence in most churches of such a canon (the word is not inappropriate) of foundational Jesus tradition" ("Can the Third Quest Hope to Succeed?," in Chilton and Evans, *Authenticating the Activities of Jesus*, p. 39).

42. Most general introductions to the New Testament discuss the authorship, composition, and dating of the Gospels. A lucid summary is given in Sanders, *Historical Figure*, pp. 57-66, to which I am indebted here.

43. A generation ago, most scholars assumed that the stories of Jesus' life and teaching circulated for perhaps a generation or longer in oral form, prior to the composition of any written records. This question cannot be answered with certainty, yet some have argued that Jesus' disciples like those of first-century rabbis did rely on written renderings of their master's teaching. See Rainer Reiser, *Jesus als Lehrer* (Tübingen: Mohr, 1981), and Robert Stein, *The Method and Message of Jesus' Teaching*, rev. ed. (Louisville: Westminster John Knox, 1994), pp. 1-32.

44. There is a much-debated statement by the second-century author Papias, quoted in Eusebius's *Ecclesiastical History* (3.39.16), regarding an Aramaic or Hebrew version of the Gospel of Matthew that preceded the Greek. See F. C. Grant, "Matthew, Gospel of," in *Interpreter's Dictionary of the Bible*, ed. George Arthur Buttrick, 4 vols. (New York and Nashville: Abingdon, 1962), 3:303-4, and William R. Schoedel, "Papias," in *Anchor Bible Dictionary*,

5:140-42. A recent defense of Matthean priority is contained in John Wenham, *Redating Matthew, Mark, and Luke: A Fresh Assault on the Synoptic Problem* (Downers Grove, Ill.: InterVarsity Press, 1992).

45. Robert H. Gundry, in his monumental study *Mark: A Commentary on His Apology for the Cross* (Grand Rapids: Eerdmans, 1993), sifts the available evidence and concludes that the Gospel of Mark was probably composed prior to the outbreak of the Jewish War in 66 C.E., and possibly as early as 60-62 C.E. (pp. 1026-45, esp. p. 1042). John A. T. Robinson, in *Redating the New Testament* (Philadelphia: Westminster Press, 1976), argued that some of the Gospels were written as early as the 50s, based on his judgment that the fall of Jerusalem in 70 C.E. is never alluded to in the New Testament, and that therefore the entire canon of the New Testament was completed by 70 C.E. The early dates are also favored in Wenham, *Redating Matthew, Mark, and Luke*. D. A. Carson, Douglas J. Moo, and Leon Morris, in *An Introduction to the New Testament* (Grand Rapids, Mich.: Zondervan, 1992), date Mark in the late 50s, Luke in the early 60s, and Matthew before 70 and probably in the 60s.

46. Sanders, *Historical Figure*, p. 65. Martin Hengel argues that the four canonical Gospels were circulated with titles attached beginning in the first decades after their composition. See Hengel's essay and book, "The Titles of the Gospels and the Gospel of Mark," in *Studies in the Gospel of Mark* (Philadelphia: Fortress, 1985), pp. 64-84, esp. pp. 81-84, and *The Four Gospels and the One Gospel of Jesus Christ: An Investigation of the Collection and Origin of the Canonical Gospels* (Harrisburg, Pa.: Trinity Press International, 2000), pp. 48-56, esp. p. 54.

47. See the discussion in Crossan, *The Historical Jesus*, pp. xxvii-xxxiv, 427-66; Meier, *A Marginal Jew*, 1:168-84; Dale C. Allison, *Jesus of Nazareth: Millenarian Prophet* (Minneapolis: Fortress, 1998), pp. 1-77; Craig A. Evans, "Authenticity Criteria in Life of Jesus Research," *Christian Scholars' Review* 19 (1986): 6-31; and Stanley E. Porter, *The Criteria for Authenticity in Historical-Jesus Research*. Other important discussions of authenticity criteria are found in Norman Perrin, *Rediscovering the Teaching of Jesus* (New York and Evanston: Harper & Row, 1967), pp. 39-47; D. G. A. Calvert, "An Examination of the Criteria for Distinguishing the Authentic Words of Jesus," *New Testament Studies* 18 (1972): 209-19; Morna D. Hooker, "On Using the Wrong Tool," *Theology* 75 (1972): 570-81; Richard N. Longenecker, "Literary Criteria in Life of Jesus Research: An Evaluation and Proposal," in *Current Issues in Biblical and Patristic Interpretation*, ed. Gerald F. Hawthorne (Grand Rapids: Eerdmans, 1975), pp. 217-29; Robert H. Stein, "The 'Criteria' for Authenticity," in *Gospel Perspectives: Studies of History and Tradition in the Four Gospels*, vol. 1, ed. R. T. France and David Wenham (Sheffield: JSOT, 1980), pp. 225-63; Gerd Theissen, "Historical Skepticism and the Criteria of Jesus Research *or* My Attempt to Leap Across Lessing's Yawning Gulf," *Scottish Journal of Theology* 49 (1996): 147-76; and G. Theissen and D. Winter, *Der Kriterienfrage in der Jesusforschung: Vom Differenzkriterium zum Plausibilitaetskriterium* (Freiburg: Universitätsverlag/Göttingen: Vandenhoek & Ruprecht, 1997), esp. pp. 175-232.

48. See Dickinson W. Adams, ed., *Jefferson's Extracts from the Gospels* (Princeton, N.J.: Princeton University Press, 1983), and the discussion in Stephen Prothero, *American Jesus*, pp. 19-42. Jefferson produced two different texts: "The Philosophy of Jesus of Nazareth," no longer extant and consisting only of Gospel sayings, and "The Life and Morals of Jesus of Nazareth," dating from 1819-20 and including selected sayings and non-miraculous narra-

tives from the New Testament Gospels. Jefferson commented to John Adams that the true sayings of Jesus were "as easily distinguishable as diamonds in a dunghill" (Adams, *Jefferson's Extracts*, p. 352). Prothero argues that Jefferson should not be seen as an irreligious man, and that his attachment to Jesus was as deep as it was non-traditional.

49. Evans, "Authenticity Criteria," pp. 7-8.

50. Perrin, *Rediscovering*, p. 39.

51. Bultmann, *Synoptic Tradition*, p. 205. Perrin's description of the criterion is quite similar to Bultmann's: "The earliest form of a saying we can reach may be regarded as authentic if it can be shown to be dissimilar to characteristic emphases both of ancient Judaism and of the early church" (*Rediscovering*, p. 39).

52. Charlesworth, *Jesus within Judaism*, p. 167.

53. Hooker, "On Using the Wrong Tool," pp. 570-81. Raymond Brown writes that the criterion of dissimilarity gives rise to a "monstrosity: a Jesus who never said, thought, or did anything that other Jews said, thought, or did, and a Jesus who had no connection or relationship to what his followers said, thought, or did in reference to him after he died" (Raymond E. Brown, *An Introduction to the New Testament*, Anchor Bible Reference Library [New York: Doubleday, 1997], p. 827; cited in Porter, *The Criteria for Authenticity in Historical-Jesus Research*, p. 57). Christopher Tuckett notes that the criterion of dissimilarity reverses the basic thrust of the "third quest," which situates Jesus in the context of first-century Palestine and views him as a part of — and not dissimilar to — Judaism ("Sources and Methods," in Bockmuehl, *The Cambridge Companion to Jesus*, pp. 132-33). Marianne Meye Thompson also criticizes the criterion of dissimilarity, and, based on N. T. Wright, suggests a "criterion of double similarity" that "favours the authenticity of that material which can be credibly located within first-century Judaism, and which can credibly explain the rise of beliefs or practices in the early church, while allowing for differences from both Judaism and the early church" ("Jesus and His God," in Bockmuehl, *The Cambridge Companion to Jesus*, p. 43; citing N. T. Wright, *Jesus and the Victory of God*, pp. 131-32). Tom Holmen, in "Doubts About Double Dissimilarity: Restructuring the Main Criterion of Jesus-of-History Research," in Bruce Chilton and Craig A. Evans, *Authenticating the Words of Jesus* (Boston and Leiden: Brill, 2002), pp. 47-80, discusses the criterion of dissimilarity at length, and concludes that "dissimilarity to Judaism furnishes no indication of authenticity and has . . . nothing to do with the question of authenticity" (p. 75). Holmen accepts dissimilarity from Christianity as a criterion for authentic sayings of Jesus, and yet sees this kind of dissimilarity as a new form of the criterion of embarrassment (pp. 75-76) — to be discussed presently.

54. Norman Perrin, *What Is Redaction Criticism?* (Philadelphia: Fortress, 1969), p. 71.

55. Meier, *A Marginal Jew*, 1:176. Similarly Gerd Theissen writes: "We have to develop a historical sense for the degree of coherence and incoherence which we may expect in a given epoch and in the writings of an individual author or in his orally transmitted words" ("Historical Scepticism and the Criteria of Jesus Research," p. 156 n. 10).

56. Ernst Käsemann, "The Problem of the Historical Jesus," in *Essays on New Testamant Themes*, Studies in Biblical Theology (London: SCM, 1964), pp. 15-47, citing p. 35.

57. Sanders, *Historical Figure*, p. 56.

58. E. P. Sanders, *The Tendencies of the Synoptic Tradition* (Cambridge: Cambridge

University Press, 1969), p. 272. Sanders draws from this the conclusion, underlined in the original: "For this reason, dogmatic statements that a certain characteristic proves a certain passage to be earlier than another are never justified" (p. 272).

59. Stanley Porter, in *The Criteria for Authenticity in Historical-Jesus Research* (pp. 240-42), expresses skepticism regarding many of the alleged new criteria of authenticity, which appear on inspection to be reworked versions of old criteria. His three proposals — for a criterion of the Greek language and its context, a criterion of Greek textual variants, and a criterion of discourse features (pp. 126-237) — are too new to have been evaluated by other scholars.

60. See Crossan, *The Historical Jesus*, pp. xxvii-xxxiv, 427-66.

61. Allison, *Jesus of Nazareth*, p. 16. See Allison's entire critique of Crossan's method on pp. 10-33, and N. T. Wright discussion of Crossan in *Jesus and the Victory of God*, pp. 48-52.

62. Crossan, *The Historical Jesus*, p. Xxxiv.

63. Allison, *Jesus of Nazareth*, pp. 29-33.

64. Crossan, "Materials and Methods in Historical Jesus Research," *Forum* 4 (1988): 10, quoted in Allison, p. 36.

65. Sanders, *Jesus and Judaism*, p. 10.

66. Charlesworth, *Jesus within Judaism*, pp. 167, 3. Against the notion that Paul departed from Jesus, David Wenham argues for substantial continuity between the two in *Paul: Follower of Jesus or Founder of Christianity?* (Grand Rapids, Mich.: Eerdmans, 1995).

67. Sanders, *Historical Figure*, p. 193.

Notes to "The Palestinian Context"

1. Eliahu Elath, "Israel," in *The New Encyclopaedia Britannica*, 30 vols. (Chicago: Encyclopaedia Britannica, 1983), 9:1059-60 (Macropaedia).

2. Robert H. Gundry notes that there is another explanation for the disappearance of the forests: with the introduction of the railroads, Palestinian forests were cut down for firewood to burn in locomotives (letter to the author, September 8, 1999).

3. For my description of the economic, political, and cultural context of first-century Palestine, I am dependent on Freyne, "Geography," pp. 75-121.

4. At the same time, it seems from the phrasing of Luke 17:11 that Luke has located Samaria alongside of Galilee, and not between Galilee and Judea.

5. Jesus' possible connection with the city of Sepphoris has significance in one's overall interpretation of his life, as Jonathan Reed explains: "Those portraying him as a rural and Torah-abiding Jew tend to point out the absence of Sepphoris in the New Testament as evidence for his avoidance of a presumably Hellenistic and gentile city. Scholars stressing Hellenistic or cosmopolitan traits in the Jesus tradition tend to identify Sepphoris as their source, believe Sepphoris's absence in the tradition to be accidental, and assume Jesus visited it during his youth" (*Archaeology and the Galilean Jesus: A Re-examination of the Evidence* [Harrisburg, Pa.: Trinity Press International, 2000], p. 102). Reed suggests that it is "likely" that Jesus visited Sepphoris during his youth but perhaps not during his ministry, and that he may

have avoided it because Herod Antipas was a more immediate threat in that city (p. 138). For further background on Sepphoris, see Richard A. Batey, *Jesus and the Forgotten City* (Grand Rapids, Mich.: Baker Book House, 1991), and "Sepphoris: An Urban Portrait of Jesus," *Biblical Archaeology Review* 18 (May/June 1992): pp. 50-62.

6. Josephus, *Jewish War* 2.556-65.

7. Josephus, *Antiquities* 17.318-20; *Jewish War* 2.94-100.

8. Josephus, *Antiquities* 17.200-205; 17.304-14.

9. Josephus, *Antiquities* 14.271-76.

10. Josephus, *Antiquities* 14.406-12.

11. Josephus, *Antiquities* 17.304-14.

12. Josephus, *Antiquities* 18.261-309; *Jewish War* 2.184-203.

13. Frederick C. Grant, *The Economic Background of the Gospels* (New York: Russell & Russell, 1973 [1926]), pp. 87-110, esp. p. 105. Some scholars think Grant's figure of 35 percent is too high.

14. Borg, *Jesus*, p. 85.

15. Freyne, "Geography," p. 90.

16. Richard A. Horsley, *Jesus and the Spiral of Violence: Popular Jewish Resistance in Roman Palestine* (San Francisco: Harper & Row, 1987), and Horsley and John S. Hanson, *Bandits, Prophets, and Messiahs: Popular Movements in the Time of Jesus* (Minneapolis: Winston Press, 1985).

17. Horsley, *Jesus*, pp. 37-43.

18. Freyne, "Geography," p. 95; see also Freyne, "Bandits in Galilee: A Contribution to the Study of Social Conditions in First-Century Palestine," in *The Social World of Formative Christianity and Judaism, Essays in Tribute to Howard Clark Kee*, ed. Jacob Neusner et al. (Philadelphia: Fortress, 1988), pp. 50-68.

19. Reed speaks of the "economic strain on Galilean peasants" (*Archaeology and the Galilean Jesus*, p. 96) caused by the cities of Sepphoris and Tiberias.

20. Stanley E. Porter, "Jesus and the Use of Greek in Galilee," in *Studying the Historical Jesus*, pp. 123-54.

21. Joseph A. Fitzmyer, in "Did Jesus Speak Greek?," *Biblical Archaeology Review* 18 (Sept./Oct. 1992): 58-63, argues that Jesus probably spoke Greek on certain occasions but might not have taught in Greek.

22. Porter, "Jesus and the Use of Greek," p. 135.

23. A brief summary of scholarship on first-century Judaism may be found in the articles of the *Anchor Bible Dictionary*, including the following: J. Andrew Overman and William Scott Green, "Judaism (Greco-Roman Period)," 3:1027-54; Anthony Saldarini, "Pharisees," 5:289-303; Saldarini, "Sanhedrin," 5:975-80; Saldarini, "Scribes," 5:1012-16; Gary G. Porton, "Sadducees," 5:892-95. A lengthier treatment is given in Anthony J. Saldarini, *Pharisees, Scribes, and Sadducees in Palestinian Society: A Sociological Approach* (Wilmington, Del.: Michael Glazier, 1988), and Martin Hengel, *Judaism and Hellenism*, 2 vols. (Philadelphia: Fortress, 1974). On the major Jewish groups in the first century, see also N. T. Wright, *Christian Origins and the Question of God*, vol. 1, *The New Testament and the People of God*, pp. 181-203, and Meier, *A Marginal Jew*, 3:289-560. A truly monumental study of the period is found in Emil Schürer, *The History of the Jewish People in the Age of Jesus Christ* (175 B.C.E.–A.D. 135),

rev. and ed. Geza Vermès and Fergus Millar, 3 vols. (Edinburgh: T&T Clark, 1973-87). This new edition of an old classic removes some of the anti-Judaic bias found in Schürer's nineteenth-century text, and incorporates new material from more recent scholarship.

24. George Foot Moore, *Judaism in the First Centuries of the Christian Era: The Age of the Tannaim*, 3 vols. (Cambridge: Harvard University Press, 1927-30).

25. Jacob Neusner has written literally hundreds of works on Judaism, and has largely set the agenda in this field of study during the last generation. Among his more important and recent works on Judaism are: *The Way of Torah: An Introduction to Judaism*, 6th ed. (Belmont, Calif.: Wadsworth, 1997), *The Four Stages of Rabbinic Judaism* (New York: Routledge, 1999), and *Judaism: An Introduction* (London and New York: Penguin, 2002). Neusner has presented his reflections on Christianity in *Children of the Flesh, Children of the Promise: A Rabbi Talks with Paul* (Cleveland: Pilgrim Press, 1995), *A Rabbi Talks with Jesus*, rev. ed. (Montreal: McGill-Queen's University Press, 2000), and, with Andrew M. Greeley, *Common Ground: A Priest and a Rabbi Read Scripture Together* (Cleveland: Pilgrim Press, 1996).

26. Jonathan Z. Smith, *Imagining Religion: From Babylon to Jonestown* (Chicago and London: University of Chicago Press, 1982), pp. 9-14.

27. Jacob Neusner, William Scott Green, and Ernest S. Frerichs, eds., *Judaisms and Their Messiahs at the Turn of the Christian Era* (New York: Cambridge University Press, 1987). With Bruce Chilton, Neusner has authored numerous studies comparing Judaism and Christianity, including *Judaism in the New Testament: Practices and Beliefs* (New York: Routledge, 1995), *Trading Places: The Intersecting Histories of Judaism and Christianity* (Cleveland: Pilgrim Press, 1996), *The Body of Faith: Israel and the Church* (Valley Forge, Pa.: Trinity Press International, 1996), *God in the World* (Harrisburg, Pa.: Trinity Press International, 1997), *Jewish-Christian Debates: God, Kingdom, Messiah* (Minneapolis: Fortress, 1998), *Types of Authority in Formative Christianity and Judaism* (New York: Routledge, 1999), *Jewish and Christian Doctrines: The Classics Compared* (New York: Routledge, 2000), and *Comparing Spiritualities: Formative Christianity and Judaism on Finding Life and Meeting Death* (Harrisburg, Pa.: Trinity Press International, 2000).

28. Chilton, *Rabbi Jesus*, p. 24.

29. Overman and Green, "Judaism," p. 1039.

30. See *Pss. Sol.* 1:8; 2:3-13; 4:1, 8, 12; 8:11ff.; *T. Levi* 10:3; 16:2-4; 14:4-6; *Liv. Pro.* 3:15ff.; these texts are included in James H. Charlesworth, ed., *The Old Testament Pseudepigrapha*, 2 vols. (Garden City, N.Y.: Doubleday, 1983-85). References from Overman and Green, p. 1040.

31. Despite the instruction in the book of Deuteronomy that all sacrifices were to be offered at "the place that the Lord your God will choose" (Deut. 12:5, and parallels) — assumed to be Jerusalem — some groups built temples in other localities. Mount Gerizim, outside of Shechem, was an ancient site of worship that may have antedated the establishment of the Temple in Jerusalem. The Samaritans claimed that this mountain, rather than Mount Zion in Jerusalem, was the divinely appointed spot for worship, and they produced a version of the Hebrew Bible that supported their claim. In Egypt a priest named Onias (either III or IV) built a temple at Leontopolis sometime in the second century B.C.E., and it re-

mained in operation until it was closed by the Romans in 74 C.E. (Overman and Green, "Judaism," p. 1040).

32. Overman and Green, "Judaism," p. 1051.

33. A seminary professor is said to have preached to a rural congregation from one of the newer Bible translations, and evoked this response from a disapproving parishioner: "If the King James Version was good enough for the apostle Paul, then it's good enough for me!"

34. Josephus, *Life* 9-12; Phil. 3:4-6.

35. Josephus, *Jewish War* 2.119-66; *Antiquities* 18.11-25.

36. Overman and Green, "Judaism," pp. 1041-42.

37. *m. Dem.* 2:2-3.

38. Meier, *A Marginal Jew*, 3:411.

39. Saldarini, *Pharisees*, p. 301.

40. Josephus, *Antiquities* 18.16; Mark 12:18; *Abot de-Rabbi Nathan* A.5.

41. Overman and Green, "Judaism," p. 1042.

42. A thorough discussion of the basic issues and debates regarding the Dead Sea Scrolls, written in the light of the most recently published texts, is found in Geza Vermès' introduction to *The Complete Dead Sea Scrolls in English* (New York and London: Allen Lane/ Penguin Press, 1997), pp. 1-90.

43. Meier writes: "Despite sensationalistic claims to the contrary, the Qumran documents never mention or allude to Jesus of Nazareth" (*A Marginal Jew*, 3:489).

44. Vermès, *Complete Dead Sea Scrolls*, Damascus Document 5.2 (p. 131), Thanksgiving Hymn 12 (p. 263).

45. Overman and Green, "Judaism," pp. 1039, 1043.

46. Josephus, *Jewish War* 2.118, cited in Overman and Green, "Judaism," p. 1044.

47. Josephus, *Life* 77; *Jewish War* 4.84-120.

48. Josephus, *Antiquities* 17.271-85.

49. Josephus, *Antiquities* 20.97-98.

50. Josephus, *Jewish War* 2.261-63.

51. Overman and Green, pp. 1044-45. These authors note (p. 1045) that there is only slender evidence for a distinctive "charismatic Judaism" in the persons of Honi the Circle-Maker (*m. Ta'an.* 3.8; *b. Ta'an.* 23a), Hananiah ben Dosa (*m. Ber.* 5.5; *t. Ber.* 3.20; *m. Sota* 9.15), and possibly Jesus of Nazareth. The rabbinic traditions attribute to the former two figures an unusual efficacy in prayer (for rain, or for healing) but not a special form of Judaism. Their actions do not set them apart from other Jewish figures of the era. Thus, contrary to Geza Vermès in *Jesus the Jew*, pp. 58-82, the accounts regarding Honi and Hananiah do not attest to a distinctive "charismatic Judaism" that can serve as a category within which to understand Jesus. Vermès' recent work, *The Changing Faces of Jesus* (London: Allen Lane/The Penguin Press, 2000), lays less emphasis on "charismatic Judaism" in interpreting Jesus than was the case in *Jesus the Jew*.

52. Saldarini, "Sanhedrin," pp. 975-77.

53. Saldarini, "Sanhedrin," p. 979.

54. Ellis Rivkin, *What Crucified Jesus? Messianism, Pharisaism, and the Development of Christianity* (New York: UAHC Press, 1997), pp. 50, 62-63, 72-73. Sean Freyne concludes that

the Gospel narratives appear to give the Sanhedrin as a court greater importance and a more permanent role than in fact it possessed. This strengthens an impression that the death of Jesus was the formal responsibility of the Jewish establishment (Freyne, *Geography*, p. 100).

55. Overman and Green, "Judaism," p. 1045. A detailed study of Jesus-centered Judaism is contained in Jean Daniélou, *The Theology of Jewish Christianity*, trans. John A. Baker (London: Darton, Longman & Todd; Chicago: Henry Regnery, 1964).

Notes to "The Forerunner"

1. On John the Baptist, see Meier, *A Marginal Jew*, 2:19-99; Robert L. Webb, "John the Baptist and His Relationship to Jesus," in *Studying the Historical Jesus*, pp. 179-229; and Joan E. Taylor, *The Immerser: John the Baptist Within Second Temple Judaism* (Grand Rapids, Mich.: Eerdmans, 1997).

2. Meier, *A Marginal Jew*, 2:7. Hendrikus Boers argued that Jesus viewed John and not himself as the pivotal figure in the coming of God's kingdom. Thus Jesus points to John rather than the reverse. See Boers, *Who Was Jesus? The Historical Jesus and the Synoptic Gospels* (San Francisco: Harper & Row, 1989), pp. xii, 35, passim.

3. The image of John the Baptist has played a role in the development of Christianity and specifically the monastic tradition, as discussed by Edmondo F. Lupieri, "John the Baptist: The First Monk," in Jordan Aumann et al., *Monasticism: A Historical Overview*, Word and Spirit 6 (Still River, Mass.: St. Bede's Publications, 1984), pp. 11-23.

4. Josephus, like the Gospels, portrays John as a preacher of divine judgment and repentance. See *Antiquities* 18.116-19.

5. Luke 1:80 says John "was in the wilderness until the day he appeared publicly to Israel," and some have connected this with Josephus's statement about the celibate Essenes who adopted and raised other people's children (*Jewish War* 282). Yet Webb observes: "Concrete evidence of John's membership in the Qumran community is lacking. And even if John had been a member at one time, aspects of his teaching are sufficiently different from that found in the Qumran scrolls, that one would be forced to conclude that John had broken away from them" ("John the Baptist," p. 207).

6. Webb, "John the Baptist," p. 184.

7. Josephus, *Antiquities* 18.116-19.

8. Meier, *A Marginal Jew*, 2:24-25.

9. Meier, *A Marginal Jew*, 2:52-53. Regarding Jewish proselytes, there are abundant references to circumcision in Philo, Josephus, the New Testament, and the text on conversion to Judaism, *Joseph and Asenath*. Consequently the lack of reference to proselyte baptism seems to be a significant silence.

10. Meier, *A Marginal Jew*, 2:32-35.

11. Webb, "John the Baptist," pp. 226-27.

12. Paul W. Hollenbach has argued that Jesus was a kind of lapsed or apostate follower of John, and that Jesus' ministry changed when he realized that he had the power to exorcise and to heal (Webb, "John the Baptist," p. 224). See Hollenbach, "Social Aspects of John the Baptizer's Preaching Mission in the Context of Palestinian Judaism," in *Aufstieg und*

Niedergang der römischen Welt, ed. W. Haase and E. Temporini (Berlin: Walter de Gruyter, 1979-), 2.19.1 (1979), pp. 850-75, and "John the Baptist," in *Anchor Bible Dictionary,* 3:887-99.

13. Webb, "John the Baptist," p. 224.

14. Meier, *A Marginal Jew,* 2:108-9.

15. Webb, "John the Baptist," pp. 225-26. The apostle Paul seems to have laid great stress on his private vision of Jesus as a basis for his authority as an apostle (Gal. 1:1, 11-17).

Notes to "The Central Message"

1. Joachim Jeremias, *New Testament Theology: The Proclamation of Jesus* (New York: Scribner, 1971), p. 96. Compare the statements of Rudolf Bultmann, that "the dominant concept of Jesus' message is the *Reign of God"* (*Theology of the New Testament,* 2 vols. [New York: Scribner, 1951], 1:4), and of John Meier that "the kingdom of God is a central part of Jesus' proclamation" (*A Marginal Jew,* 2:289).

2. Perrin, *Rediscovering,* p. 54.

3. For a summary of the different views, see Wendell Willis, ed., *The Kingdom of God in Twentieth-Century Interpretation* (Peabody, Mass.: Hendrickson, 1987).

4. G. B. Caird, *The Language and Imagery of the Bible* (Grand Rapids, Mich., and Cambridge, U.K.: Eerdmans, 1997 [1980]), p. 250. For a careful elaboration on the uses of the word "eschatology," see the whole section on "The Language of Eschatology" (pp. 243-71).

5. Albert Schweitzer, *Paul and His Interpreters* (London: A. and C. Black, 1912), p. 228; Caird, *The Language and Imagery of the Bible,* p. 250.

6. Borg, *Jesus,* p. 11, emphasis in original. The disavowal of "eschatology" is seen in Borg's essay "A Temperate Case for a Non-Eschatological Jesus," in *Jesus in Contemporary Scholarship,* pp. 47-68. At the same time, Borg qualifies his rejection of the term when he writes: "Though I deny imminent eschatology, I do not exclude eschatology altogether from Jesus' message. In addition to speaking of the kingdom of God as a present power, Jesus apparently used kingdom language to refer to the eschatological banquet with Abraham, Isaac, and Jacob . . . and seems to have affirmed a life beyond death . . . [and] a last judgment" (*Jesus in Contemporary Scholarship,* pp. 41-42 n. 79).

7. Crossan, *Jesus,* pp. 52-53.

8. Caird, p. 243, notes that the word was first used in Germany, and then carried over into English. The first recorded use in the *Oxford English Dictionary* was in 1845, by the American author G. Bush. Gerhard Sauter, in "The Concept and Task of Eschatology — Theological and Philosophical Reflections," *Scottish Journal of Theology* 41 (1988): 499-515, traces the term back to Abraham Calov, who used the rubric *eschatologia* for the final section of his *Systema locorum Theologicorum* (1677).

9. David Aune, "Eschatology (Early Christian)," in *Anchor Bible Dictionary,* 2:594-609, quoting p. 594.

10. Aune, "Eschatology (Early Christian)," pp. 594-95. See Rev. 14:1-5; 20:1-10; 21:1–22:5.

11. See Jean Daniélou, *The Theology of Jewish Christianity,* trans. and ed. John A. Baker (London: Darton, Longman & Todd; Chicago: Henry Regnery, 1964), pp. 377-404.

12. Some writers distinguish "apocalyptic" as a literary genre (e.g., the book of Daniel, the *Book of Enoch*, the book of Revelation) from "apocalypticism" as a thought world or worldview (including belief in the predetermination of history, the conflict of good and evil, etc.). See the helpful treatment in Charlesworth, *Jesus within Judaism*, pp. 34-38. In this brief discussion I am not distinguishing the texts from the worldview or social context that engendered them. For a thorough treatment of the issues, see Bernard McGinn, John Joseph Collins, and Stephen J. Stein, eds., *The Encyclopedia of Apocalypticism*, 3 vols. (New York: Continuum, 1998).

13. Norman Perrin, *The Kingdom of God in the Teaching of Jesus* (Philadelphia: Westminster, 1963), pp. 176-77.

14. Aune, "Eschatology (Early Christian)," pp. 595-96. Once again there is a possibility of confusion over terms, since I began this discussion by asking about the relationship between "eschatology" and "apocalypticism," and now have resorted to a different usage, according to which "eschatology" is a larger term that embraces both "prophetic eschatology" and "apocalyptic eschatology." From this point on I will follow this latter convention.

15. Charlesworth, *Jesus within Judaism*, pp. 34-39.

16. Because of this prevailing idea of apocalypticism as escapist, many scholars have reacted against Schweitzer's portrayal of Jesus as a Jewish apocalpyticist, as Walter P. Weaver explains: "There also remained a fundamental suspicion of apocalypticism and frequent efforts to disassociate Jesus from it. Apocalpyticism was regarded as largely a retreat from the world, or, even worse, the rantings of maniacs. Little effort was extended toward seeing how an apocalyptic worldview could also be associated with a pronounced social concern" (*The Historical Jesus in the Twentieth Century, 1900-1950*, pp. 360-61). Though Weaver is describing the scholarship on Jesus during the early twentieth century, the same attitudes continue today.

17. References from Sanders, *Jesus and Judaism*, p. 79.

18. References from Sanders, *Jesus and Judaism*, pp. 96-97.

19. While there is a saying attributed to R. Eliezer the Great that Gentiles are excluded from the life to come, it is opposed in the same passage by the saying of R. Joshua that the righteous Gentiles will indeed have a share in the life to come (*t. Sanh.* 13.2).

20. Sanders, *Jesus and Judaism*, pp. 97-98.

21. Meier, *A Marginal Jew*, 2:9-10, 238-39, 244, 274 n. 18, 277.

22. Meier, *A Marginal Jew*, 2:240.

23. The parables of Jesus will be discussed below, but two classic studies relate Jesus' parables to differing conceptions of the kingdom of God as present or as future, respectively: C. H. Dodd, *The Parables of the Kingdom* (New York: Scribner, 1961), and Joachim Jeremias, *The Parables of Jesus*, trans. S. H. Hooke, 3rd rev. ed. (London: SCM, 1972).

24. The concluding petition, "lead us not into temptation" (Matt. 6:13, RSV), might also have eschatological significance if the word "temptation" (Gk. *peirasmos*) refers to the final time of testing for the world.

25. See the discussion of this saying that John Meier judges to be authentic: "There is no hint of Jesus' death as atoning sacrifice, to say nothing of an explicit affirmation of his resurrection, exaltation, or parousia. In all this there is something disconcerting to Christian expectations" (*A Marginal Jew*, 2:308).

26. References from Aune, "Eschatology (Early Christian)," p. 601.

27. Marcus Borg reports that 80 percent of the voting members of the Jesus Seminar have judged the coming "Son of Man" sayings to be inauthentic (Borg, *Jesus in Contemporary Scholarship*, p. 40 n. 53). The "Son of Man" theme will be taken up again in "Wisdom, Apocalypse, and the Identity of Jesus."

28. Schweitzer, *Quest*, p. 357.

29. Sanders, *Jesus and Judaism*, pp. 153-54. Sanders qualifies this somewhat by adding: "Just as we cannot say precisely what Jesus thought would happen in the future, so also we cannot say just what he thought was taking place in the present" (p. 154).

30. A good deal of debate centered on a single Greek word, *eggizei* (Matt. 3:2; 4:17; 10:7; Mark 1:15; Luke 10:9, 11), which some translated as "the kingdom of God *draws near*" and others as "the kingdom of God *is upon* you."

31. Dodd, *Parables of the Kingdom*, pp. 34-35, 159.

32. Aune, "Eschatology (Early Christian)," p. 600.

33. G. B. Caird seems to hold that there is not a tension between these two aspects of the kingdom of God, but rather a semantic confusion in the discussion regarding them: "The debate between those who hold that Jesus declared the kingdom of God to have arrived and those who hold that he declared it to be imminent is reducible to its simplest terms when we recognise that the parties to the debate have differently identified the referent. If Jesus was referring to the final vindication of God's purposes in the reign of justice and peace, where the righteous are to banquet with Abraham, Isaac and Jacob (Matt. 8:11; Luke 13:28-29), it is mere nonsense even to suggest that this was present on earth when Caiaphas was High Priest and Pilate Governor of Judaea. On the other hand, if Jesus was referring to the redemptive sovereignty of God let loose for the destruction of Satan and all his works (Matt. 12:28; Luke 11:20), it makes nonsense of the whole record of his ministry to argue that for him this lay still in the future. And we have only so to state the matter to see that on various occasions Jesus referred to both" (Caird, p. 12).

34. Aune, "Eschatology (Early Christian)," p. 601. See the discussion of the differing aspects of the kingdom's presence and futurity in Scot McKnight, *A New Vision for Israel: The Teachings of Jesus in National Context* (Grand Rapids, Mich., and Cambridge, U.K.: Eerdmans, 1999), pp. 70-155. Another interpretation of Jesus' eschatological language, not discussed in the main text, is the "preterist" view supported by N. T. Wright and in the nineteenth century by J. Stuart Russell (1816-1895). Russell's major work has recently been republished as *The Parousia: The New Testament Doctrine of our Lord's Second Coming* (Grand Rapids, Mich.: Baker Books, 1999). According to this perspective, at least some of Jesus' apocalyptic statements in Matthew 24 and elsewhere in the Gospels related to the near-term destruction of the Temple that occurred in 70 C.E. Thus Jesus' apocalyptic language refers to impending historical events, and the earliest Christians were not mistaken in expecting earth-shattering changes within their own lifetime. The events connected with the siege of Jerusalem and destruction of the Temple were a fulfillment of Jesus' words, though not always in the most literal sense. I am indebted to Jonathan Barlow for informing me regarding the preterist view.

35. Norman Perrin, *Jesus and the Language of the Kingdom: Symbol and Metaphor in New Testament Interpretation* (Philadelphia: Fortress, 1976), p. 40.

36. Perrin, *Jesus*, p. 43. Willem S. Vorster seems close to Perrin's perspective when he writes that "Jesus used metaphoric and apocalyptic language functionally . . . to resocialize his hearers by offering them a new symbolic universe" ("The Function of Metaphorical and Apocalyptic Language About the Unobservable in the Teaching of Jesus," in *Speaking of Jesus: Essays on Biblical Language, Gospel, Narrative and the Historical Jesus*, ed. J. Eugene Botha [Leiden: Brill, 1999], pp. 3-19, citing p. 19).

37. Perrin, *Jesus*, pp. 29-32.

38. Borg, *Conflict*, pp. 253-54, 259, 261. Borg acknowledges his debt to Huston Smith's "primordial tradition," and uses this as a framework for understanding Jesus (*Jesus in Contemporary Scholarship*, pp. 127-39). Somewhat like Perrin and Borg, Bernard Brandon Scott asserts that "kingdom" has no conceptual content, and that Jesus "experienced Kingdom" — an experience that cannot be expressed in discursive speech (*Jesus, Symbol-Maker for the Kingdom* [Philadelphia: Fortress, 1983], pp. 10-12, 29, cited in Sanders, *Jesus and Judaism*, p. 125).

39. Borg, *Jesus*, p. 28.

40. Crossan, *Jesus*, p. 197.

41. Crossan, *Jesus*, p. 56.

42. When I say to my friend "I follow you," the physical act of coming after something else stands for the intellectual act of understanding her statement. George Lakoff and Mark Johnson, in *Metaphors We Live By* (Chicago: University of Chicago Press, 1980), make the following claim: "Most people think they can get along perfectly well without metaphor. We have found, on the contrary, that metaphor is pervasive in everyday life. . . . Our ordinary conceptual system, in terms of which we both think and act, is fundamentally metaphorical in nature" (p. 3).

43. Meier, *A Marginal Jew*, 2:242.

44. Bruce Chilton, "The Kingdom of God in Recent Discussion," in *Studying the Historical Jesus*, pp. 255-80, citing p. 265.

Notes to "The Man of Power"

1. Bultmann, "New Testament and Mythology," p. 5.

2. Gerd Theissen, *The Miracle Stories of the Early Christian Tradition*, trans. Francis McDonagh, ed. John Riches (Philadelphia: Fortress, 1983), p. 34. Gerd Lüdemann makes the same sort of sweeping statement as Gerd Theissen: "Today no one seriously accepts that Jesus in fact walked on the sea, stilled a storm, multiplied bread, turned water into wine and raised the dead. Rather, these actions were invented for Jesus only after his death or his supposed resurrection in order to heighten his importance" (*Jesus After Two Thousand Years*, p. 1). Paula Fredriksen writes: "I do not believe that God occasionally suspends the operation of what Hume called 'natural law.' What I think Jesus might possibly have done, in other words, must conform to what I think is possible in any case" (*Jesus of Nazareth*, p. 114).

3. Crossan, *Jesus*, p. 85.

4. Though Bultmann denied that modern people can believe in miracles, he seems to have had no problem affirming this for the ancients. After admitting that the miracle stories

in the Gospels have "embellishments," he added: "But there can be no doubt that Jesus did the kinds of deeds which were miracles to his mind and to the minds of his contemporaries, that is, deeds which were attributed to a supernatural, divine cause; undoubtedly he healed the sick and cast out demons" (*Jesus and the Word*, p. 173).

5. Ernst Troeltsch, "Über historische und dogmatische Methode in der Theologie" (1898), in *Gesammelte Schriften* (Tübingen: J. C. B. Mohr, 1922), 2:729-53.

6. Alex De Jong, *The Life and Times of Grigorii Rasputin* (London: Collins, 1982), pp. 136-42.

7. Josephus, *Antiquities* 18.3.3. Among the notable recent discussions of Jesus' miracles are the following: Meier, *A Marginal Jew*, 2:509-1038; Barry L. Blackburn, "The Miracles of Jesus," in *Studying the Historical Jesus*, pp. 353-94; Harold E. Remus, "Miracles (NT)," in *Anchor Bible Dictionary*, 4:856-69; Sanders, *Historical Figure*, pp. 132-68; Reginald H. Fuller, *Interpreting the Miracles* (Philadelphia: Westminster, 1963); Morton Smith, *Jesus the Magician* (New York: Harper & Row, 1977); David Wenham and Craig Blomberg, eds., *Gospel Perspectives*, vol. 6, *The Miracles of Jesus* (Sheffield: JSOT Press, 1986); and Graham H. Twelftree, *Jesus: The Miracle Worker* (Downers Grove, Ill.: InterVarsity Press, 1999). A discussion of the philosophical issues involved in the debate over miracles is contained in Colin Brown, *Miracles and the Critical Mind* (Grand Rapids, Mich.: Eerdmans, 1984), and R. Douglas Geivett and Gary R. Habermas, eds., *In Defense of Miracles: A Comprehensive Case for God's Action in History* (Downers Grove, Ill.: InterVarsity Press, 1997).

8. Early Christian texts indicate that both Jewish and pagan opponents derided Jesus as a magician: Justin, *Dialogue* 69.5; *First Apology* 30; Origen, *Contra Celsum* 1.6, 28, 38, 68, 71; 2.9, 14, 16, 48-49; 3.27; 5.51, 57; 6.77; 7.77; Tertullian, *Apologeticus* 21.17; 23.7; Arnobius, *Adversus nationes* 1.43; Lactantius, *Divine Institutes* 4.15.1. Jewish sources refer to Jesus' "sorcery": b. *Sanh.* 43a; b. *'Abod. Zar.* 27b; y. *Shabb.* 14.4, 14d; t. *Hul.* 2:22-23; y. *'Abod. Zar.* 2.2, 40d-41a. References from Blackburn, "The Miracles of Jesus," p. 361 n. 40, and Remus, "Miracles (NT)," p. 861.

9. J. M. Cohen and M. J. Cohen, *The Penguin Dictionary of Quotations* (Harmondsworth, Middlesex, England: Penguin Books, 1960), p. 3.

10. Sanders, *Historical Figure*, p. 135.

11. b. *Berakot* 34b.

12. For a fuller discussion see Emma Jeannette Levy Edelstein, *Asclepius: A Collection and Interpretation of the Testimonies*, 2 vols. (Baltimore: Johns Hopkins University Press, 1945); K. H. Rengstorff, *Die Anfänge der Auseinandersetzung zwischen Christusglaube und Asklepiosfrömmigkeit* (Münster, 1953), and "Asklepios the Healer," in Howard Clark Kee, *Miracle in the Early Christian World: A Study in Sociohistorical Method* (New Haven and London: Yale University Press, 1983), pp. 78-104.

13. Fuller, p. 22.

14. Josephus, *Antiquities* 8.46-49.

15. Hans Dieter Betz, ed., *The Greek Magical Papyri in Translation*, 2 vols. (Chicago: University of Chicago Press, 1986), 1:96 (lines 3019-20), cited in Blackburn, "The Miracles of Jesus," p. 361.

16. Sanders, *Historical Figure*, pp. 137-38.

17. Blackburn, "The Miracles of Jesus," pp. 353-54. This also does not include the mi-

raculous catches of fish (Luke 5:1-11; John 21:1-11; Matt. 17:24-27), which might be seen as due to supernatural knowledge.

18. Theissen, *Miracle Stories,* pp. 85-86.

19. Borg, *Jesus,* pp. 61-62, 65, 73 n. 28.

20. The evil spirit that tormented King Saul is an exception to the rule (1 Sam. 16:14-23; 18:10-11; 19:9-10), but even here there is no exorcism, properly speaking.

21. Sanders, *Historical Figure,* pp. 149-50 (for biblical references), and 152-53.

22. Meier, *A Marginal Jew,* 2:874-77.

23. Gerd Lüdemann proposes as one of his "criteria of inauthenticity" that any alleged action of Jesus is fictitious if it involves a violation of natural laws, as is the case with the so-called "nature miracles": "Those actions are unhistorical which presuppose that the laws of nature are broken. Here it makes no difference that people at the time of Jesus did not know these laws or did not think in scientific categories" (*Jesus After Two Thousand Years,* p. 4). Bruce J. Malina interprets the Gospel narratives of Jesus' walking on water in terms of the disciples' "altered state of consciousness" — a familiar phenomenon in the history of religions ("Assessing the Historicity of Jesus' Walking on the Sea: Insights from Cross-Cultural Psychology," in Chilton and Evans, *Authenticating the Activities of Jesus,* pp. 351-71). Along the same lines, Bruce Chilton states that Jesus' alleged stilling of the storm "had more to do with . . . visionary practice than with a miraculous event" (*Rabbi Jesus,* p. 157).

24. Blackburn, "The Miracles of Jesus," pp. 370-71, with n. 78.

25. Sanders, *Jesus and Judaism,* p. 164.

26. Borg, *Jesus,* p. 71.

27. Burton Mack is one of the very few who hold that Jesus in his lifetime was not known as a wonder-worker. According to Mack, nothing in the Gospel miracle tradition has any basis in Jesus' life (*A Myth of Innocence,* esp. pp. 75-77, 91-93, 215-24).

28. Meier, *A Marginal Jew,* 2:4.

29. Bultmann, *Synoptic Tradition,* p. 162.

30. Theissen, *Miracle Stories,* p. 278. "Jesus sees his own miracles as events leading to something unprecedented. They anticipate a new world" (p. 280).

31. Geza Vermès, *Jesus the Jew,* pp. 58-82, interprets Jesus on analogy with other charismatic Jewish healers. Yet this misses the connection between Jesus' miracles and the kingdom of God. His interpretation suffers from other difficulties as well (Blackburn, "The Miracles of Jesus," pp. 376 n. 101, 379). (1) Only two figures are clearly Galilean — Jesus and Hanina — and this is hardly enough to create a whole category of Galilean miracle worker. (2) The source for Hanina's life (i.e., the Palestinian Talmud) dates to about three hundred years after his life. (3) Miracle working was probably only incidental to the lives of these Jewish sages. In fact, miracles were attributed to other Jewish sages as well, and so the boundaries of Vermès' religious type are blurry. Successful prayers for rain were attributed to Rabbi Aqiba as well. (4) Jesus never procured rain, which is the only miracle common to the other figures belonging to Vermès' type. (5) There is no evidence that any of them except Jesus conducted an itinerant ministry. (6) In the whole Gospel tradition, Jesus is only once portrayed as *praying* prior to the miracle, while for Honi and Hanina the situation is just the reverse. Meier notes that a person who prays for and awaits a miracle by God is not in the

strict sense a "miracle-*worker*" (*A Marginal Jew*, 2:536). The Gospels present Jesus as working wonders by his own power.

32. Crossan, *Jesus*, p. 104. Robert Grant writes: "In polemical writing, your magic is my miracle, and vice versa" (*Gnosticism and Early Christianity*, 2nd ed. [New York, 1966], p. 93, cited in Remus, "Miracles (NT)," p. 859).

33. A classic sociological discussion of the entrepreneurial character of magic and magicians is contained in Max Weber, *The Sociology of Religion*, trans. Ephraim Fischoff (Boston: Beacon Press, 1963), esp. pp. 28-30.

34. Kee, *Miracle*, pp. 62-64, 170, 211-18, and Howard Clark Kee, *Medicine, Miracle, and Magic in New Testament Times*, Society for New Testament Studies Monograph Series, 55 (Cambridge and New York: Cambridge University Press, 1986), pp. 95-125.

35. Ernst Käsemann (*Essays*, p. 96) notes that the same notion of a healing garment later occurs with reference to Paul (Acts 19:12), and that even the shadow cast by Peter was thought to be able to heal the sick (Acts 5:15).

36. Meier, *A Marginal Jew*, 2:11-12.

37. Did Jesus heal while he was in some kind of altered state of consciousness? There is a reference in Mark 3:20-21 to Jesus being "beside himself" (RSV). This could denote some kind of trance or visionary state, although the context in Mark does not make it altogether clear. Morton Smith takes this as a reference to Jesus' "abnormal behavior": "Magicians who want to make demons obey often scream their spells, gesticulate, and match the mad in fury" (*Jesus the Magician*, p. 32). Yet these verses in Mark are a rather slender basis for Smith's claim. For a critique of Smith's views, see Walter Wink, "Jesus as Magician," *Union Seminary Quarterly Review* 30 (1974): 3-14.

38. Crossan, *Jesus*, p. 90.

39. Borg, *Jesus*, p. 72 n. 12.

40. Sanders, *Historical Figure*, p. 132.

41. Josephus, *Antiquities* 18.3.3.

Notes to "The Teacher"

1. See the comparative study of Jesus with the great first-century Jewish sage Hillel: James H. Charlesworth and Loren L. Johns, eds., *Hillel and Jesus: Comparative Studies of Two Major Religious Leaders* (Minneapolis: Fortress, 1997). Perhaps the best-known point of comparison is between Jesus' "golden rule" ("Do to others as you would have them do to you," Matt. 7:12) and Hillel's reported response to a Gentile convert to Judaism who wanted a short summary of the Torah: "What is hateful to you, do not to your neighbor: that is the whole Torah, while the rest is the commentary thereof; go and learn it" (*b. Shabb.* 31a).

2. Scot McKnight's *A New Vision for Israel* argues that the proper context for interpreting Jesus' teaching is that of "ancient Jewish nationalism and Jesus' conviction that Israel had to repent to avoid a national disaster." He set forth a "vision of the proper religious life centered on the restoration of the Jewish nation and on the fulfillment of the covenants that God had made with the nation" (p. 10).

3. Pheme Perkins, *Jesus as Teacher* (Cambridge: Cambridge University Press, 1990), pp. 1-2.

4. Meier, *A Marginal Jew*, 3:52-53.

5. Perkins, *Jesus as Teacher*, pp. 27-28. See also the discussion of Jesus' itinerancy as a teacher in Martin Hengel, *The Charismatic Leader and His Followers*, trans. J. C. G. Greig (Edinburgh: T&T Clark, 1981), pp. 35-37.

6. Perkins, *Jesus as Teacher*, pp. 28-29.

7. In the following paragraphs I am indebted to the penetrating discussion in Borg, *Jesus*, pp. 81-91.

8. Borg, *Jesus*, p. 86.

9. While the authenticity of the sayings in Matt. 23 is contested by scholars, it is not very plausible to imagine that the early Christians would have invented a saying in which Jesus says to "do whatever" the Pharisees say.

10. Borg, *Jesus*, p. 104.

11. Crossan, *Jesus*, p. 59.

12. See the discussion of Luke 9:59-60 in Sanders, *Jesus and Judaism*, pp. 252-55, and in Perrin, *Rediscovering*, p. 144.

13. Jesus' sayings regarding the family have the effect of focusing attention on Jesus himself, as Jacob Neusner has noted: "Here is a Torah-teacher who says in his own name what the Torah says in God's name." Jesus' form of address is distinctive, since "sages . . . say things in their own names, but without claiming to improve upon the Torah. The prophet, Moses, speaks not in his own name but in God's name, saying what God has told him to say. Jesus speaks not as a sage nor as a prophet" (*A Rabbi Talks with Jesus: An Intermillennial, Interfaith Exchange* [New York: Doubleday, 1993], pp. 30-31). The attributed teachings of Jesus raise many challenging questions of interpretation: What exactly is the basis of Jesus' ethical claims? In what way does God's reign hold priority over other interests and loyalties? Does Jesus disparage the importance of human relationships if they are not somehow brought within the scope of God's reign? If the kingdom is God's kingdom, then is it Jesus' too? Or what relationship of Jesus to God is implied in Jesus' reported words? Why does Jesus speak in the way that he does? Some of these questions will be taken up again in the last two chapters, which treat the issues of Jesus' identity, self-understanding, and claims upon his followers.

14. Borg, *Jesus*, pp. 104-5. For a fuller discussion of Jesus and money, see Thomas E. Schmidt, *Hostility to Wealth in the Synoptic Gospels* (Sheffield, England: JSOT, 1987).

15. Borg, *Jesus*, p. 105.

16. Borg, *Jesus*, pp. 105-6.

17. Borg, *Jesus*, pp. 108-16.

18. See Friedrich Baumgärtel and Johannes Behm, "*kardia*, etc.," in *Theological Dictionary of the New Testament*, ed. Gerhard Kittel, 10 vols. (Grand Rapids, Mich.: Eerdmans, 1964-74), 3:605-14.

19. Borg, *Jesus*, p. 113.

20. Borg, *Jesus*, p. 114.

21. William E. Phipps, *Was Jesus Married? The Distortion of Sexuality in the Christian Tradition* (New York: Harper & Row, 1970), argued that Jesus may have been married as a

youth and that his wife may have died before his ministry began. The most important argument is from the consideration that this was the normal pattern for Jewish males. Yet, as we have already noted, some of the Essenes did not marry, and there are traditions about some of the biblical prophets (Jer. 16:1-4) and later rabbis (e.g., Ben Azzai; b. Yeb. 63b) remaining unmarried. So there were exceptions to the practice of early marriage, and in any case it is not very sound to argue that a general custom must apply to every individual within a society. See Meier, A Marginal Jew, 1:332-45. Bruce Chilton suggests that Jesus may have had sex outside of marriage, and that Mary Magdalene is "the most likely candidate [i.e., sex partner] if he did so, because she is the only woman, apart from his mother, with whom he had persistent contact" (Rabbi Jesus, p. 145). Yet Chilton's assertion is unsubstantiated, and the canonical and extracanonical traditions about Jesus lack any references to sexual activity on his part.

22. See Allison, Jesus of Nazareth, pp. 172-216. Allison defines "asceticism" as "the practice of the denial of the physical or psychological desires in order to attain a spiritual ideal or goal" (p. 172), and this description surely applies to Jesus' teaching. Yet such a definition is probably too broad to be useful, for almost all religious groups would thereby qualify as "ascetic." Vincent L. Wimbush, Richard Valantasis, and Elizabeth Clark stress the difficulty in providing a useful cross-cultural definition of the term "asceticism," in Wimbush and Valantasis, eds., Asceticism (New York: Oxford University Press, 1995), pp. xix-xxxiii, 505-10.

23. C. H. Dodd, The Founder of Christianity (New York: Macmillan, 1970), pp. 37, 39.

24. Dodd, The Founder of Christianity, p. 41.

25. One of the few studies of this subject is Jakob Jonsson, Humour and Irony in the New Testament; Illuminated by Parallels in Talmud and Midrash (Leiden: Brill, 1985).

26. For a brief treatment of the role of humor in religion, see Michael J. McClymond, "The Wit and Wisdom of The Door," in Colleen McDannell, ed., Religions of the United States in Practice, 2 vols. (Princeton, N.J.: Princeton University Press, 2001), 2:433-35.

27. Krister Stendahl, foreword to Jonsson, p. 6. Stendahl adds: "Perhaps there is a good deal of continuity between the Sages of the Synagogue and Woody Allen. . . . And even between Jesus and Woody Allen — although a student of the Western theological tradition must wonder where the humor went" (p. 6).

28. Some readers may have had the experience of going to a film or theater performance in a foreign country and finding that everyone else was laughing at things that were not funny and not laughing at things that were funny.

29. This saying may refer to the desire on the Sabbath day to avoid all killing (thus straining one's beverages before drinking them), since killing could be considered a form of work.

30. Jonsson, Humour and Irony, p. 176. Some other possibly humorous texts include the lamp (probably a Sabbath light) placed under a basket to be hidden (Matt. 5:15); the man who loses both coat (himation) and cloak (chiton) — and so is rendered naked (Matt. 5:40); giving children not bread but a stone, a serpent, or a scorpion to eat (Matt. 7:9-10; Luke 11:11-12); the gathering of grapes from thornbushes (Matt. 7:16); a house foolishly built on sand (perhaps in a dried-out riverbed; Matt. 7:26-27); looking in the Judean desert for a dandy dressed in fine clothes (Matt. 11:8); a person who started to build a house with no plan for it

(Luke 14:28-30); a slave who sits to eat before the master does (Luke 17:7-10); a judge who is at the mercy of a pesky and persistent widow (Luke 18:1-8).

31. On Jesus' parables see Bernard B. Scott, *Hear Then the Parable* (Minneapolis: Fortress, 1989); J. Dominic Crossan, "Parable," in *Anchor Bible Dictionary*, 5:146-52; Craig L. Blomberg, "The Parables of Jesus: Current Trends and Needs in Research," in *Studying the Historical Jesus*, pp. 213-54; and the previously mentioned standard works, Jeremias, *The Parables of Jesus*, and Dodd, *The Parables of the Kingdom*.

32. See David Stern, *Parables in Midrash* (Cambridge: Harvard University Press, 1991), and Craig A. Evans, "Parables in Early Judaism," in Richard N. Longenecker, ed., *The Challenge of Jesus' Parables* (Grand Rapids, Mich., and Cambridge, U.K.: Eerdmans, 2000), pp. 51-75.

33. Crossan, "Parable," p. 147.

34. Adolf Jülicher, *Die Gleichnisreden Jesu im allgemeinen* (Freiburg: J. C. B. Mohr, 1899). A recent examination of the issues of allegory in the parables is Klyne R. Snodgrass, "From Allegorizing to Allegorizing: A History of the Interpretation of the Parables of Jesus," in Richard N. Longenecker, ed., *The Challenge of Jesus' Parables*, pp. 3-29. While "theological allegorizing" is absent from academic study today, Snodgrass sees a return to "sociological and ideological allegorizing." While noting the "banality" of simplistic readings of the parables, he is critical of Craig Blomberg, John Dominic Crossan, and Mary Ann Tolbert, and others who see the parables as "polyvalent" and subject to a plurality of interpretations (pp. 21-22, 27).

35. Blomberg, p. 235, based on David Stern's study of the Jewish *mashal*, notes that the typical pattern of the *mashal* was a division into two components — the *mashal* proper and the *nimshal*, an appended explanation that usually identifies or otherwise enables an identification of the main characters, objects, or events with God, Israel, historical events, etc. This may help to account for the parabolic explanations that occasionally occur in the Gospels (e.g., Matt. 13:3-8 with 13:18-23, and 13:24-30 with 13:36-43). "Such explanatory material fell well within the range of what Jewish interpreters expected the *mashal* to do, [and] ought not to be viewed as misrepresenting original intent" (p. 235).

36. Crossan, "Parable," pp. 147-50.

37. Borg, *Jesus*, pp. 156-58.

38. John Meier, "Reflections on Jesus-of-History Research Today," in *Jesus' Jewishness: Exploring the Place of Jesus in Early Judaism*, ed. James H. Charlesworth, The American Interfaith Institute (New York: Crossroad, 1991), p. 92.

39. Abraham Heschel, in his classic study *The Prophets*, 2 vols. (New York: Harper & Row, 1962), shows how these individuals not only *saw* the world differently than others but *felt* differently as well (esp. 1:ix-xv, 3-26). They not only knew God intellectually but felt the feelings of God — including God's anger at sin and compassion for those who suffer. Jesus appears much like a Hebrew prophet when he sees the city of Jerusalem and weeps at the thought of the coming judgment (Luke 19:41-44).

40. Bruce Chilton and Craig A. Evans, "Jesus and Israel's Scriptures," in *Studying the Historical Jesus*, pp. 281-335, citing p. 281.

41. See the discussion in Graham Stanton, "Matthew," in *It Is Written: Scripture Citing*

Scripture, Essays in Honour of Barnabas Lindars, ed. D. A. Carson and H. G. M. Williamson (Cambridge: Cambridge University Press, 1988), pp. 205-19.

42. Meier, *A Marginal Jew,* 1:171-72. See the rabbinical discussion of divorce in *b. Gittin* 90a; *m. Gittin* 9:10.

43. Borg, *Jesus,* p. 98.

44. Chilton and Evans, "Jesus and Israel's Scriptures," pp. 287-96.

45. Chilton and Evans, "Jesus and Israel's Scriptures," p. 296.

46. John A. T. Robinson, "Did Jesus Have a Distinctive Use of Scripture?" in *Twelve More New Testament Studies* (London: SCM, 1984), pp. 35-43.

47. Chilton and Evans, "Jesus and Israel's Scriptures," pp. 309-10.

Notes to "The Public Figure"

1. It is highly unlikely that the tradition regarding Jesus as "the king of the Jews" originated with the early disciples. See the discussion in Nils Alstrup Dahl, *The Crucified Messiah and Other Essays* (Minneapolis: Augsburg, 1974), pp. 23-24, and especially Ernst Bammel, "The *Titulus*," in *Jesus and the Politics of His Day,* pp. 353-64.

2. Meier goes so far as to suggest that the fact of Jesus' death could be the basis for a new "criterion of Jesus' rejection and execution." Every reconstruction of Jesus' life can be tested as to whether it can account for his death by crucifixion, and thus "a Jesus whose words and deeds did not threaten or alienate people, especially powerful people, is not the historical Jesus" (*A Marginal Jew,* 3:11-12). A problem with the Cynic-sage depiction of Jesus is that such a figure would hardly come across as threatening to the Jewish and/or Roman authorities.

3. By contrast Henry Cadbury suggested that "Jesus probably had no definite, unified, conscious purpose," that he was "much more of a vagabond or gipsy than many another in the land," and that "we can hardly make a picture of Jesus' life and that of his contemporaries that will be too casual for the facts" (Cadbury, *Peril,* pp. 141, 124). Cf. Mack, *A Myth of Innocence,* pp. 53-77, 353-57. Mack states: "Jesus' social critique, though pointed and sharp in particular cases of human event, did not include polemic against specific institutions. He did not name those who were at fault, nor did he suggest an alternative program to set things right. . . . He did not propose to do battle with Pharisees or synagogue leaders for the control or cleansing of a religious institution. He did not philosophize about the *polis,* how to legislate a better law, what to do about tyranny, or the chances of finding a perfect king. . . . He proposed no political program. He did not organize a church" (p. 64). Jesus' life is to be understood on analogy with the Cynics' "unconventional way of life" (p. 68). Yet some of Jesus' undisputed actions (e.g., the choice of the Twelve, the trip to Jerusalem at festival time, the action at the Temple) do not comport with the image of Jesus as an unreflective vagabond. Ben F. Meyer, *The Aims of Jesus,* seeks to construct the possible purposes or intentions of Jesus' ministry, and is summarized in Meyer's essay "Appointed Deeds, Appointed Doer: Jesus and the Scriptures," in Chilton and Evans, *Authenticating the Activities of Jesus,* pp. 155-76. See also N. T. Wright's discussion of Jesus' aims in *Jesus and the Victory of God,* pp. 99-105.

4. Sanders, *Historical Figure,* pp. 106-8.

5. Meier observes that relatively little has been written about Jesus' web of relationships — a major focus in the third volume of *A Marginal Jew* — and he attributes this to the dominant individualism of Western and especially American culture (*A Marginal Jew,* 3:2). In my comparative study of five religious founders, I found that the same kind of individualistic interpretation affects modern readings of Moses, Buddha, Confucius, and Muhammad as well as Jesus ("Prophet or Loss? Reassessing Max Weber's Theory of Religious Leadership," in David Noel Freedman and Michael J. McClymond, eds., *The Rivers of Paradise: Moses, Buddha, Confucius, Jesus, and Muhammad as Religious Founders* [Grand Rapids, Mich.: Eerdmans, 2001], pp. 649-55). I argue that one cannot understand prophetic "charisma" in its historical and sociological context apart from a community that may recognize, respond, oppose, support, qualify, or redirect the impulses originating from the prophet or founder.

6. Borg, *Jesus,* p. 128.

7. Sanders, *Historical Figure,* pp. 108-9.

8. Sanders, *Historical Figure,* pp. 107-10.

9. For a discussion of the issues, see Elisabeth Schüssler Fiorenza, *In Memory of Her: A Feminist Theological Reconstruction of Christian Origins* (New York: Crossroad, 1983), esp. pp. 118-54, and more recently, *Jesus, Miriam's Child, Sophia's Prophet* (New York: Continuum, 1999) and *Jesus and the Politics of Interpretation* (New York: Crossroad, 2000).

10. "R. Eliezer says: If any man gives his daughter a knowledge of the Law it is as though he taught her lechery" (*m. Sot.* 3.4). Yet there is a reference in *m. Ned.* 4.3 to one who "may teach Scripture to his sons and to his daughters."

11. Kathleen E. Corley, "Jesus' Table Practice: Dining with 'Tax Collectors and Sinners,' Including Women," in *Society of Biblical Literature Seminar Papers, 1993* (Atlanta: Scholars Press, 1993), pp. 444-59.

12. John Meier notes that the term "disciple" is never actually used in the Gospels in relation to a female, and yet, given the other sorts of evidence one finds, he observes: "Whatever the problems of vocabulary, the most probable conclusion is that Jesus viewed and treated these women as disciples" (*A Marginal Jew,* 3:73-80, citing p. 80).

13. Meier, "Reflections," pp. 90-91. See also John P. Meier, "The Circle of the Twelve: Did It Exist During Jesus' Public Ministry?", *Journal of Biblical Literature* 116 (1997): 635-72. Meier notes that the Twelve had multiple symbolic meanings, and were equally a "standing exemplar of what being a disciple meant," "symbols of the regathering of the twelve tribes of Israel," and "prophetic missionaries to Israel" (*A Marginal Jew,* 3:126-63, esp. pp. 148, 154). Some scholars in the Jesus Seminar reject the idea of Jesus' appointment of the Twelve, perhaps in part because it strongly suggests a Jewish (rather than Hellenistic) context for understanding Jesus and underscores Jesus' mission to restore and renew the nation of Israel (Evans, "Authenticating the Activities of Jesus," in Chilton and Evans, *Authenticating the Activities of Jesus,* pp. 5-6).

14. Sanders, *Historical Figure,* p. 123.

15. Sanders, *Historical Figure,* p. 123.

16. Daniel J. Harrington, "The Jewishness of Jesus: Facing Some Problems," *Catholic Biblical Quarterly* 49 (1987): 1-13, esp. 12.

17. In what follows I am indebted to Sanders, *Historical Figure*, pp. 205-37, and *Jesus and Judaism*, pp. 174-97, but have also taken note of the discussion of the Pharisees in Jacob Neusner, *From Politics to Piety: The Emergence of Pharisaic Judaism* (Englewood Cliffs, N.J.: Prentice-Hall, 1973), pp. 67-80, and the critique of Sanders's positions in James D. G. Dunn, "Pharisees, Sinners, and Jesus," in *The Social World of Formative Christianity and Judaism*, pp. 264-89, and Bruce D. Chilton, "Jesus and the Repentance of E. P. Sanders," *Tyndale Bulletin* 39 (1988): 1-18.

18. Sanders, *Historical Figure*, pp. 212-13.

19. Sanders, *Historical Figure*, pp. 206-7.

20. The Palestinian Talmud contains the story of a certain Elisha ben Abujah who deliberately rode his horse in front of the Temple mount on a Day of Atonement that also happened to fall on a Sabbath. According to the story, a voice came forth from the Temple, saying: "Repent, children, except for Elisha ben Abujah, for he knew my power yet rebelled against me!" (*y. Hag.* 2.1). There is nothing even remotely comparable to this in the Gospels' portrayal of Jesus.

21. Paula Fredriksen notes that Jesus' disputes with fellow Jews over legal issues do not show him to have been a careless or defiant Jew, but instead an observant one: "This is not to say that Jesus did not dispute with other Jews over the correct way to be Jewish. As our brief survey of Second Temple Judaism has shown, few things are more antecedently plausible, even probable: This is what Jews did. By comparison with what some of the Qumran texts and later rabbinic literature have to say about the Jerusalem priesthood, or what the houses of Hillel and Shammai, debating points of Pharisaic interpretation, occasionally say about each other, what passes between the scribes and Jesus is fairly mild. Further, the very fact of argument implies the opposite of rejection or indifference. Argument here implies mutual involvement, common concern, shared values, religious passion. If one party or the other had thought the issues unimportant, there would have been no fight" (*Jesus of Nazareth*, p. 107).

22. "James" is a modernization of the New Testament name "Jacob," and there are two important figures in the earliest church by the name of "Jacob" — (1) Jacob, son of Zebedee and brother of John, who was among the Twelve, and (2) Jacob, the brother (or some say kinsman) of Jesus. Here we refer to the second.

23. Maccoby, *Judaism in the First Century*, p. 35.

24. In the Epistle to the Galatians, Paul comes into conflict with Peter for not sharing meals with Gentiles (Gal. 2:11-14). Yet one argument that Paul does not use in this dispute is that Jesus abolished the dietary laws, and this militates against supposing that Jesus taught anything along these lines.

25. Sanders, *Jesus and Judaism*, pp. 264-67. "Pharisees did not organize themselves into groups to spend their Sabbaths in Galilean cornfields in the hope of catching someone transgressing" (p. 265; cf. pp. 178, 199, 209). Paul Winter supports this position: "In historical reality Jesus was a Pharisee. His teaching was Pharisaic teaching. In the whole of the New Testament we are unable to find a single historically reliable instance of religious differences between Jesus and the members of the Pharisaic guild" (*On the Trial of Jesus* [Berlin and New York: Walter de Gruyter, 1961], p. 133, quoted in D. R. Catchpole, "The Problem of the Historicity of the Sanhedrin Trial," in *The Trial of Jesus*, Cambridge Studies in Honor of

C. F. D. Moule, ed. Ernst Bammel, Studies in Biblical Theology 2/13 [Naperville, Ill.: Alec R. Allenson, 1970] p. 48). Similarly, Paula Fredriksen sees "polemical caricature, not realistic portraiture" in the representation of Jesus' controversies with scribes and Pharisees in the Gospel of Mark (*Jesus of Nazareth,* pp. 107-8).

26. Neusner, *From Politics to Piety,* p. 80.

27. James Dunn ("Pharisees, Sinners, and Jesus," esp. pp. 274-75, 282-83) sees Sanders's argument as a response to the traditional stereotype of Judaism as legalistic and Jesus as a kind of liberator from this legalism. Yet Sanders may have overreached in asserting that Jesus and the Pharisees had no disputes over ritual purity. N. T. Wright speaks of his disagreement with E. P. Sanders on this point as "oblique, rather than head-on." There was indeed a clash between Jesus and the Pharisees, says Wright, but "it was because of Jesus' eschatological beliefs and agenda, rather than because of . . . religious or moral values or teachings" (*Jesus and the Victory of God,* pp. 371-83, citing p. 377).

28. As argued, for instance, in Jeremias, *New Testament Theology,* pp. 108-21, esp. p. 112.

29. Peter Farb and George Armelagos, *Consuming Passions: The Anthropology of Eating* (Boston: Houghton Mifflin, 1980), pp. 4, 211, cited in Crossan, *Jesus,* p. 68.

30. Crossan, *Jesus,* p. 70.

31. Dunn, "Pharisees, Sinners, and Jesus," p. 283. David Noel Freedman makes an intriguing observation: "One thing [shown by] the reaction to Jesus' fellowship with sinners is that the opponents considered Jesus to be different from those he associated with, namely to be more like themselves (the opponents) — they grouped him with them, i.e., as a Pharisee, or like a Pharisee and expected him to maintain their standards — an important inference or induction. If they had considered him to be one of 'them,' i.e., outsiders, they would not have bothered or even noticed his associations" (letter to the author, August 5, 1999).

32. Sanders, *Jesus and Judaism,* p. 174.

33. Strictly speaking, the Temple sacrifices were to atone for inadvertent sins and not serious and deliberate violations of the Torah. For weighty transgressions there was no ritual or sacrifice, except the Day of Atonement (Yom Kippur) ritual for the entire nation. The point here is that Jesus' proclamation of forgiveness was not tied to either the regular Temple sacrifices or the Day of Atonement rituals.

34. Sanders, *Jesus and Judaism,* pp. 207, 210; cf. p. 255. Meier agrees with Sanders on this general point (*A Marginal Jew,* 2:149-50).

Notes to "Approaching the End"

1. This is Sanders's estimate (*Historical Figure,* p. 249). Josephus gives much larger numbers for attendance at the Passover, on the order of 2.5 to 3 million, but these figures are generally thought to be rather unrealistic (*Jewish War* 6.420-27; 2.280).

2. Schweitzer, *Quest,* pp. 387-92.

3. N. T. Wright comments: "The way of the servant was to take upon himself the exile of the nation as a whole," and "Jesus, then, went to Jerusalem not just to preach, but to die.

Schweitzer was right: Jesus believed that the messianic woes were about to burst upon Israel, and that he had to take them upon himself, solo" (*Jesus and the Victory of God*, pp. 608-9).

4. Borg, *Jesus*, p. 172.

5. Borg, *Jesus*, pp. 173-74.

6. Sanders, *Historical Figure*, pp. 252-53.

7. Borg, *Jesus*, p. 174.

8. Joseph Klausner, *Jesus of Nazareth: His Life, Times, and Teaching*, trans. Herbert Danby (New York: Macmillan, 1953), p. 312.

9. Borg, *Jesus*, pp. 174-75.

10. Dodd, *The Founder of Christianity*, p. 145.

11. Meier seems to agree with Sanders that the Temple action "was probably not a call for reform but a prophecy that the present Temple would be destroyed" ("Reflections," p. 101).

12. Sanders, *Jesus and Judaism*, pp. 301-5, and *Historical Figure*, pp. 254-62. Crossan agrees with Sanders that it is likely that "what led immediately to Jesus' arrest and execution in Jerusalem at Passover was that act of symbolic destruction, in deed and word, against the Temple" (*Who Killed Jesus? Exposing the Roots of Anti-Semitism in the Gospel Story of the Death of Jesus* [San Francisco: HarperSanFrancisco, 1995], p. 65).

13. Craig A. Evans, "Jesus' Action in the Temple: Cleansing or Portent of Destruction?" *Catholic Biblical Quarterly* 51 (1989): 237-70; and Evans, "Jesus and the 'Cave of Robbers': Toward a Jewish Context for the Temple Action," *Bulletin for Biblical Research* 3 (1993): 93-110.

14. Wright, *Jesus and the Victory of God*, pp. 417, 490.

15. Crossan takes an opposing view that there was no "solemn, formal, and final institution by Jesus himself" of a ritual meal. Instead certain groups of followers ritualized the "open commensality" that had characterized Jesus during his ministry (*Jesus*, p. 130). See also Crossan's discussion of bread-and-fish meals (pp. 179-80).

16. Since the Gospel of John speaks of the "preparation of the Passover" (Gk., *paraskeue tou pascha*, John 19:14) on the day of Jesus' death, scholars have generally concluded that the Passover meal took place after Jesus' death, and that Jesus' final meal with his disciples in the Gospel of John could not have been a Passover meal. John would be consistent with the Synoptics if the Jews celebrated the Passover on two different days, and this has in fact been suggested: "Ingenious attempts have been made to reconcile the differences by suggesting that Jesus and his disciples, along with the Essenes of the Dead Sea Scrolls, may have celebrated the Passover according to an ancient solar calendar different from that observed by the Jews of Jerusalem" (Ian Wilson, *Jesus: The Evidence* [San Francisco: HarperSanFrancisco, 1996], p. 120). For a full discussion of this possibility, see A. Jaubert, *The Date of the Last Supper* (New York: Alba House, 1965). Craig Blomberg may offer a better resolution of the calendrical problem when he notes that the Greek term *paraskeue*, "preparation," was the common word for Fridays among the Jews, since it was the day on which one prepared for the Sabbath (i.e., Saturday). On this account, *paraskeu tou pascha* means "the day of preparation for the Sabbath during Passover week," or simply "Friday in Passover week." Blomberg's fuller explanation is best presented in his own words: "The most plausible harmonization of John and the Synoptics therefore requires a closer look at the specific

terms which John uses in his apparently contradictory verses and the contexts in which they are found. . . . In 13:29, then, when some of the disciples think that Judas left in order to buy provisions for 'the feast', the word that is used would refer to the week-long festival. Which particular meal during those seven days the provisions were required for is left unspecified. If the meal in progress were the first night's banquet, then 'the feast' would quite naturally refer to part or all of the remaining six days. This explanation makes equally good sense of 18:28, where the Jewish leaders wish to avoid defilement which would prevent them from eating the Passover. In fact defilement incurred during the daylight hours would expire at sundown and would not prevent their celebration of an evening dinner, so it is more likely that John has in mind the lunchtime meal known as the *chagigah*, celebrated during midday after the first evening of Passover. 19:14 and 31 do not contradict this by their labelling the day of Jesus' death 'the day of Preparation of the Passover' since the Greek word *paraskeue* translated 'day of Preparation', was (and still is) the standard name for Friday in Greek. Since Friday was always Preparation Day for the Sabbath (Saturday), it came to be called by that name. John's language is thus a natural shorthand for saying 'the day of preparation for the Sabbath during Passover week' or simply 'Friday in Passover week'. Mark 15:42 confirms the appropriateness of this interpretation, since Mark also calls the day of Jesus' death 'the day of Preparation' but then immediately explains, 'that is, the day before the Sabbath'" (*The Historical Reliability of the Gospels* [Downers Grove, Ill.: InterVarsity Press, 1987], pp. 177-78). I am indebted to Michael Farley for calling my attention to Blomberg's calendrical explanation.

17. Meier, "Reflections," p. 103.

18. Bruce Chilton holds that Jesus held a final Passover meal with his disciples, but that the Jewish ban on the drinking of blood was so compelling that any idea of partaking in Jesus' blood would have been unthinkable to Jesus' followers. For this reason, Chilton is skeptical of the Gospel accounts regarding the institution of the eucharist, and argues that the Christian eucharist "owes more to the thought of the Hellenistic world of the Gospels than to Rabbi Jesus' revolutionary teaching" (*Rabbi Jesus*, pp. 250-54, citing p. 251). Yet the opposite conclusion would seem to follow. Since the Gospel texts originated in a largely Jewish rather than Gentile context, the criterion of dissimilarity suggests that any tradition regarding the drinking of blood would not have been invented by the earliest Jewish disciples but rather derived from Jesus himself.

19. Binyamin Eliav, "Anti-Semitism," in *Encyclopedia Judaica* (Jerusalem: Macmillan/ Keter Publishing, 1971), 3:87-160.

20. The encyclical *Nostra Aetate* (1965), in the Vatican II documents, contains an explicit repudiation of the notion of Jewish guilt for the death of Jesus (Austin Flannery, ed., *Vatican II Council: The Conciliar and Post-Conciliar Documents* [Northport, N.Y.: Costello Publishing, 1975], p. 741).

21. This becomes evident in the harsh tone of the mid-second-century work by Justin Martyr, *Dialogue with Trypho, A Jew,* in *The Ante-Nicene Fathers*, 1:194-272.

22. See especially the following verses: John 2:18-20; 5:10-18; 6:41, 52; 7:1, 13; 8:48, 52, 57; 9:18, 22; 10:31-33; 11:8; 18:36; 19:7, 12, 38; 20:19. Other texts in the Gospel of John speak of Jesus' followers as Jews and of a "division" among the Jews over Jesus, but the designation of Jesus' opponents simply as "Jews" is frequent.

23. Ernst Bammel, "The Trial before Pilate," in *Jesus and the Politics of His Day*, pp. 415-51, citing p. 449.

24. Raymond E. Brown, *The Death of the Messiah: From Gethsemane to the Grave*, 2 vols., Anchor Bible Reference Library, ed. David Noel Freedman (New York: Doubleday, 1994). Brown forthrightly discusses the questions of responsibility for Jesus' death, and anti-Judaism in the Gospel narratives, at 1:383-97.

25. Raymond Brown, *Death of the Messiah*, 1:14.

26. Crossan, *Jesus*, p. 145; highlighted in the original. In *Who Killed Jesus?*, Crossan presents at length his spirited dissent with Raymond Brown.

27. Josephus, *Antiquities* 18.63.

28. Crossan, *Who Killed Jesus?* p. 147.

29. Catchpole, "Problem of Historicity," p. 54.

30. See the following discussions: William Riley Wilson, *The Execution of Jesus: A Judicial, Literary, and Historical Investigation* (New York: Scribner, 1970); Bammel, *The Trial of Jesus*, including especially Catchpole, "The Problem of the Historicity of the Sanhedrin Trial," pp. 47-65; Bammel, "The Trial before Pilate," pp. 415-51; Richard A. Horsley, "The Death of Jesus," in *Studying the Historical Jesus*, pp. 395-422; Raymond Brown, *Death of the Messiah*, 1:237-877.

31. Paul Winter, *On the Trial of Jesus*, 2nd ed. (Berlin and New York: Walter de Gruyter, 1974). Vis-à-vis the guidelines in the Mishnah, the trial as described in Mark violated five principles: (1) a night session, (2) a trial on a feast day, (3) the omission of the statutory second session, (4) meeting in the house of the high priest, and (5) a discrepancy between the understanding of "blasphemy" in the Gospel account and in *m. Sanh.* 7.5 (Catchpole, "The Problem of the Historicity of the Sanhedrin Trial," p. 58).

32. Meier, "Reflections," pp. 103-4.

33. John 18:31 implies that the Jewish leaders did not have the right to capital punishment. Some support for this is given in Josephus's treatment of the death of James, the brother or kinsman of Jesus and a leader in the early church (*Antiquities* 20.200-203), an event that aroused the ire of the Romans perhaps because it involved a capital sentence being carried out without prior Roman approval.

34. Philo wrote of "the briberies, the insults, the robberies, the outrages and wanton injuries, the executions without trial constantly repeated, the ceaseless and supremely grievous cruelty" that marked Pilate's rule (*Embassy to Gaius* 302, quoted in Sanders, *Historical Figure*, p. 274). Josephus recounts an episode in which Pilate sought to bring Roman military standards, bearing the emperor's image, into the Holy City, and he backed down before a multitude of protesters willing to face death (*Jewish War* 2.169-71; *Antiquities* 18.55-59). He also took money from the Temple fund to build an aqueduct into the city (*Jewish War* 2.175-76; *Antiquities* 18.60-62). Pilate was eventually dismissed from office because of his large-scale and ill-advised executions of political agitators (*Antiquities* 18.88-89). And the high priest Caiaphas, who had an extraordinarily long tenure in office that ended in the same year (36 C.E.) as Pilate's did (*Antiquities* 18.95), may have been a political partner to the Roman governor who fell from grace when Pilate did.

35. Against the viewpoint that Jesus was misunderstood by the Romans and died because they took him to be a potential revolutionary, Sanders writes (*Historical Figure*,

p. 268): "The solitary execution of the leader shows that they feared that Jesus could rouse the mob, not that he had created a secret army. In other words, they understood Jesus and his followers very well."

36. The ancient Jewish authors Philo (*Against Flaccus* 72, 84) and Josephus (*Antiquities* 12.256; *Jewish War* 2.306-8; 5.446-51) commented on the scourging that accompanied Roman crucifixion. For a thoroughly documented study of the ancient practice of crucifixion, see Martin Hengel, *Crucifixion in the Ancient World and the Folly of the Message of the Cross* (Philadelphia: Fortress, 1977).

37. Meier, "Reflections," pp. 104-6. On the discovery of the corpse of the crucified man, see Charlesworth, *Jesus within Judaism*, pp. 122-23, and Joseph Zias and Eliezer Sekeles, "The Crucified Man from Giv'ar ha-Mivtar: A Reappraisal," *Israel Exploration Journal* 35 (1985): 22-27.

38. Hengel, *Crucifixion*, p. 87.

39. Josephus, *Jewish War* 5.447-51.

40. Meier, "Reflections," p. 106. Crossan holds that the disciples had no knowledge of what happened to Jesus' body: "By Easter Sunday morning, those who cared did not know where it was, and those who knew did not care" (*Jesus*, p. 158). He suggests further that the body was probably devoured by dogs — an idea that may be linked with his viewpoint regarding the resurrection (discussed in the notes to "A New Beginning"). Yet there is archaeological evidence that the body of a first-century victim of crucifixion, Jehochanan, was honorably interred in an ossuary and tomb, and so it is not true that crucifixion victims were never buried (Charlesworth, *Jesus within Judaism*, pp. 122-23; and Zias and Sekeles, "The Crucified Man," pp. 22-27). Moreover, Mark 6:29 indicates that the disciples of John the Baptist were able to retrieve his body for burial as well. While it is a "peculiar circumstance" that Jesus' body should be turned over for burial to a nonrelative, i.e., Joseph of Arimathea, John 19:31 attributes this to the religious motive of insuring that the corpse did not remain on the cross during the Sabbath day (Pheme Perkins, "The Resurrection of Jesus of Nazareth," in *Studying the Historical Jesus*, pp. 423-42, esp. pp. 431-32, 437). Crossan, despite his skepticism regarding the biblical reports of Jesus' burial, notes that the Old Testament Apocryphal text of *Tobit* stresses the solemn responsibility of the pious Jew to provide for proper burial of a fellow Jew, and adds: "Joseph of Arimathea could have been a pious Jew like Tobit . . . a few centuries before Jesus" ("Historical Jesus as Risen Lord," in John Dominic Crossan et al., *The Jesus Controversy: Perspectives in Conflict* [Harrisburg, Pa.: Trinity Press International, 1999], p. 20). Bruce Chilton argues in favor of the traditional burial account, noting that the Gospel authors generally tried to shift blame for Jesus' death onto the Jewish Sanhedrin, and so they were not likely to have invented a story about Jesus' burial by Joseph of Arimathea (*Rabbi Jesus*, p. 270).

Notes to "A New Beginning"

1. On the general topic of Jesus' resurrection, see the extensive bibliography of about 1200 books and articles in Watson E. Mills, ed., *Bibliographies on the Life and Teachings of Jesus*, vol. 8, *The Resurrection* (Lewiston, N.Y.: Edwin Mellen, 2002). N. T. Wright published his

major work on the resurrection of Jesus as *The Resurrection of the Son of God* (Minneapolis: Fortress Press, 2003), which is the third in the series *Christian Origins and the Question of God* (Minneapolis: Fortress Press, 1992-).

2. Sanders, *Historical Figure*, pp. 276-77.

3. This phrase "spiritual body" has evoked a good deal of discussion, as in the following: Robert H. Gundry, *Soma in Biblical Theology*, Society for New Testament Studies Monograph Series (Cambridge: Cambridge University Press, 1976), and Gundry, "The Essential Physicality of Jesus' Resurrection according to the New Testament," in *Jesus of Nazareth, Lord and Christ; Essays on the Historical Jesus and New Testament Christology*, ed. Joel B. Green and Max Turner (Grand Rapids: Eerdmans; Carlisle, U.K.: Paternoster Press, 1994), pp. 204-19; Murray J. Harris, *Raised Immortal: Resurrection and Immortality in the New Testament* (Grand Rapids: Eerdmans, 1983), and Harris, *From Grave to Glory: Resurrection in the New Testament* (Grand Rapids, Mich.: Zondervan, 1990).

4. As one might expect, the resurrection is a hotly debated topic among scholars. Gerd Lüdemann claims that "we can no longer take the statements about the resurrection of Jesus literally . . . the tomb of Jesus was not empty, but full, and his body did not disappear but rotted away" (*What Really Happened to Jesus? A Historical Approach to the Resurrection*, trans. John Bowden [Louisville: Westminster/John Knox, 1995], pp. 134-35). William Lane Craig presents his counterarguments in *Assessing the New Testament Evidence for the Historicity of the Resurrection of Jesus* (Lewiston, N.Y.: Edwin Mellen, 1989), and more concisely in the proceedings of his debate with Gerd Lüdemann, in Paul Copan and Ronald K. Tacelli, eds., *Jesus' Resurrection: Fact or Figment? A Debate Between William Lane Craig and Gerd Lüdemann* (Downers Grove, Ill.: InterVarsity Press, 2000), esp. pp. 31-39, 46-51, 162-206.

5. Borg, *Jesus*, p. 189 n. 44; Crossan, *Who Killed Jesus?*, p. 216. Crossan adds: "Empty tomb stories and physical appearance stories . . . are, for me, parables of resurrection, not the resurrection itself." Basically "resurrection" means "the continuing experience of God's presence in and through Jesus." Compare Bruce Chilton's idea that "the resurrection was an angelic, nonmaterial event" grounded in the disciples' visionary experiences (*Rabbi Jesus*, pp. 283, 272-74).

6. Perkins, "Resurrection," p. 436. N. T. Wright argues that apart from the resurrection, Jesus after his crucifixion would have been regarded as a "remarkable but tragic memory," like other would-be messiahs such as Judas the Galilean or Simeon ben Kosiba (*Jesus and the Victory of God*, pp. 658-59). By contrast, John Dominic Crossan claims that the author of the Gospel of Mark invented both the burial story concerning Jesus and the notion of an empty tomb, maintains that Paul's emphasis on the postresurrection appearances of Jesus is missing from the Gospel of Mark, and claims that "bodily resurrection has nothing to do with a resuscitated body coming out of its tomb" ("Historical Jesus as Risen Lord," in Crossan, *The Jesus Controversy: Perspectives in Conflict*, pp. 16-18, citing p. 46). For further discussion see: Markus Bockmuehl, "Resurrection," in Markus Bockmuehl, ed., *The Cambridge Companion to Jesus*, pp. 102-18; Gerald O'Collins, "Is the Resurrection an 'Historical Event'?" *Heythrop Journal* 8 (1967): 381-87; Pheme Perkins, *Resurrection: New Testament Witness and Contemporary Reflection* (Garden City, N.Y.: Doubleday, 1984); and the discussion on the resurrection between Marcus J. Borg and N. T. Wright, *The Meaning of Jesus*, pp. 111-42.

Notes to "Wisdom, Apocalypse, and the Identity of Jesus"

1. A number of recent writers make this distinction, and a few suggest that the two categories could be united. Willem S. Vorster noted that "there are currently two opposing images of Jesus among New Testament scholars . . . as an eschatological prophet or a wisdom teacher" (*Speaking of Jesus*, p. 301), yet claimed that "it is too early to make final judgements as to whether Jesus was an eschatological prophet or a wisdom teacher" (p. 316) — thus ruling out the possibility of Jesus being both. Michael O. Wise, in *The First Messiah: Investigating the Savior Before Jesus* (San Francisco: HarperSanFrancisco, 1999), suggests that Jesus should be understood on analogy with the "Teacher of Righteousness" in the Dead Sea Scrolls (perhaps named Judah), and he concludes: "What have previously been separate portrayals of the historical Jesus — that of wise man or sage, and that of apocalyptic prophet — ought to be merged. Many Gospel data support this merged portrait, but historians have previously dismissed some as unhistorical or have separated them into distinct, incompatible piles. . . . For we know from Judah's hymns that he was both wisdom teacher and prophet of the apocalypse. If Judah, why not Jesus?" (p. 275). Ben Witherington III argues that is plausible to understand Jesus in terms of multiple categories: "Jesus lived at a time when the rivers of the prophetic, apocalyptic, and sapiential traditions had already flowed together; indeed, apocalyptic was itself a hybrid of wisdom and prophetic materials. It is not surprising that Jesus himself reflected the situation in his words and deeds and in his self-understanding as a messianic prophet, a northern prophet, an apocalyptic eschatological sage, a Son of Man" (*Jesus the Seer: The Progress of Prophecy* [Peabody, Mass.: Hendrickson Publishers, 1999], p. 291).

2. Borg, "Reflections on a Discipline," in *Studying the Historical Jesus*, p. 20.

3. N. T. Wright uses the phrase "sapiential prophet" to denote a specific aspect of Jesus' ministry, namely the ways in which Jesus "made the interpretation of scripture . . . a significant part of his work" (*Jesus and the Victory of God*, p. 164). My emphasis is different, and while I agree with N. T. Wright regarding Jesus' appeal to the Hebrew scriptures, I am using the word "sapiential" to refer to Jesus' teaching for everyday living, which may or may not have involved an interpretation of, or reference to, the Jewish scriptures.

4. See the following: James H. Charlesworth, "Jesus' Concept of God and His Self-Understanding," in *Jesus within Judaism*, pp. 131-64; Ben Witherington III, *The Christology of Jesus* (Minneapolis: Fortress, 1990), esp. pp. 118-43, 215-33; John C. O'Neill, *Who Did Jesus Think He Was?* (Leiden: Brill, 1995); and Christopher M. Tuckett, *Christology and the New Testament: Jesus and His Earliest Followers* (Louisville: Westminster/John Knox, 2001), pp. 202-26.

5. Joachim Jeremias, *The Prayers of Jesus* (Philadelphia: Fortress, 1967), pp. 11-65, esp. pp. 57, 60, 62, argues that Jesus' address to God as *Abba* is unique to him, while this claim is disputed in Vermès, *Jesus the Jew*, pp. 210-13, and accepted in a qualified fashion in James D. G. Dunn, *Christology in the Making: A New Testament Inquiry into the Origins of the Doctrine of the Incarnation*, 2nd ed. (Grand Rapids: Eerdmans, 1996), pp. 26-28. See also: Meier, *A Marginal Jew*, 2:358-59; Wright, *Jesus and the Victory of God*, pp. 649-50; and Allison, *Jesus of Nazareth*, pp. 47-50. Mary Rose D'Angelo, impelled in part by the feminist challenge to male terminology for God, has argued that the term *Abba* was not unique to Jesus or characteristic of him, and perhaps was never used by him ("*Abba* and 'Father': Imperial Theology and the Jesus Traditions," *Journal of Biblical Literature* 111 [1992]: 616). Marianne Meye

Thompson provides a full discussion in *The Promise of the Father: Jesus and God in the New Testament* (Louisville: Westminster/John Knox, 2000), noting that "Jeremias did not argue that Jesus' *view of God* was novel or unique but that Jesus' *mode of address* to God was novel and unique because *his experience of God* was distinctive" (p. 25). In the end, Thompson concludes that "we simply lack the data to conclude that such address gives us access to Jesus' sense of Sonship or to his experience of God. The relevant texts of the New Testament do not answer the question why Jesus used the term Father for God, however much both biblical scholars and theologians have hastened to fill in the silences with various sorts of historical and dogmatic explanations" (p. 172).

6. In addition to the works already cited by Witherington and Dunn, see also Martin Hengel, *The Son of God: The Origin of Christology and the History of Jewish-Hellenistic Religion* (London: SCM, 1976), and C. F. D. Moule, *The Origin of Christology* (Cambridge: Cambridge University Press, 1977).

7. Sanders, *Historical Figure*, pp. 239-40.

8. Bultmann (*Jesus and the Word*, pp. 38-39, 49) held that Jesus did actually use the phrase, but possibly of some other figure still to come rather than of himself. Like Bultmann, Adela Yarbro Collins comments: "Jesus expected a radical transformation of the world and that this would involve the coming of a heavenly figure . . . [but] Jesus did not believe himself to be this figure" (in Ostling, "Who Was Jesus?," p. 40).

9. Barnabas Lindars, "Re-enter the Apocalyptic Son of Man," *New Testament Studies* 22 (1976): 52-72, and *Jesus Son of Man* (Grand Rapids: Eerdmans, 1983).

10. Meier, "Reflections," pp. 100-101. Christopher Tuckett argues that the abundant references to Jesus as "Son of Man" in the synoptic Gospels but not in other parts of the New Testament or postbiblical Christian tradition suggest that this designation was not invented by the earliest Christians but rather was an authentic part of Jesus' teaching about himself (*Christology and the New Testament*, pp. 216-19).

11. Norman Perrin argued that the term as applied to Jesus was simply a creation of early Christianity, in *A Modern Pilgrimage in New Testament Christology* (Philadelphia: Fortress, 1974), esp. pp. 65-66, 77-78.

12. Meier, "Reflections," p. 98. Along the same lines, N. T. Wright states that Jesus intended to "embody in himself the returning and redeeming action of the covenant God" (*Jesus and the Victory of God*, p. 653). Daniel Doriani argues that the Gospels seek to make an implicit case for Jesus' divinity, in "The Deity of Christ in the Synoptic Gospels," *Journal of the Evangelical Theological Society* 37 (1994): 333-50.

13. Sanders, *Historical Figure*, pp. 236-37.

14. Sanders, *Historical Figure*, pp. 238, 242. David Flusser, perhaps the leading contemporary Jewish interpreter of Jesus, concluded that Jesus identified himself as the Messiah and "came to the conclusion that he himself would eventually be revealed as the divine Son of Man" (*Jesus*, pp. 273-74). Along different lines, Michael O. Wise (*The First Messiah*, p. 263) distinguishes the "free prophet" who "claims to receive divine revelation without extensive interaction with . . . written tradition," from the "scripture prophet" who "derives his self-understanding in large measure via prolonged meditation on earlier written revelation," and identifies Jesus as "scripture prophet." Yet Wise seems to underestimate the degree to which Jesus claimed personal authority and the power to act and speak directly on God's behalf,

independent of written authorization and attestation. Christopher Tuckett uses the category of "prophet" as a step toward grasping Jesus' self-understanding, and yet he notes that Jesus' willingness to speak by his own authority makes him unlike the traditional sort of "prophet" (*Christology and the New Testament*, pp. 213-15).

15. See Neusner, *Rabbi*, pp. 30-31, and Koester, *Introduction*, 2:78. Achad Ha'am was pointed in his criticism of Jesus' "I": "Israel cannot accept with religious enthusiasm, as the Word of God, the utterances of a man who speaks in his own name — not 'thus saith the Lord' but 'I say unto you.' This 'I' is in itself sufficient to drive Judaism away from the Gospels for ever" (*Ten Essays on Zionism and Judaism* [London, 1922], p. 232, quoted in Catchpole, "Problem of Historicity," p. 50). Ben Witherington III concurs that "Jesus could not simply be seen as standing in the line of the classical prophets," inasmuch as "the form of most of his probably authentic utterances does not allow this conclusion," "his utterances lack a messenger formula," and "he was certainly not among the writing prophets" (*Jesus the Seer*, p. 246).

Notes to "Thinking Outside the Boxes"

1. Albert Schweitzer, *The Quest of the Historical Jesus: A Critical Study of Its Progress from Reimarus to Wrede* (New York: Macmillan, 1978), p. 4.

2. Henry Cadbury wrote of "the peril of modernizing Jesus," and noted that "we are anxious to secure his authority for our own point of view. We flatter ourselves by praising his universality, his modernness, his insight, since we mean by these things merely our own judgments in the areas where we are quoting him" (*Peril*, p. 43).

3. George Tyrrell, *Christianity at the Cross Roads* (London: Longmans, 1909), p. 44.

4. Funk et al., *The Five Gospels*, p. 5.

5. N. T. Wright, *The Challenge of Jesus: Rediscovering Who Jesus Was and Is* (Downers Grove, Ill.: InterVarsity Press, 1999), p. 11.

6. Crossan, *Jesus*, pp. 58-60.

7. *The Didache*, 10.6, in Cyril Richardson, ed., *Early Christian Fathers* (New York: Macmillan, 1970), p. 176.

8. Richard T. France, "On Being Ready," in Longenecker, ed., *The Challenge of Jesus' Parables*, pp. 177-95, citing p. 193. My purpose here is not to resolve the issue of Matthew 25 and salvation by grace. A Christian who regards the whole of the New Testament as authoritative will read Matthew 25 alongside of the Epistle to the Romans and other texts that teach that human works are not the basis for salvation. Yet Matthew 25 challenges an imbalanced theology that focuses on divine grace and neglects God's call to radical discipleship.

9. Cited in Edward M. Gerlock, "Foreword," in José Ignacio López Vigil and María López Vigil, *Just Jesus*, 3 vols. (New York: Crossroad, 2000), 1:vii.

10. John 7:53–8:11 is a textual variant and almost certainly was not a part of the Gospel of John in its original form. Yet the passage illustrates an important point about Jesus' ministry, and in any case my concern in this conclusion is not with textual authenticity but rather with contemporary understandings of Jesus that have often appealed to this text.

11. I am drawing on Professor Marty's Lenten chapel message, given at Washington University in St. Louis in Spring 2001.

12. Robert N. Bellah et al., *Habits of the Heart: Individualism and Commitment in American Life* (Berkeley: University of California Press, 1985), pp. 220-21, 235.

13. Wade Clark Roof, *A Generation of Seekers: The Spiritual Journeys of the Baby Boom Generation* (San Francisco: HarperSanFrancisco, 1993), and *Spiritual Marketplace: Baby Boomers and the Remaking of American Religion* (Princeton: Princeton University Press, 1999).

14. Scot McKnight rejects the image of Jesus as spiritual master because he regards Jesus' ministry as outward and public rather than inward and individualistic: "Jesus cannot be understood if he is described exclusively, or even primarily, in the category of spiritual master, or as one who was primarily concerned with the inner religious life" (*A New Vision for Israel*, p. 10). McKnight equally finds fault with the individualistic interpretation of Jesus' teaching in German liberalism, as in Rudolf Bultmann, *Theology of the New Testament*, trans. K. Grobel, 2 vols. (New York: Scribners, 1951-55), 1:25-26, and Adolf von Harnack, *What is Christianity?*, trans. Thomas B. Saunders (New York: Harper, 1957), p. 60.

15. John Meier expresses the point well: "Although Jesus rarely spoke directly about his own status, he implicitly made himself *the* pivotal figure in the final drama he was announcing and inaugurating. The Kingdom was somehow already present in his person and ministry, and on the last day he would be the criterion by which people would be judged" ("Reflections," p. 98).

16. Sanders, *Historical Figure*, pp. 236-37.

17. Neusner, *Rabbi*, pp. 30-31.

18. Achad Ha'am, *Ten Essays on Zionism and Judaism* (London, 1922), p. 232.

19. The larger context of C. S. Lewis's statement is worth reproducing: "I am trying to prevent anyone saying the really foolish thing that people often say about Him: 'I'm ready to accept Jesus as a great moral teacher, but I don't accept His claim to be God.' That is the one thing we must not say. A man who was merely a man and said the sort of things Jesus said would not be a great moral teacher. He would either be a lunatic — on the level with the man who says he is a poached egg — or else he would be the Devil of Hell. You must make your choice. Either this man was, and is, the Son of God: or else a madman or something worse" (*Mere Christianity* [New York: Macmillan, 1960], pp. 55-56).

20. A discussion of some similarities as well as differences between Jesus and Buddha, along with Moses, Confucius, and Muhammad, is given in Michael J. McClymond, "Prophet or Loss? Reassessing Max Weber's Theory of Religious Leadership," in David Noel Freedman and Michael J. McClymond, eds., *The Rivers of Paradise: Moses, Buddha, Confucius, Jesus, and Muhammed as Religious Founders* (Grand Rapids, Mich.: Eerdmans, 2001), pp. 613-58.

21. The great historian of Christianity, Jaroslav Pelikan, describes eighteen successive images of Jesus that dominated at one time or other in the history of the church, in *Jesus Through the Centuries: His Place in the History of Culture* (New Haven: Yale University Press, 1985). Anyone who is convinced that his or her viewpoint on Jesus is not conditioned by cultural context would benefit from a reading of this book.

22. Ben Witherington III, *Jesus the Seer: The Progress of Prophecy* (Peabody, Mass.: Hendrickson, 1999), p. 246.

23. Robert M. Price, in *Deconstructing Jesus* (Amherst, N.Y.: Prometheus Books, 2000), p. 16.

Index of Subjects and Names

Agrapha, 26, 30-31
Allison, Dale, 7, 12, 22, 42, 101, 184n.22
Anti-Jewish bias in early church, 124-25
Antiochus Epiphanes, 53, 96
Apocalypticism, 6, 69-71, 177nn.12, 16.
  See also Eschatology; Kingdom of
  God
Apollonius, 85
Aune, David, 78

Barth, Karl, 13
Barton, Bruce, 22-23
Bauer, Bruno, 24, 163n.68
Bellah, Robert, 150
Benjamin, Joshua M., 163n.70
Blackburn, Barry L., 91
Blomberg, Craig, 7, 34, 167n.40,
  185nn.34, 35, 190n.16
Boers, Hendrikus, 175n.2
Bolingbroke, Lord, 24
Borg, Marcus: and apocalyptic/
  sapiential eschatologies, 133; and the
  "end-of-the-world" Jesus, 143; and es-
  chatological language, 68, 78, 80,
  176n.6; and historical Jesus research,
  7, 18, 19, 156n.4, 160n.39, 178n.27; and
  Jesus' final week, 120, 122; and Jesus'
  sayings and parables, 99, 100, 107;
  and "the politics of holiness," 95; and
  the resurrection, 131

Boring, M. Eugene, 168n.41
Bornkamm, Günther, 14-15
Brown, Raymond E., 7, 125, 126, 153n.3,
  170n.53
Brunner, Emil, 13
Bultmann, Rudolf: and apocryphal
  texts, 31; and criteria of authenticity,
  38-39; and early Jesus research, 7, 8,
  13-14, 18, 78, 159n.26; and miracles, 10,
  82, 88, 179n.4; and "Son of Man" title, 196n.8

Cadbury, Henry, 136, 186n.3, 197n.2
Caiaphas, 5, 126, 192n.34
Caird, G. B., 68, 176n.8, 178n.33
Career of Jesus, 109-19; and conflicts
  with Jewish opponents, 114-19;
  controversiality and reasons for Jesus' death, 112-19, 123; female followers, 110-11, 146-47, 187n.12; followers
  and disciples, 110-12, 146-47, 164n.12,
  187nn.12, 13; and forgiveness for
  nonobservant Jews, 118-19, 189n.33;
  intentions of Jesus' ministry and
  mission, 2-4, 109-10, 186n.3; and the
  Pharisees, 113, 114, 115, 116-17, 188n.25,
  189n.27; as prophet and wisdom
  teacher, 6, 43, 133-36, 195n.1; and social intimacy with nonobservant

Jews, 117-18, 189n.31; Torah disputes and legal issues, 115-16, 188n.21

Celsus, 28

Charlesworth, James H., 7, 43, 70

Chilton, Bruce: and burial of Jesus, 193n.40; and historical Jesus research, 7, 22, 160n.35; and Jesus' identity, 162n.62; and Jesus Seminar, 160n.35; and Jesus' sexual activity, 183n.21; on Jesus' teachings and Hebrew tradition, 106, 108; and kingdom of God, 81; and Last Supper, 191n.18; and miracles, 181n.23; and paternity of Jesus, 153n.3; and the resurrection, 194n.5; and the Temple, 53

Christology, origins of, 136-38

Cleage, Albert, 23

Collins, Adela Yarbro, 196n.8

Controversiality of Jesus. See Career of Jesus

Corley, Kathleen, 111

Craig, William Lane, 131

Crossan, John Dominic: and apocryphal gospels, 32, 166n.30; and contemporary images of Jesus, 141, 148; and Cynic philosophy, 16, 17; dating and classification of Gospels, 42, 43; on eschatology, 68; and historical Jesus research, 7, 9, 10, 15, 16, 17, 19; and infancy narratives, 153n.3; on Jesus and inclusive community, 118, 135, 148; and Jesus as revolutionary, 158n.16; and Jesus' attack on the family, 97, 141; on Jesus' death, and his followers, 125-26, 193n.40; and Jesus' message to sinners, 118; and kingdom of God, 79, 80, 118, 148; and miracles, 89; on parables, 103, 104, 185n.34; and the resurrection, 131, 194nn.5, 6; on synoptic Gospels, 33; and Temple incident, 190n.12

Cullmann, Oscar, 77

Cynic philosophy, 16-18, 160n.42, 186n.2

D'Angelo, Mary Rose, 195n.5

Davies, Stevan L., 166n.32

Dead Sea Scrolls, 54, 57-58, 73, 165n.21, 195n.1

Death of Jesus: and burial, 4, 128, 193n.40; and the crucifixion, 4, 125-28; dating of, 5, 123-24; Jesus' controversiality and reasons for, 112-19, 123; and Jesus' followers, 125-26, 193n.40; Jewish involvement in, 29, 60, 113-14, 124-27, 174n.54, 192n.33; in non-Christian sources, 29; in rabbinical writings, 27. See also Final week of Jesus; Resurrection of Jesus

Dodd, C. H., 77, 79, 80, 101

Doriani, Daniel, 196n.12

Douglas-Klotz, Neil, 163n.70

Dowling, Levi H., 23

Downing, F. G., 7, 16, 17

Dungan, David L., 159n.20

Dunn, James D. G., 7, 168n.41, 189n.27

Dupuis, Charles Francois, 24

Ehrmann, Bart, 7, 12, 22

Eisenman, Robert H., 165n.21

Eschatology, 6, 67-81, 133-35; and apocalypticism, 69-71; consistent/realized, 77, 78, 79; and contemporary images of Jesus, 143-46; defining, 68-69, 176n.8; in early Christianity, 69; and Hebrew scriptures, 71-73; of Jesus, 43, 133-36, 143-46, 195n.1; and Jesus research, 11-12, 21-22, 69-71, 74, 76-81; and Jesus' teachings, 6, 67-81, 133-35; and Jewish postbiblical literature, 72-73; and John the Baptist's message, 2, 62-63, 65, 175n.4; and kingdom of God teachings, 67-81; and metaphorical language, 78, 80, 179n.36; and mysticism, 78; and parables, 3-4; "proleptic" or "inaugurated" model, 77-78, 79, 178n.33; prophetic, 70, 71-73; and Second Temple

Judaism, 73-74; symbolic/metaphorical function, 78-79, 80, 179nn.36, 38; and temporal references, 78, 79-80. *See also* Kingdom of God

Essenes, 56, 57-58, 183n.21

Evans, Craig, 7, 106, 108, 123

Exorcisms. *See* Miracles of Jesus

Faber-Kaiser, A., 24

Falk, Harvey, 7

Family, Jesus' attack on, 94-95, 96-97, 112, 141-42

Final week of Jesus, 4, 120-28; and ironic parables/sayings, 103; and Jesus' followers, 125-26, 193n.40; journey to Jerusalem, 4, 120-22, 189n.3; Last Supper Passover meal, 123-24, 190nn.15, 16, 191n.18; prophetic actions of, 121-22; and Sanhedrin, 60, 126-27; Temple incident, 4, 20, 121, 122-23, 190nn.11, 12; the trial, 4, 60, 126-27, 192nn.31, 35. *See also* Death of Jesus

Flusser, David, 196n.14

France, R. T., 145

Fredriksen, Paul, 7, 22, 179n.2, 188nn.21, 25

Freedman, David Noel, 189n.31

Freyne, Sean, 7, 47, 50, 160n.42, 174n.54

Funk, Robert, 7, 15-16, 139

Galilee. *See* Palestine, first-century

Gogarten, Friedrich, 13

Gospel of Peter, 31, 166n.30

Gospel of Philip, 31

Gospel of Thomas, 21, 30, 31-32, 166n.32, 167nn.33, 34

Grant, Robert, 182n.32

Greco-Roman world: demonic possession and exorcism in, 84-86, 87; miraculous healings in, 84, 90, 91-92; and noncanonical sources on Jesus,

27-29, 165n.15. *See also* Palestine, first-century

Green, William Scott, 55, 61, 174n.51

Gundry, Robert H., 169n.45, 171n.2

Gutiérrez, Gustavo, 149

Ha'am, Achad, 150-51, 197n.15

Hanina ben Dosa, 84, 87, 174n.51, 181n.31

Harnack, Adolf von, 139

Harvey, A. E., 7, 19

Heidegger, Martin, 14

Hengel, Martin, 37, 128, 169n.46

Herod Antipas, 2-3, 47, 48, 50

Herod the Great, 5, 49, 50, 59, 155n.7

Heschel, Abraham, 185n.39

Hillel, 93, 107, 182n.1

Hofius, O., 30

Hollenbach, Paul W., 175n.12

Holmen, Tom, 170n.53

Holtzmann, H. J., 11, 159n.20

Honi the Circlemaker, 87, 174n.51, 181n.31

Horsley, Richard, 7, 50

Identity of Jesus, 133-38; as both prophet and wisdom teacher, 6, 43, 133-36, 195n.1; as eschatological prophet, 43, 133, 134, 195n.1; and Jesus' self-presentation, 137-38, 196nn.12, 14, 197n.15; and Jesus' self-understanding, 136-38, 195n.5; and Jesus' titles for himself, 5-6, 137, 196nn.8, 10; and kingdom of God teachings, 133-36; and origins of Christology, 136-38; and parables, 133-35; as sapiential wisdom teacher, 43, 79, 133, 195n.3; scholarly debate about Jesus' wisdom and authority, 5-6, 43, 133-34, 183n.13, 195n.1; "Son of Man," 5-6, 137, 196nn.8, 10, 11. *See also* Jesus, contemporary images of

Islamic sources on Jesus, 164n.9

Jefferson, Thomas, 38, 169n.48
Jenkins, Philip, 160n.32, 163n.70
Jeremias, Joachim, 30, 67, 77, 195n.5
Jerusalem, Jesus' final journey to, 4, 120-22, 189n.3
Jesus, contemporary images of, 139-52; the "end-of-the-world Jesus," 143-46; eschatological teachings, 143-46; the "family values Jesus," 140-43; fire-and-brimstone preaching, 147-48; the "global spirituality Jesus," 148-51; as homewrecker, 141-42; and popular culture images, 11, 22-23; and self-transformation, 148-51; siding with the poor, 144-46; the "socially inclusive Jesus," 146-48; and temptation to eclecticism, 149-50; totalitarianism/claims to authority, 150-51, 198nn.15, 19
Jesus as teacher. See Kingdom of God; Parables and sayings of Jesus
Jesus' life, 1-6; crucifixion and death, 4-5; dating issues, 5, 123-24, 155n.7; differing scholarly opinions on, 153n.3, 154n.4; early life, 1-3, 155n.5; and family, 1-2, 112, 154n.4; John the Baptist and baptism of Jesus, 2-3, 40, 62, 66; and marriage, 100, 183n.21; ministry in Galilee, 2-4; and virginal conception, 153n.3, 154n.4. See also Career of Jesus
Jesus research, 7-25; apocalyptic and eschatological interpretations, 11-12, 21-22, 69-71, 74, 76-81, 177n.16; and Cynic philosophy, 16-18, 160n.42; debate about Jesus' wisdom and authority, 5-6, 43, 133-34, 195n.1; of first half of twentieth century, 12-15; "first quest" for historical Jesus, 10; form criticism and demythologization, 13-14; German existential and dialectical thinkers, 13-14; and Jesus' first-century Jewish context, 8-9, 18-22,
160n.45; and the Jesus Seminar, 15-16; on kingdom of God, 11-12, 21, 69-71, 74, 76-81; and miracles, 82, 89-91, 179n.2; mythmaking and romanticism, 10-11; of nineteenth century, 9-12, 77, 82, 136; and popular culture images of Jesus, 11, 22-23; pseudoscholarship, 23-25, 163nn.68, 70; recent changes in, 7-9, 156nn.3, 4; Schweitzer and, 9, 12-13, 18, 22, 139; and "Son of Man" title, 137, 178n.27, 196nn.8, 10, 11; "third quest" for historical Jesus, 9, 18-22, 160n.45. See also Jesus, contemporary images of
Jesus Seminar, 15-16, 167n.40, 178n.27; criticism of, 21, 159n.31, 160nn.32, 35
Johnson, Luke Timothy, 7, 159n.31
Johnson, Mark, 179n.42
John the Baptist, 62-66; apocalyptic/eschatological message of, 2, 62-63, 65, 175n.4; baptism and repentance/forgiveness, 63; and baptism customs, 63, 64; and the "Coming One," 64, 65; and infancy narratives, 153n.3; and Jesus, 2-3, 40, 62, 64, 65-66, 100, 175nn.2, 12; and Jesus' baptism, 2-3, 40, 62, 66; and miracles/exorcisms, 87, 88; mission of, 63-65; and prophetic movements in Palestine, 59; and Qumran, 63, 175n.5
Josephus, 28-29; on first-century Palestine, 47, 49, 50; and Jesus' death, 29, 126; on Jewish exorcisms, 85, 87; on John the Baptist, 63, 175n.4; on Passover attendance, 189n.1; on Pilate, 192n.34; on Roman crucifixions, 128, 193n.36; on sects/popular movements, 55-56, 57, 59
Jülicher, Adolf, 103, 185n.34
Justin Martyr, 28

Käsemann, Ernst, 14, 41, 182n.35
Kazantzakis, Nikos, 23

Kee, Howard Clark, 90
Kingdom of God, 3, 67-81; and apocalypticism, 69-71, 177nn.12, 16; and command to love one's neighbor/one's enemies, 4, 71; definitions of, 74-76; future arrival of, 76, 77, 81; and Jesus' attack on the family, 97; and Jesus' departure from John the Baptist, 66; and Jesus' eschatological teachings, 67-81, 133-35; Jesus' meaning of, 3, 74-78, 80-81, 133-35, 178nn.29, 33, 34; and Jesus research, 11-12, 21, 69-71, 74, 76-81; and Last Supper, 124; and miracles, 88-89, 92; and parables, 3-4, 75-77, 102, 105, 108, 133-35; presence of, 3, 71, 75, 76-77, 78, 80, 81; Second Temple Judaism and eschatological expectations, 73-74; and "Son of Man" sayings, 76-77, 144-45, 177n.25, 178n.27. *See also* Eschatology
Klausner, Joseph, 122
Koester, Helmut, 6, 26, 155n.5, 167n.33
Kümmel, W. G., 77

Ladd, G. E., 77
Lakoff, George, 179n.42
Last Supper, 123-24, 190nn.15, 16, 191n.18
Lawrence, D. H., 23
Left Behind novels, 146
Lewis, C. S., 151, 198n.19
The Life of Brian (film), 23
Lindars, Barnabas, 137
Lucian of Samosata, 165n.15
Lüdemann, Gerd, 179n.2, 181n.23, 194n.4
Luther, Martin, 134

Mack, Burton L.: and historical Jesus research, 7, 9, 16-17, 160n.39, 163n.68; on Jesus' mission and social critique, 186n.3; and miracles, 181n.27; and

non-Christian sources on Jesus' death, 29
Malina, Bruce J., 181n.23
Marty, Martin, 150
Marx, Karl, 24
Mary, mother of Jesus, 1, 27, 112, 153n.3, 154n.4
Mary Magdalene, 24, 128, 129, 183n.21
Maurin, Peter, 146
McKnight, Edgar V., 156n.3
McKnight, Scot, 7, 77, 182n.2, 198n.14
Meier, John P.: on followers of Jesus, 111, 187nn.12, 13; and historical Jesus research, 7, 9, 18, 20-21; on Jesus' audacity, 198n.15; and Jesus' career, 186n.2, 187n.5; on Jesus' identity and Christology, 137-38; and Jesus' self-presentation, 137-38; on John the Baptist, 62, 63-64, 66, 88; on kingdom of God, 74, 80; and Last Supper, 124; and miracles, 87, 88, 181n.31; and parables, 105; on Sadducees, 57; and sources on Jesus' life and sayings, 29, 32-33, 41; on synoptic Gospels, 167n.33; and Temple incident, 190n.11; and twelve disciples, 111
Meyer, Ben F., 7-8, 18
Miracles of Jesus, 3, 82-92; canonical Gospels on, 86-91; contemporary views and popular beliefs, 82-83, 179n.2; and the crowds, 88; faith healings, 89; and Greco-Roman context, 84-86, 90, 91-92; healings and exorcisms, 3, 65-66, 86-87, 89, 90-91, 175n.12, 182n.37; and Hebrew Bible, 87-88; and Jesus as sorcerer, 28, 83; and Jesus research, 82, 89-91, 179n.2; and Jesus' uniqueness, 87, 88, 181n.31; and John the Baptist, 65-66, 87, 175n.12; and kingdom of God teachings, 88-89, 92; magic and miracles, 89-91; nature miracles, 87-88, 181n.23; revivification miracles, 87-88; sym-

bolic significance of, 91; and the twelve disciples, 112
Moore, George Foot, 52

Nag Hammadi library, 31, 33-34
Nelson-Pallmeyer, Jack, 163n.68
Neusner, Jacob, 52, 116-17, 150, 183n.13

Olrik, Axel, 104
Overman, J. Andrew, 55, 61, 174n.51

Palestine, first-century, 44-61; cultural and cosmopolitan character, 51-52; diversity of, 51-53, 61; economic system of, 48-51; and female followers of Jesus, 110-11; Gospels on, 46-48; and Hellenistic culture, 51-52; and historical Jesus research, 8-9, 18-22, 160n.45; Jewish and Gentile relations in, 47-48; Jewish diversity in, 52-53, 113, 115-16; Jewish law and authority in, 55, 59-61; languages of, 51-52; natural features of, 44-47; political life of, 48-51, 59-61; and "politics of holiness," 95-96; sects and popular movements in, 55-59, 174n.51; social banditry in, 50-51; the Temple in, 53-54, 117, 173n.31; travel and trade in, 47-48
Parables and sayings of Jesus, 3-4, 93-108; and allegory, 103-4, 185n.34; and asceticism, 100-101, 184n.22; call to transformation/renunciation, 99-101; criteria of authenticity for, 37-42, 170nn.51, 53, 171n.59; and criticism of the family, 94-95, 96-97, 112; and criticism of wealth, 97-98; critiques of conventional wisdom, 96-99; and early Christians, 168n.41; on everyday life and human affairs, 101, 104, 133-34; and first-century Palestinian context, 94-98; Gospel parables, 103-6, 168n.41; and Hebrew Bible tradition, 103, 104, 106-8, 185n.35; on honor, 98;

and humor, 98, 101-2, 184nn.27, 28, 30; and irony, 102-3; and Jesus as prophet and wisdom teacher, 133-35; and Jesus' distinctiveness as teacher, 93-95, 96-97, 182nn.1, 2; judgment and challenging tone of, 104-6; and kingdom of God, 3-4, 75-77, 102, 105, 108, 133-35; and oral storytelling features, 104; paradoxes and surprise in, 3-4, 102; on religion/pious practices, 98-99; on sexuality, 100-101, 141
Pelikan, Jaroslav, 198n.21
Perkins, Pheme, 8, 94, 131
Perrin, Norman, 38, 41, 67, 78, 80, 170n.51, 196n.11
Pharisees, 55-57, 61, 113; Jesus' conflicts with, 56, 96, 99, 113-17, 188n.25, 189n.27; and ritual purity, 55-56, 117
Philo, 57, 192n.34, 193n.36
Philostratus, 85
Phipps, William E., 183n.21
Pliny the Elder, 46, 57
Pliny the Younger, 27-28
Pontius Pilate, 4, 5, 113, 121, 127, 192n.34
Porter, Stanley E., 51, 160n.45, 171n.59
Price, Robert M., 152, 163n.68
Prophet, Elizabeth Clare, 23

The Quest of the Historical Jesus (Schweitzer), 9, 12, 76
Quirinius, 5, 155n.7
Qumran, 54, 57-58, 63, 73, 175n.5

Reed, Jonathan L., 8, 171n.5
Reimarus, Hermann Samuel, 9, 10, 82, 158n.14
Reinhartz, Adele, 23
Renan, Ernest, 11
Resurrection of Jesus, 4-5, 129-32; and afterdeath appearances, 4, 130, 131-32; Christian differences of emphasis regarding, 130-32; Paul and, 130, 131, 132; scholarly debate over, 131,

194nn.4, 6; Scripture accounts of, 129-30

Riches, John, 8

Ridderbos, Herman, 77

Ritschl, Albrecht, 12

Rivkin, Ellis, 8, 61

Robinson, John A. T., 108, 169n.45

Roof, Wade Clark, 150

Russell, J. Stuart, 178n.34

Sadducees, 56, 57, 61, 117

Saldarini, Anthony, 60-61

Sanders, E. P.: on apocryphal gospels, 167n.34; and Gospel authors, 37; and historical Jesus research, 7, 9, 18, 19-20; and Jesus' attack on the family, 142; and Jesus' audacity, 150; on Jesus' conflicts with Jewish opponents, 114-15, 116, 117, 118, 189n.27; on Jesus' identity, 137, 138; on Jesus' message to sinners, 118; and Jesus' self-presentation, 138; on Jewish eschatology, 43; on kingdom of God, 77, 118, 178n.29; and miracles, 91; on origin of Christology, 137; on Synoptic tradition and sources, 41, 43; and Temple incident, 20, 122-23, 190nn.11, 12; and trial of Jesus, 192n.35

Sanhedrin, 59-61, 110, 113, 126-27, 174n.54

Sayings of Jesus. *See* Parables and sayings of Jesus

Scholarship. *See* Jesus research

Schonfield, Hugh, 23

Schweitzer, Albert: and eschatology, 12, 68, 134; and historical Jesus scholarship, 9, 12-13, 18, 22, 139; and Jesus' trip to Jerusalem, 120; and kingdom of God, 76, 77

Scott, Bernard Brandon, 179n.38

Seeley, David, 29

Sepphoris, 2, 47, 48, 51, 59, 171n.5

Smith, Huston, 179n.38

Smith, Morton, 8, 89, 182n.37

Snodgrass, Klyne R, 185n.34

"Son of Man," 5-6, 120-21, 137, 178n.27, 196nn.8, 10, 11

Sources and methods, 26-43; agrapha, 26, 30-31; apocryphal gospels, 26, 31-33, 167n.34; canonical Gospels, 33-38, 41-43, 167n.33; classical Roman authors, 27-29, 165n.15; and criteria of authenticity, 37-42, 170nn.51, 53, 171n.59; Dead Sea Scrolls, 165n.21; Gospel authorship, 37; Gospel contexts, 35-37; Gospel dating, 36-37, 42, 43, 169n.45; Islamic sources, 164n.9; and Josephus, 28-29; and methods of inquiry, 33-43; noncanonical sources, 26-33; non-Christian sources, 26-29, 164n.9, 165nn.15, 21; proto-Gospels, 36-37, 168n.44; rabbinical writings, 27; redaction criticism, 34; reliability and authenticity questions, 33-34, 35-43

Stendahl, Krister, 184n.27

Strabo, 46

Strauss, David Friedrich, 10-11, 82

Suetonius, 27

Tacitus, 46, 165n.15

Temple: in first-century Judaism, 53-54, 117, 173n.31; Jesus and Temple incident, 4, 20, 121, 122-23, 190nn.11, 12; leadership of, 54, 58; sacrifices and atonement in, 118, 189n.33

Theissen, Gerd, 82, 88, 170n.55, 179n.2

Thiering, Barbara, 24

Thompson, Marianne Meye, 170n.53, 195n.5

Tiberias, 5, 47, 48, 51

Tolbert, Mary Ann, 185n.34

Troeltsch, Ernst, 83

Tuckett, Christopher, 167n.34, 170n.53, 196n.10

Van Voorst, Robert E., 30, 167n.34
Vermès, Geza, 8, 174n.51, 181n.31
Volney, Constantin-Francois, 24
Voltaire, 24
Vorster, Willem S., 179n.36, 195n.1

Weaver, Walter P., 177n.16
Webb, Robert, 63, 175n.5
Weiss, Johannes, 11-12, 77
Wells, George A., 24, 163n.68
Wenham, David, 8
Williams, Rowan, 164n.12
Winter, Paul, 7, 126, 188n.25
Wise, Michael O., 195n.1, 196n.14

Witherington, Ben, III, 8, 151, 195n.1, 197n.15
Wright, N. T.: and contemporary images of Jesus, 139; and historical Jesus research, 8, 9, 12, 18, 21-22, 160n.45; and Jesus as sapiential prophet, 195n.3; and Jesus' conflicts with Pharisees, 189n.27; and Jesus' eschatological language, 178n.34; and Jesus' final trip to Jerusalem, 120, 189n.3; and Jesus' self-presentation, 196n.12; and Last Supper, 190n.15; on the resurrection, 194n.6; and Temple incident, 123

Index of Scripture and Other Ancient Literature

HEBREW BIBLE

Genesis

12:1-3	69

Exodus

3:14-15	107

Leviticus

19:18	4

Deuteronomy

12:5	173n.31
21:22-23	128

2 Samuel

8:17	57
15:24	57

1 Kings

17:17-24	88

2 Kings

4:8-44	88

Job

38:8-11	88

Psalms

65:7	88
89:9	88
93	74
96	74
99	74
107:23-32	88

Isaiah

5:1-7	103
5:3	103
11:6	70
20:3	121
29:13	99, 149
40–66	71
44:28	72
49:5-6	71
54:3	72
56:1-8	71
56:7	107, 121
59–66	63
60:3-14	71
60:16	72
61:6	72
66:18-24	72

Jeremiah

7:11	107, 121
16:1-4	183n.21
19:1-13	121
27–28	121
31	63
31:31-34	72

Ezekiel

4–5	121
12:1-16	121
24:15-24	121
34	72
36	63
36:24-27	72
37	72
40–43	72
47:13–48:29	72

Hosea

11:8-9	106

Micah

4	72

Zechariah

9:9-10	122

APOCRYPHA

Sirach

36:11	72
48:10	72

Baruch

4:37	72
5:5	72

1 Maccabees	52

2 Maccabees	
1:27ff.	72
2:18	72

NEW TESTAMENT

Matthew
1:22-23	106
1:25	154n.4
2:15	106
2:17-18	106
2:23	106
3:2	178n.30
3:4	65
3:10	63
3:11-12	64
3:13–4:11	66
4:14-16	106
4:17	178n.30
4:23	65
4:23-24	86
4:24	86
5-7	11
5:3-11	133
5:4-8	76
5:13	105
5:13-14	105
5:14-16	105
5:15	184n.30
5:20	76
5:22	60
5:27-30	101
5:32	140
5:36	102
5:40	184n.30
5:44	4, 71
6:1-6	98
6:1-18	32
6:2	98
6:5-6	98
6:10	76, 81
6:13, RSV	177n.24

6:16-18	98
6:26	100, 107
6:28	100
6:28-30	71
6:30	107
7:4	102
7:9-10	184n.30
7:11	106
7:12	182n.1
7:16	184n.30
7:18	99, 149
7:21	76
7:22	85
7:24-27	150
7:26-27	184n.30
8:4	116
8:5-13	84, 86, 146
8:11	178n.33
8:11-12	76, 147
8:12	147
8:16	65, 86
8:16-17	86
8:17	106
8:28-34	86
9:1	46
9:14	65
9:14-17	65
9:32-34	86
10:1	85
10:1-4	111
10:5-6	48
10:7	178n.30
10:8	85
10:9-13	110
10:17	60
10:23	76, 134
10:25	147
10:34-38	141
10:37-39	97
10:39	100, 149
11:3	62, 64
11:4-5	75
11:8	51, 184n.30
11:16-19	100

11:18	87
11:18-19	65
11:19	146
11:20	109
11:23	46
12:3	108
12:5	108
12:17-21	106
12:22-32	28
12:22-37	87
12:27	85
12:28	75, 88, 90, 92, 178n.33
12:33	99, 149
12:43	87
12:46-50	40
12:48-50	95
13:1-9	141
13:1-53	94
13:3-8	185n.35
13:3-23	75
13:16-17	75
13:18-23	185n.35
13:23	135
13:24-30	104, 185n.35
13:24-50	75
13:30	4, 135
13:31	105
13:31-32	134
13:33	105, 135
13:35	106
13:36-43	185n.35
13:40-42	105
13:40-43	147
13:43	133
13:44	75, 105
13:45	105
13:45-46	75
13:47	105
13:55	2
14:14	86
14:35-36	86
15:1-20	56
15:2	115

15:13-14	105	23:24	102	2:15-17	110
15:14	102	23:25	96	2:18	65
15:21-28	86, 146	23:27	96	2:18-22	114
15:24	48	23:29	96	2:23-28	114
15:30-31	86	24	178n.34	2:25	108
17:9	120	24:27	76	3:1-6	86, 114
17:18	86	24:37	76	3:8	46
17:22-23	120	24:45-51	105	3:10-12	86
17:24-27	87, 116	25	145, 197n.8	3:11	86
17:25-26	50	25:1-13	75, 104, 105	3:13-19	40, 111
18:23-35	75	25:31-46	144	3:15	85
19:3-8	108	25:34	147	3:20-21	182n.37
19:4	108	25:41	147	3:20-30	87
19:12	101, 141	26:52-54	4	3:21	40, 94, 112
19:14	140	26:55	102	3:27	75
19:28	76, 111	26:66	60	3:33	112
20:1-16	3, 75	27:9	106	3:35	112
20:16	133, 146	27:25	125	4	104
20:17-19	120	27:57-60	125	4:2	104
21–27	4	28:7	129	4:3-8	104
21:4-5	106	28:9	129	4:9	104
21:9	121	28:16	129	4:21	104
21:14	86	28:16-20	129	4:23	104
21:16	108			4:24	104
21:25	103	**Mark**		4:26-27	75
21:33-44	105	1:4	63	4:26-29	3, 75, 104, 135
21:42	108	1:6	65	4:30-32	104
22:1-13	104	1:7-8	64	4:30-34	75
22:1-14	75, 105	1:9-11	2	4:33	104
22:3	75	1:9-13	66	4:35-41	87
22:10	4	1:12	45	5	91
22:13	147	1:13	46	5:1-5	86
22:30	143	1:14-20	45	5:1-20	86
22:31	108	1:15	66, 178n.30	5:5	91
22:41-46	103	1:23-28	86	5:9	89
22:42	108	1:29-31	86	5:15	86
22:43	108	1:32-34	65, 86	5:17	48
23	96, 183n.9	1:35-37	148	5:19	91
23:3	96	1:38-39	65	5:20	86
23:6	98	1:39	86	5:21-24	87
23:7	98	1:40-45	86	5:24-34	86
23:13	96	2:1-12	86, 89, 114	5:26	84
23:15	96	2:5	89	5:34	89
23:23	96	2:13-17	114	5:35-43	87

6:1-6	109	11–15	4	2:21	153n.3
6:5	86, 89	11:12-14	87	2:25-38	153n.3
6:7	85	11:15-19	121	2:40-52	153n.3
6:13	85	11:17	107, 121	3:1	5
6:29	193n.40	11:20-21	87	3:10-14	65
6:30-44	87	12:10	108	3:15-17	64
6:45-52	87	12:26	108	3:21-22	66
6:52	112	12:28-34	107	4:1-13	66
6:55-56	86	12:31	4	4:16-20	2, 51
7:1-23	56	12:34	125	4:21	75, 108
7:6	99, 149	12:35	108	4:23	102
7:19	116	12:41-44	102	4:31-37	86
7:24-30	86	13:2	54	4:40-41	65, 86
7:31-37	86, 90	13:9	60	4:41	86
8:1-10	87	13:24-27	143	4:43-44	65
8:11-13	89	13:26	76	5:33	65
8:14-21	40	14:22-25	121	5:33-35	65
8:22-26	86	14:25	76	6:3	108
8:27–9:1	11	14:33	112	6:12-16	111
8:31-33	40	14:43-64	121	6:18	86
8:34	100, 149	14:62	76	6:18-19	86
8:34-35	4	14:64	60	7:1-10	86
8:38	76	14:66-72	40	7:11-17	87
9:1	76	15	121	7:19	62
9:2-8	112	15:1	60	7:21	86
9:12	108	15:21	127	7:33	87
9:13	50	15:38	54	7:33-34	65
9:25	86	15:42	190n.16	7:36-50	110, 146
9:31	120	15:42-47	110	8:1-3	98, 110
9:38	85	15:43	98, 125	8:2	86
9:38-40	85	16:7	129	8:19	142
9:43-48	76, 147	16:14	40	8:19-21	97
9:48	147			8:26-39	86
10:2-9	108	**Luke**		9:1	85
10:11-12	106	1:5-25	153n.3	9:1-11	112
10:15	76, 141	1:5-80	63	9:11	86
10:23	76, 98	1:26-38	153n.3	9:22	120
10:25	98	1:52-53	146	9:42	86
10:28-30	142	1:57-58	153n.3	9:44	120
10:32-34	120	1:59-63	153n.3	9:49	85
10:35-45	40	1:65-79	153n.3	9:51-52	46
10:38-40	100	1:80	153n.3, 175n.5	9:58	109
10:44	102	2:2	155n.7	9:59-60	97
10:46-52	86	2:7-14	153n.3	9:60	142

9:62	4	16:19-31	104	4:5	46
10:1-20	112	17:7-10	184n.30	4:46	46
10:9	178n.30	17:11-19	86	5:10-18	191n.22
10:11	178n.30	17:20-21	75	6:35	34
10:17	85	17:21	80	6:41	191n.22
10:25-37	104, 146	17:24	76	6:52	191n.22
10:29-37	101, 104	17:26	76	7:1	191n.22
10:38-42	111, 147	18:1-8	184n.30	7:1-9	40
10:42	111	18:9-14	3, 146	7:5	142
11:1	65	18:10-13	104	7:13	191n.22
11:5-8	101	18:11-12	99	7:53–8:11	197n.10
11:11-12	184n.30	18:31-33	120	8:7	147
11:13	107	19–23	4	8:11	147
11:14-23	87	19:1-10	110, 146	8:12	34
11:19	85	19:11-17	104	8:48	191n.22
11:20	66, 88, 92,	19:11-27	105, 141	8:52	191n.22
	178n.33	19:17	147	8:57	191n.22
11:24	87	19:38	121	9:6-7	90
11:27-28	97	20:41	108	9:16	125
11:28	142	22:50-51	86	9:18	191n.22
11:37-44	110	22:71	60	9:22	191n.22
12:8-9	76	23:28-29	76	10:20	94
12:16-21	97	23:50-53	125	10:31-33	191n.22
12:24	107	24:1-12	130	10:41	65
12:28	107	24:9-11	40	11:1-44	87
12:50	100	24:13-35	79, 130	11:8	191n.22
13:4-5	76	24:33-36	129	11:47-53	60
13:6-9	105	24:36-49	130	11:51	125
13:10-17	86	24:42-43	129	12:24	100, 149
13:16	146	24:50-53	129	13:29	190n.16
13:20-21	75	27:39	129	14:6	151
13:21	75			15:1	34
13:28-29	178n.33	**John**		18:28	190n.16
13:32	86	1:25-27	64	18:31	192n.33
13:33	120	1:35-42	65	18:36	191n.22
14:1-6	86	2:1-2	46	19:7	191n.22
14:7-11	98	2:1-11	87	19:12	191n.22
14:26	4	2:12	46	19:14	190n.16
14:28-30	184n.30	2:18-20	191n.22	19:31	190n.16
14:33	4, 97	2:23	86	19:38	191n.22
15:3-7	101	3:1	125	19:38-42	125
15:11-32	3, 101, 103, 104	3:22–4:2	62	20:19	40, 191n.22
15:20	4, 106	3:23	46	20:19-20	129
16:1-9	3, 101	4:1-4	46	20:20	129

20:26-29	40
21:1-3	110
21:13	129

Acts

1:3	130
1:6-11	129
1:13	111
1:14	112
2:22	91
4–6	60
4:32-37	110
5:21	60
5:33-40	125
5:34	60
6:7	125
6:13-14	54
7:48-53	54
10:14	116
11:8	116
19:13-17	85
20:35	30
22:30	60
23	60
23:6-8	57
25:19, NASB	132

Romans

1:4	130
9:4-5	98

1 Corinthians

9:14	110
15	130
15:3-8	130
15:17	131
15:20	130
15:23	130
15:44	130

2 Corinthians

5:16	13
12:7-9	168n.41

Galatians

1:11	176n.15
1:11-17	176n.15

Hebrews

8:2	54
8:5	54
9:24	54
11:8-16	69

Revelations

1:11	70
2:9	125
10:4	70
12:7-12	70
21:1	143
21:12	73

POSTBIBLICAL LITERATURE

1 Clement	30
Gospel of the Nazoreans	30
Liber Graduum	30
Acts of Peter	30
Gospel of Thomas	21, 30, 31-32
Gospel of Philip	31
Gospel of Peter	31

RABBINICAL WRITINGS

Tractate Sanhedrin	
13:10	73

Psalms of Solomon

8:34	72
11	72
17:28-31	72
17:50	73

Testament of Moses

3:4	73
4:9	73
10:7	73

Testament of Levi	54

Lives of the Prophets	54

QUMRAN DOCUMENTS

1QM

1:2	73
2:2ff.	73
2:7ff.	73
3:13	73
5:1	73
11:13	73
13:13f.	73

4Q285	165n.21
4Q491	165n.21

1QpHab (Commentary on Habakkuk)

2:6	73
5:3-6	73

11QTemple (Temple Scroll)

18:14-16	73
57:5f.	73